Portrait of
BIRMINGHAM

VIVIAN BIRD

*Illustrated
and with maps*

ROBERT HALE · LONDON

ISBN 0 7091 1871 6

Robert Hale & Company
63 Old Brompton Road
London S.W.7

PRINTED IN GREAT BRITAIN
BY RICHARD CLAY (THE CHAUCER PRESS), LTD.,
BUNGAY, SUFFOLK

PORTRAIT OF BIRMINGHAM

I dedicate this book to

SAM BATTERSBY

who defected to Manchester but
retained a friendship in Birmingham

"One has no great hope of Birmingham. I always say there is something direful in the sound."

JANE AUSTEN's Mrs. Elton in Emma

"Birmingham is not my native town—I wish it were."

JOSEPH CHAMBERLAIN

". . . the best-governed city in the world."

J. RALPH, Harper's Monthly Magazine 1890

"We believe that everything points inflexibly to the fact that Birmingham's expansion will have to be stopped at some point or other."

The Birmingham Post, 1969

CONTENTS

ILLUSTRATIONS

MAPS

INTRODUCTION

Poor old Spiceal Street's half gone,
And the poor Old Church stands all alone;
And poor old I stand here to groan,
For I can't find Brummagem.

IN 1828 the comedian James Dodds sang in the Theatre Royal,
Birmingham, this verse of his own song "I Can't Find Brummagem", because after an absence of "full twenty years" he
could no longer recognise the town. Today, of course, he wouldn't
even find the Theatre Royal. That went in 1957 at the beginning
of an upheaval far more catastrophic than any changes of 150
years ago.

If Dodds craved the sympathy of his audience, I crave my
readers' indulgence with even more justification. The Birmingham which is my subject matter has not only been disappearing
before my eyes, it has simultaneously been constantly renewed.
So, while waxing nostalgic about the past, I have had to keep my
eyes open round every corner for some new development—no
easy task. Birmingham is regularly described as the most dynamic
city in the world today, and if any city is more dynamic Heaven
help it.

Mercifully, attempts to make Birmingham a 'swinging city'
have not been conspicuously successful.

Preparing this book has given me a new respect for the Birmingham of the past. I have been amazed at the number of things
which Birmingham has pioneered—from building societies to
rationing in the First World War. Previously I had merely
accepted the city's motto of "Forward", laughed at it occasionally
as all Brummies have, but now I feel it to be justified.

Though born in Warwick, twenty miles distant, I have lived in
Birmingham for fifty-three years. I am not sure that there is a

residential qualification to be a Brummie in the strict sense of the word. Nor, unlike the Cockney born within sound of Bow Bells, is it a matter of being born here—unless incidentally. Accent confers Brummiehood, an uncongenial regional accent which is being retained on radio and television, but which, happily, is tending to die. The visitor is more likely to hear the Welsh accents of immigrants from India than indigenous Brummie today.

Throughout this book I use the term Brummie in the wider sense of one who has lived in the city long enough to feel involved in it—as I have. In this sense I am proud enough to proclaim myself as Brummie. If it confers no particular distinction, it connotes nothing unworthy—as Liverpudlian implies an involvement in raucous pop discord, for instance.

The label Brummie at least identifies my habitat, and I'm satisfied enough with this not to want it confused with the Black Country, which laps our western and north-western borders. Phil Drabble writes in *Black Country* (Robert Hale, 1952): "One insult that no Black Countryman will tolerate is to be mistaken for a Brummie." This intolerance is a two-way traffic. Both areas are made up of a vast majority of ordinary people with no striking regional characteristics, but when you do unearth a thorough-going Black Country character he surely sounds the most uncouth caricature among regional types in Britain. The greatest insult that can be levelled at a Brummie is to equate him with a Black Countryman, and here I take my stand squarely with my fellow-citizens.

The Brummie is no longer cloth-capped, collarless, and with a choker round his neck as he carries a basket of pigeons. More often he wears a waterproof or a wind-cheater and loads his car with expensive fishing equipment. The Birmingham Anglers' Association has an aggregate membership of over 40,000 from more than 1,000 clubs, and its annual contest attracts more entries than any fishing contest in the world.

My modern chapters will be contentious. I am no believer in objective reporting when it can be enlivened with personal opinion, and he would be a poor soul, caught up in the maelstrom of Birmingham's redevelopment, who did not react noticeably. "Controversy; for ever a characteristic of Birmingham history..." wrote John Sanders in *Birmingham* (Longman, 1969). So, controversy it is when dealing with the city's traffic, housing, and immigration problems, and I have the satisfaction of knowing that this is no parish-pump controversy—even though the 'parish' be Britain's 'second city' with a population estimated in June 1967 at 1,101,990.

Birmingham may not impinge on British history so frequently and dramatically as lesser places, but the city's expansion, diesel fumes, and integration worries are common to most towns and cities in the kingdom. While these problems cannot be ignored— and by Heaven they cannot—I feel that my historical chapters are more authentically Birmingham. Its history is peculiar to the city; it shares its modern problems with countless communities throughout the world.

Generally this book is chronologically progressive, but I have chosen in Chapters IV to VII, inclusive, to isolate several topics. I have included material which involved some fairly original research on my part, but fact is fact, and history is history, so I am indebted to many who have written before me, particularly that indispensable trio of bygone Birmingham historians, John A. Langford, Robert K. Dent, and Samuel Timmins. Among more modern works I owe particular thanks to Gill and Briggs *History of Birmingham*; Pevsner's *Warwickshire* in the Buildings of England series; the Victoria County History of Warwickshire, Volume VII; John Sanders' *Birmingham*, mentioned above, and, over the years, to many church guide books, including a recent one on King's Norton by J. E. Vaughan.

Miss D. M. Norris, now retired, and her staff in the Birmingham section of the Central Reference Library could always be relied on to produce the most abstruse material, and I have been fortunate that my office is just across a corridor from the splendid *Birmingham Post and Mail* library of press cuttings so comprehensively and comprehensibly marshalled by Mr. Leslie Withers during his term as chief librarian, and so ably staffed by various obliging young ladies. Once again I have to thank my friend Norman Williams for reading the draft of a book of mine and for making helpful suggestions.

I

DIRTY DERIDED RIVER

ROMANCE is where you find it, and I found it at two points on the insignificant Rea, Birmingham's laughing-stock of a river.

At Hazelwell Mills, Stirchley, the rubber-component manufacturers now occupying the site believe that swords which flashed during the Charge of the Light Brigade were ground at a blade mill there in the middle of last century. This could well be so, though mills downstream of Hazelwell on the Rea and its tributaries were turning earlier in the nineteenth century from blade mills to rolling mills, from merely processing material manufactured elsewhere to becoming an integral part of the factory. Even so, the tithe map of Edgbaston Parish in 1843 still shows Speedwell Mill and Edgbaston Mill on the Rea, Pebble Mill on the Bourn Brook, and Over Mill below Edgbaston Pool on the Chad Brook, as blade mills.

With greater certainty we can link the Rea with Equatorial Africa. It is often said, whether with more contempt for Birmingham or the offending foreign countries I am never sure, that most of the metal souvenirs of travel throughout the world are made in Birmingham. The city's detractors may find it more legitimate that bus tickets issued at Accra in Ghana are made in Birmingham, and that 88 per cent of their raw material is actually water extracted from the River Rea at the Cranemore Street Paper Mills by Smith, Stone, and Knight Ltd. In addition, this firm also makes cartridge paper for Australia and wrapping and pastel paper for Ceylon, Pakistan, and the West Indies, each with its quota of Rea water.

Rivers have always been a major factor in determining the

position of towns and cities, and have continued thereafter to give them purpose and character. Birmingham owes its existence to the Rea. The settlements which became the nucleii of the town grew up where the ridge roads from Redditch, Warwick, and Coventry in the south dipped to the ford at Deritend on the way to Lichfield, Tamworth, and Walsall. Duddeston, barely a mile downstream, also had its ford, and another community sprang up there. It would be false to say that the Rea has given purpose or character to Birmingham, but the image of the river has become that of the city—dirty, derided, even turbulent on occasions, but useful.

All but the first of the Rea's meagre eleven miles are within the city boundary, and its course constitutes a microcosm of Birmingham, a synopsis of this book, touching on nearly every facet explored in the following chapters, though not necessarily in sequence.

The Rea rises below the slopes of Windmill Hill on the ridge which extends south-westward of Birmingham for six miles between the city's two hill playgrounds, the Lickeys and the Clent Hills, giving a magnificent panorama from the Black Mountains and the Brecon Beacons to the exquisite Shropshire hills around and beyond Church Stretton, balm to eyes tired of brick and mortar. Travellers in more primitive days sought to outflank this ridge, and were thus forced nearer to Deritend ford. Had the Rea sprung half a mile westward on the other side of this watershed, it would have pursued a rural course to the Severn— and Birmingham might never have been.

At one of its springs in Gannow Green Farm the Rea's crystal stream was piped as the domestic and farm water until the M5 Motorway construction cut off the supply. For centuries this spring provided life-giving water for man and beast—a chastening thought when we see what man has done to the despised River Rea. Within two miles of its source industry hits the river with shattering impact at the Longbridge Works of British Leyland Motors Corporation, still much better known to Birmingham as 'the Austin'. Herbert Austin installed his motor-car works in a derelict printing premises at Longbridge in 1901, and for good or ill struck the keynote for the Birmingham of the twentieth century. Originating in Buckinghamshire, Austin emigrated to Australia, coming back to Birmingham in 1893 to take charge of the Wolseley Sheep-Shearing Company. His passion for mechanised transport flowered in the design of a tiller-steered, three-wheeled car which the newly formed Wolseley Motors Ltd. bought from him in 1901 for £40,000. A four-cylinder tourer was the first Austin car turned out from the Longbridge factory in 1906, and in 1923 came the famous Austin Seven, costing £165.

Member of Parliament for the King's Norton Division of Birmingham, elevated to the peerage in 1936, Lord Austin died in 1941 and lies in Lickey churchyard, a mile from the colossus he created, which today turns out some 8,000 vehicles in an average week and employs 25,000, who, together with their fellow car workers in Coventry and local ancillary industries, render both B.B.C. and A.T.V. Midland news broadcasts inexpressibly boring and irritating with their interminable strikes.

Escaping around the fringe of this hotbed of internal combustion and shop stewards' hot air, the Rea flows between Northfield and King's Norton, two of the medieval manors ultimately absorbed into Birmingham, each with its church.

The mills farther down the Rea were an important part of local economy, so safeguards were necessary to keep the wheels turning when the cutting of canals threatened to upset the distribution of water. The companies promoting the Worcester and Birmingham Canal and other canals 150 years ago had to construct reservoirs at Wychall and Lifford on the Rea, and at Harborne on its tributary, the Bourn Brook, in order to conserve water. Beside Lifford Reservoir the Rea is a pleasant tree-embowered stream. A bridge crosses the river to Lifford Hall, now a chemical manufacturer's canteen, but 200 years ago the house of James Hewitt, who became Lord Chancellor of Ireland and took the title of Viscount Lifford of Lifford in Donegal. Thus this town on the River Foyle, near the border with Northern Ireland, shares its name with a house, a reservoir, and a district on Birmingham's River Rea. John Dobbs, the engineer who worked on the Worcester and Birmingham Canal near by, was a later resident at Lifford Hall.

On past Hazelwell Mills and through the district of Selly Park, the Rea receives its major tributary, the Bourn Brook, where the

Pebble Mill of olden times has given place to Birmingham Zoo. The Bourn Brook has skirted the city's campus quarter overlooked by the Chamberlain Tower of the University of Birmingham. Near by rises the clock tower of the justly famed Queen Elizabeth Hospital, and King Edward's School, which moved from the city centre in 1936 to temporary quarters which were burned down that same year, and, after dispersal for four years, into the new buildings in 1940.

The Bourn Brook has also trickled below the site of some Roman forts in the campus complex, while its tributary, the Stonehouse Brook—which gives a name to the Stonehouse Gang, one of Birmingham's prouder achievements in boys' club work—has made close acquaintance with Birmingham's 'principal ancient monument', Weoley Castle. The place-name Weoley derives from the Old English for a wood or a clearing with a heathen temple, and in 1264 Roger de Somery was granted a licence to fortify and crenellate his manor house of Weoley, and to enclose it with a stone wall and moat—from the Stonehouse Brook. In the mid-seventeenth century some particulars in a sale document described Weoley as a ruined castle. Excavations were begun on the site in 1932 by the King Edward's School Archaeological Society and some Birmingham University students under the supervision of the Birmingham Archaeological Society, and with the blessing of the Corporation. Among the lesser finds was an abundance of oyster shells, suggesting speedy communications from Colchester or Bristol along the Watling Street or Ryknield Street.

Pebble Mill Road, remembered as Birmingham's first short stretch of dual carriageway with a central tramway reservation, is the site of the new B.B.C. Midlands headquarters. The Pebble Mill or King's Mill stood on the Bourn Brook near its junction with the River Rea. It played a part in the first industrial process to be mechanised in England, the fulling of woollen cloth by mallets driven by a water-wheel instead of the treading of the cloth in a bath of detergent by human 'walkers'. In 1557 John Kynge, a Birmingham fuller, bequeathed his son Roger "half my indenture and terms of one fullynge mill in Edgbaston; he to have full liberty to occupy and cullar cloth in my dyynge house". Roger also inherited Over Mill near by on the Chad Brook, where remains of it are still to be seen below Edgbaston Pool in the grounds of Edgbaston Golf Club. From being a fulling mill, Pebble Mill became later a blade mill and a corn mill, and it was occupied in 1890 by Henry Harrison, a dairyman.

Less than half a mile down the Rea from the confluence with the Bourn Brook stood the manorial mill of Edgbaston, and its old mill house still survives at the Tally Ho Tennis Club. First mentioned in 1284 as the result of a burglary, it underwent the usual vicissitudes of the Rea mills, being a corn mill for several tenants in the nineteenth century, until in 1880 John Drew moved his business from there to Ward End Mill on the River Tame to manufacture his "celebrated self-raising flour". One more mill remained on the Rea in the old Manor of Edgbaston—Speedwell or Carpenter's Mill—both names are retained in present-day roads. A map of 1816 shows there to have been a windmill adjacent to the watermill, and in 1823 the occupier was William Fox, who used Speedwell Mill as a rolling mill. Fox then had a works in New Street, Birmingham, employing 250 workers and said to be the largest of its kind in England. These rolling mills were capable of drawing "a piece of round iron three yards long into wire to the amazing extent of seven miles". Princess Road was built over the filled-in millpool of Speedwell Mill at a period of the nineteenth century given away by the names of neighbouring roads—Varna Road, after the Bulgarian Black Sea port used by the Allies in the Crimean War, and Alexandra Road, a compliment to the Danish princess who became the bride of Edward VII in 1863 when he was Prince of Wales.

Between the sites of Pebble Mill and Edgbaston Mill the Rea runs with Queen's Drive alongside Birmingham's most important public park, Cannon Hill Park, and here lorries conveniently dump snow in the river after the occasional blizzards when Birmingham motorists blame the Public Works Department for the difficulties they create for themselves by taking their cars out in such conditions.

Cannon Hill Park was given to the city by Louisa Ann Ryland, a millionairess who remained true to a youthful love and died a spinster in 1889. The Ryland family has given more names to Birmingham streets than most of the city's great families. The first Ryland to make much impact on Birmingham was John, who lived towards the end of the eighteenth century in Baskerville House, Easy Hill—forerunner of Easy Row. Of him, contemporary historian William Hutton wrote that he "had done more public business than any other within my knowledge, and not only without reward, but without a fault". John Ryland found his private business ventures more rewarding. He also married a wealthy heiress, Martha Ruston, and though his home was burned down during the Priestley Riots because he was a Unitarian, he was able to leave a considerable fortune to his only son, Samuel. Martha's maiden name is perpetuated in Ruston Street, next to Ryland Street off Broad Street.

Samuel Ryland married Anne Pemberton, daughter of Samuel Pemberton of 'The Laurels', Edgbaston, a house which became Edgbaston High School for Girls. Their only child was Louisa Ann Ryland, born on 17th January 1814, in Birmingham. The family moved to 'The Priory', Warwick, while Louisa was a girl, but when the Great Western Railway was cut through his grounds Samuel Ryland bought the Sherbourne estate south of Warwick, where he lived like a country gentleman at a house called 'Barford Hill'. He had great ambitions for Louisa of marriage into a titled family. He was thought to be in favour of Lord Brooke, but Louisa had made her own choice—Mr. Henry Smith, of whom it was written by J. Thackray Bunce, historian of the Corporation of Birmingham, that he was deserving of honoured remembrance in Birmingham for "the eminent services he rendered to local government in promoting, and afterwards, as Mayor (1851–52) in executing, the Improvement Act". Henry loved Louisa, but her father's opposition proved insuperable, and he married Maria Louisa Phipson, a relation of the Rylands.

Louisa Ryland remained faithful to Smith, and, though at Samuel Ryland's death in 1843 she was left more than £1 million, she never married, living at Barford Hill with her companion, Charlotte Randell, and making many gifts to her native Birmingham. In 1875 she gave Cannon Hill Park, laying it out at her own cost and refusing to allow it to be called Ryland Park—the same modesty being behind her refusal to allow a statue to be erected to her. In 1879 she gave Victoria Park, Small Heath, with £4,000 towards the cost of laying it out. She bequeathed £25,000 to the General Hospital in Steelhouse Lane, gave £10,000 towards the Midland Institute, and £10,000 to augment the salaries of teachers at the School of Art. What she did anonymously will never be known. Her benefactions to churches included a reredos at St. John's, Sparkhill, and in 1864 she rebuilt Sherbourne Church, where she now lies beside her old companion. Charlotte died in 1882, aged 88; Louisa on 28th January 1889, aged 75.

Faithful unto death, Louisa Ryland left her huge fortune to the son of the man she had loved all her life, on condition that he adopted the surname of Ryland. So Charles Alston Smith, born in 1859 to Henry and Maria Smith, became Charles Alston Smith-Ryland. Today, his grandson, Alderman Charles Smith-Ryland, Chairman of Warwickshire County Council, still lives at Barford Hill as squire of Sherbourne. Names from the Sherbourne Estate were duplicated on Ryland property in the Ladywood area of Birmingham, where streets are named after Northbrook Farm, Marroway Farm, Coplow Hill, Morville, and Sherbourne. Names from the family are perpetuated in several Ryland roads and streets: Alston Street, and in Sparkhill, in Ivor, Phipson, Dennis, Evelyn, Adria, Esme, and Doris roads, while even the old school of the wealthy Smith-Rylands is among them in Eton Road.

Reconstructed in Cannon Hill Park is one of Birmingham's oldest buildings, the fifteenth-century Golden Lion Inn, which stood where today a screw factory stands in Deritend.

Leaving the park behind, the Rea skirts Warwickshire County Cricket ground. The river was, in fact, the accepted boundary between Warwickshire and Worcestershire for cricket qualification purposes until 1954, although it had not been the actual county boundary since the Local Government Act of 1888. So for a batsman to have cleared the Rea from Edgbaston County Ground before 1954 was to have hit the ball out of Warwickshire and into Worcestershire cricket territory.

"One massive shot across the Rea is still recalled with bated breath," I was told by Mr. Leslie Deakin, secretary of Warwickshire County Cricket Club. "In 1932, during the first Indian tour, one of their batsmen, C. K. Nayudu, hit a leg break from Jarrett across the Rea and 80 yards up the sports field beyond the river—a wonderful stroke accomplished with all the grace of a very tall Indian."

Barely out of range of such hard hitters of a cricket ball, the
Rea moves into Birmingham's notorious Balsall Heath and
Lower Edgbaston, long the city's 'red lamp' area, more lately the
home of a large proportion of Birmingham's coloured population. Victorian houses, which were seedy theatrical lodgings in the
days of 'The Hippodrome', 'The Empire', 'The Grand', 'The
Prince of Wales', the Theatre Royal, and 'Bordesley Palace', became teeming warrens of immigrants, coloured and Irish, where
it was not unknown for the same bed to have a night-time
occupant who worked days and a daytime occupant who worked
nights. The bulldozers have now moved in over much of this
area.

Only a few doors from Edward Road bridge, where the Rea
becomes the dividing line between the grass of Calthorpe Park
and the grit of its 'black patch', a terraced dwelling-house long
did duty as a mosque, mainly for Birmingham Moslems from
Aden until they moved into more commodious quarters. Alongside the Rea in Belgrave Road, at a house named after his favourite seaside resort, 'St. Ives', one of Birmingham's most colourful
characters lived until his death in 1959. Percy Shurmer was a
laughable replacement in 1945 for Leopold Amery as M.P. for the
Sparkbrook Division. He was nevertheless a man who gave un-
stintingly of his time in local and national politics, and he was not
above going out with a broom and sweeping Belgrave Road
when he thought that Birmingham Corporation was falling down
on the litter problem. The 'Shurmer's Sparrows' organisation
gave many a poor child his only visit to the country between the
wars, and appropriately 'Our Percy' himself had much of the
pertness of a sparrow about him.

Birmingham has several Indian and Pakistani cinemas, among
them 'The Triangle' in Gooch Street, built almost above the
Rea. Not half a mile downstream, little Apollo Row preserves the
name of a stately pleasure dome of former days. Early last century,
when the "lively-tripping Rea" was fringed by meadows, cherry
orchards, and parkland which came up to the backs of houses in
Bradford Street so that residents could feed the deer from their
gardens, boats hired at Deritend bridge were rowed upstream to
"the lovely sequestered and elegant gardens of the Apollo House
in Moseley Street". If the pleasure-seekers turned instead down-

stream from Deritend it was to Vauxhall Gardens, where teas were served at the riverside in an area now intensely industrial, with railway sidings and gasworks where once the nightingale sang. Gone is all but the written memory of this sylvan stream.

Just upstream of Cannon Hill Park the Rea has been impounded in a brick channel, and so it remains to its confluence with the Tame at Salford Bridge. This part of the river is the creation of an Act of Parliament of 1929 which authorised the spending of £1,900,000 on improvements. Building encroachment on the river meant a quicker influx of storm water because a built-up area is waterproof. It also ruled out widening. So the channel had to be deepened, and this meant starting in the River Tame at Curdworth Bridge, five miles downstream of the point where the Rea enters the Tame. By 1939 Cannon Hill Park was reached— around the position of the old Pebble Mill. From this channel many firms extract water for cooling and other industrial pur- poses. The Sewers and Rivers Section of Birmingham Public Works Department is justly proud that so little pollution gets into the Rea. Some 95 per cent of Birmingham's trade effluent runs into sewers.

Rowing upstream to Apollo House, the trippers of a century and a half ago would soon pass on their right the head race to the Town Mill at a place named Vaughton's Hole, remembered today in Vaughton Street. The manorial mill, as the name Mill Lane still denotes, was around the position of Digbeth bus station, while Moat Lane, just uphill of Mill Lane, recalls the site of the moat surrounding the Manor House of Birmingham. The moat was fed by springs and overflowed into the Rea. With a lease of Town Mill to Joseph Farmer in 1728 went permission to divert this overflow into his millpool every third week to sup- plement the flow from the Rea via Vaughton's Hole. In 1816 a "delightful garden" was advertised for sale in the avenue from Deritend Brewery to Vaughton's Hole "with no probability of ever being disturbed for building". Alas, many of the buildings that gave the lie to this boast are now themselves being de- molished to make way for others.

There were, of course, considerable problems when a number of mills shared the same river, and William Hutton, the Birmingham historian, tells of one instance in 1756 when he accompanied

Will Ryland to a Mr. Horton at Duddeston Rolling Mill to have some silver rolled: "Cooper came in from Heath Mill, full of sweat and wrath, and blamed Horton in severe terms for not drawing the gates, it being a flood, declaring he had lost a guinea an hour. 'I am glad,' says Horton, 'you have so profitable a trade. I will turn my works into a corn mill.'"

Just across the Rea from the mill in Deritend was the church of St. John the Baptist. To it in the opening years of the sixteenth century went a little boy whose father was a lorimer near by. He was also a pupil at the grammar school maintained by the Gild of St. John before Edward VI founded his grammar school in Birmingham; went later to Cambridge, and became a priest. With William Tyndale and John Frith he translated the Bible into the English version known as the 'Matthew Bible'. He was also associated with Bishop Ridley and Bishop Latimer, and in 1554, like all four of them, he was burned at the stake by Mary Tudor—Birmingham's martyr, John Rogers. Today two small plaques on the wall of a screw factory commemorate both John Rogers and the Church of St. John the Baptist, which was demolished in 1947.

Through all the changes in Deritend, this "pretty streete called Dirtey", according to John Leland, topographer to Henry VIII, this focal point of Birmingham's growth, one building has stood since 1348, the quaint timbered Old Crown Inn. Between it and the Rea for many years, until a move recently to Banbury, was the works of Alfred Bird and Sons Ltd., which continued to make a custard powder first prepared by a chemist, Alfred Bird, in 1837, without eggs because his wife had a weak digestion. Also in his chemist shop, beneath the old Market Hall in Bell Street, Bird made a baking powder without yeast, thus enabling British troops in the Crimea to eat fresh bread.

The street name Stone Yard almost beside the Rea is a reminder that, to this spot in the 1880s came Walter Frederick Bannocks with his newly established business as a marble, granite, and slate mason. Little could he have known that his successors in the firm of W. F. Bannocks (Senr.) Ltd. of Hall Green, Birmingham, would be changing the face of Birmingham three-quarters of a century later. When the architects had designed the new Birmingham and the builders had constructed it, in came Bannocks with their marble 'cladding' to put a polished sheen on the façades of hotels, banks, office blocks, the Bull Ring Shopping Centre—even the walls of the underpasses—and, with true Birmingham business magnanimity, what they could do for their own city they have also done for towns and cities from Newcastle upon Tyne to Newquay in Cornwall.

From Deritend the Rea runs in its brick channel through the sombre surroundings of Vauxhall and Duddeston, close neighbour of gasworks and marshalling yards, to its confluence with the even murkier River Tame, which has come down from Bescott Junction by way of Wednesbury Forge, West Bromwich Sewage Works, and Handsworth Golf Club from its twin sources at Monmore Green, Wolverhampton, and Titford Pool, Oldbury. At the time of writing the projected course of the M6 Motorway through Birmingham runs slap across the junction of these two rivers, with half a mile to go to one of the most diabolical road planning upheavals that even Birmingham has suffered—the Gravelly Hill complex at Salford Bridge.

It is the fate of each generation to suffer that posterity shall benefit—and how Birmingham has suffered from the planners since the war. Even so, much of the 'plandalism' has been intended, rightly or wrongly, in the interest of the citizens. The M6 horror lacks even this justification. Birmingham has been torn asunder that traffic from everywhere else may thunder through the suburbs. To Birmingham citizens this Gravelly Hill intersection has been for long a barrier, surmountable only by those with the strongest nerves or the weakest sensibilities, a labyrinth penetrable only by drivers with the fortitude of Theseus, so that many who might previously have driven to Sutton Park, for instance, now recoil at the Gravelly Hill earthquake, and, having survived their first brush with it, resolve never again to pass that way. Far from facilitating driving, these monstrous traffic islands—nay, archipelagoes—with their teeming link roads, act as a wall or a moat surrounding the city and imprisoning its people. More and more as we come face to face with new enormities perpetrated since last we drove that particular way, do the older generations of Birmingham drivers turn sorrowfully back home.

Having accepted the Rea, the River Tame flows eastward

alongside Fort Dunlop, Birmingham's 'tyre town'. When John
Boyd Dunlop of Belfast took out a patent in July 1888 for his
new inflatable rubber tyre it was first produced in a Dublin
factory. The prospectus described it as "indispensable for ladies
and persons with delicate nerves", and it proved so popular that
the Dublin factory was soon inadequate. So a move was made to
Coventry, centre of the cycle industry, but these premises, too,
were outgrown and another move brought the pneumatic tyre
to Aston Cross, Birmingham. Finally, in 1916, when large-scale
expansion became necessary, 400 acres were purchased at Erdington, and there today Fort Dunlop employs its thousands.

Across the Tame from this massive factory the streets of
Bromford Bridge Estate, named after famous racehorses, are a
reminder that this was the site of Birmingham's Bromford Bridge
racecourse. The Tame flows out of the city boundary beneath the
cold unfriendly residential skyscrapers of Castle Vale Estate,
rising from what was once Castle Bromwich aerodrome.

Here, too, from 1920 to 1957, between the aerodrome and the
river, the permanent site of the British Industries Fair grew from
two acres to sixty. Birmingham Chamber of Commerce launched
the enterprise, maintained it, and ran it at a profit. Ultimately the
huge exhibition buildings were demolished to make way for
Castle Vale housing, but by 1970 Birmingham was casting greedy
eyes on a section of the green belt between Elmdon and Stonebridge on which the President of the Board of Trade had granted
the city permission to build a National Exhibition Centre.

This, then, is how modern Birmingham works—an insatiable
monster preying on the green fields surrounding it, and excreting
brick, concrete, and tarmac in its wake.

II

THE MEDIEVAL MANORS

BIRMINGHAM is a classic Saxon name—the 'ham' or home of the
'ing' or tribe, or family, of the Berms, and its early pronunciation
approximated to the modern slang term 'Brummagem'.

After the Conquest, William Fitzansculf was given Dudley
Castle, and he granted the manors of Aston, Edgbaston, Erdington, Handsworth, Selly Oak, Witton, and Birmingham to certain
of his vassals. In the mid-twelfth century the Manor of
Birmingham came to Peter de Bermingham, whose family was
to hold it for 400 years.

In Domesday Book Birmingham rated only four hides; its
other particulars being: "There is land for six ploughs. In the
demesne is one, and there are five villeins and four bordars with
two ploughs. Woodland half a league long, and two furlongs
broad. It was, and is, worth 20 shillings." Of the surrounding
manors, Selly Oak, Erdington, and Aston—today all parts of
Birmingham—had bigger populations and larger assessments.
Aston—the east town—was not east of Birmingham, being in
fact to northward. Aston was east either of Saxon Wednesbury
or of the Ryknield Street, and in Domesday Book it was assessed
at five times the value of Birmingham and had five times the
population.

Yet by 1550 Aston was Aston-juxta-Birmingham, the name by
which it is still described in its parish church guide book.
Birmingham was obviously growing in importance. A church had
been built—the forerunner of the parish church of St. Martin.
In 1166 a market had been granted to Peter de Bermingham for
the sale of livestock, and in 1251 Henry III granted William de

Bermingham the right to hold a Whitsun Fair. This William was killed fighting against Henry for Simon de Montfort in 1265. His forfeited estates were restored to his son, another William, who in 1309 proved that his ancestors levied tolls in a market they ran in Birmingham before Hastings.

In 1536 Edward de Bermingham, having probably been 'framed' by John Dudley, later Duke of Northumberland, was declared a felon and deprived by Act of Parliament of the Manor of Birmingham, which remained under the Crown for nine years until it went in 1545 to Lord Lisle, Lord Admiral to Henry VIII. A short eight years later Lisle, now Duke of Northumberland himself, was executed for high treason as sponsor of the unhappy nine-days' queen, Lady Jane Grey. After two more years under the Crown, the Manor of Birmingham was acquired by the Marrow family, who were Lords of Berkswell, near by in Warwickshire. From them it descended to the Musgraves, though by the early sixteenth century the manor house, uphill from the Rea, stood dilapidated and unoccupied in the shadow of St. Martin's, now a larger sandstone church of thirteenth-century construction.

When Leland visited Birmingham in 1538 he approached from the south, and would have been traversing the parish of Aston in the hamlet of Bordesley and until he crossed the Rea, for Aston circled eastward of Birmingham, and even in the nineteenth century it had a gaol in Bordesley behind the Brown Lion Inn. The gaol, consisting only of two cellars, was known as 'Brownell's Hole' after W. D. Brownell, the gaoler, whose wife Jemima kept the inn. Not until 1911 was Aston annexed to the City of Birmingham.

Back from the road on his left Leland had the birch plantation which gave Birchall Street its name, and proceeding down Deritend he would have passed the 'Old Leather Bottle' hostelry and continued between the Golden Lion Inn on his left and the Crown House, "a mansion house of tymber", on his right, its gardens extending to the River Rea. Passing the "propper chappell" of St. John's and the Gild Grammar School, he forded the Rea beside the bridge maintained by the Gild of the Holy Cross.

The Birmingham he entered had up to 1,500 inhabitants living in 200 or so houses in half a dozen streets. He wrote: "The beauty

The late fifteenth-century Golden Lion Inn
St. Nicolas Church above the village green at King's Norton

of Birmingham, a good market towne in the extreame parts of
Warwickshire, is one street going up alonge almost from the left
ripe of the brooke, up a meane (not very steep) hill, by the length
of a quarter of a mile." No doubt he remembered as he wrote the
pungent odour of the tanneries as he crossed the river from the
tanyards where Digbeth Institute now stands. Oak bark from
the Forest of Arden combined with Rea water to determine the
position of Tanners Row, and one factor in the early abandon-
ment of the manor house could have been its proximity to this
odour. On the left was the manorial mill, owned at the time by
William Ascrick, a man of sufficient consequence for Elizabeth,
widow of Edward de Bermingham, to take him as her third
husband.

Among the meaner sheds, barns, and lean-to workshops
lining the road and clangorous with the trade of the smiths were
the more spacious houses of the mercers, gabled and lavishly
decorated like the Old Tripe House, which endured almost to the
end of the nineteenth century. There were two more taverns in
Digbeth, the 'White Harte' and the 'Redd Lyon'. At the point
where Digbeth Police Station today rears its white minaret,
Well Street, named after a spring there, commenced in Tudor
days. To the left of it, going uphill, was the decayed manor house,
its moat overgrown with weeds, and some distance farther westward, also moated, the rectory. The buildings in Digbeth and
Well Street constituted just a strip either side of the road. Behind
those on the left the Holme Park bordered manor house and
rectory, while the Little Park stretched on the right, though one
needs a well-developed imagination to conjure the earlier sylvan
scene out of the modern Park Street, dark beneath the bridges
which carry the railway to Moor Street Station.

Moor Street, parallel then, and until recently, with Park Street,
was the home until his death in 1525 of William Lench, founder
of the Trust to repair bridges, maintain roads, and relieve the
poor, and Lench's Trust Almshouses are an honoured institution
in the city today.

Birmingham's parish church, St. Martin's, as it stood in
Leland's day, was the late-thirteenth-century building which replaced an earlier Norman church. The fabric was wearing badly
when Leland saw it; in 1690 it was encased in red brick, all but

c

'Farm', Sparkbrook

the spire, and in 1781 this was rebuilt by John Cheshire. Between 1873 and 1875 the entire building was demolished and rebuilt with the exception of the tower and spire, and a certain amount of restoration was necessary after German bombing in 1941. Through all these vicissitudes four recumbent stone figures have held a place in the church. One of them, variously described as a William de Bermingham who fought in the French Wars for Edward I and another William who was a friend of Edward II, is probably the oldest thing fashioned by the hands of man in Birmingham. The others are thought to be members of the de Bermingham family, though without any inscriptions and their identities uncertain they have nothing but antiquity to commend them, except William's shield with its bend dexter of five lozenges which is incorporated in the city arms today.

The clutter of houses and shops around St. Martin's was thicker in Tudor times than today, and no doubt the market booths even overflowed into the church. The narrow street winding round the west end of the church testified to local trade as Mercer Street, sometime Spicer Street, and eventually Spiceal Street. The continuation of Well Street past the east end of St. Martin's was Corn Cheaping, notorious for its noisome shambles, the domain of butchers, which extended right up the Bull Ring— as we knew it recently; knew it and, I think, loved it between the wars, with flower stalls on market days, and railway horses from Moor Street and Curzon Street clattering up the cobbles. As sixteenth-century Corn Cheaping it ended at its junction with High Street, where New Street came in at the Tollbooth, the seat of the town administration and of the court. Hereabouts was the Market Cross, usually a lively scene as countrywomen came in to sell their eggs and dairy produce around it.

The Tollbooth or Toll House was the headquarters of the Court Leet, and though its high and low bailiffs, headborough, con-stable, flesh conner, ale taster, and others operated from there, it was the leather sealer after whom it became known as the Leather Hall. An arched gateway led into New Street, where the old Gild Hall had become the new Free Grammar School of Edward VI—"our pious founder and benefactor" in the school prayer known to countless Edwardians of later years. New Street was but little developed, though it stretched, as it does today, as far as

Paradise Close and Udwall Lane, now the Paradise Street and Pinfold Street area.

From the Tollbooth, High Street extended for its present length to the Welch Cross, beyond which sheepfolds stretched along what is now Dale End, where a country road ran out towards Coleshill. To the south from Welch Cross a little street ran barely 100 yards to Molle or Moor Street. It bore an unusual name— God's Carte Lane—because it housed the cart on which the sacraments were taken to St. Martin's, though some say this cart was merely used as a stage for religious drama. Whatever the origin of the name, it has now become the less cumbersome Carrs Lane.

The twentieth-century Bull Street was known in Elizabethan times as Chapel Street after the chapel of St. Thomas Priory, near the present Friends Meeting House, though the Old Bull Tavern, from which the later name derived, was already there. Prior's Conigree Lane, now Steelhouse Lane, set the northern bounds to Birmingham with its westward extension now known as Colmore Row.

Surrounding Birmingham in the sixteenth century were a number of manors and parishes subsequently to be taken over. To northward lay Handsworth, with its hamlet of Perry Barr; to eastward Aston, extending as far as Water Orton and including the township of Erdington along with Bordesley, Saltley, Duddeston, and Nechells. Continuing clockwise around Birmingham were Yardley, King's Norton, Northfield, and Harborne.

The manor house of Handsworth was originally Hamstead Hall, called also Wyrleys from the family of that name who were lords of the manor. The hall stood close to Hamstead Mill on the Tame, where Frank Andrews was still grinding corn by water-power in 1920. Demolished in the late eighteenth century, the old hall was replaced by a new one, itself pulled down to make way for housing in the 1930s. Perry Hall, Erdington Hall, and Pype Hall are three other manor houses that have gone. The last of these stood on the corner of Bromford Lane and Kingsbury Road, and was known as Wood End House when it was taken down in 1932. Pype Hayes Hall, which still survives in Pype Hayes Park, was part of a quite separate estate connected mainly with the Bagot family—whose coat-of-arms with its goats embellishes the sign of the 'Bagot Arms' opposite the park. The hall itself dates only from the first half of the seventeenth century.

In Aston Hall, now a museum and art gallery, Birmingham retains an architectural jewel in Jacobean style, once the manor house of the lords of the Manor of Aston. An inscription above the door puts the visitor in the picture before he even crosses the threshold of the hall. Building, it explains, was begun in 1618 by Sir Thomas Holte, knighted as one of the delegates who welcomed James VI of Scotland to the English throne in 1603 and created a baronet in 1612—a dignity which meant he had to maintain thirty soldiers in Ulster at a cost of £1,000. Sir Thomas moved into Aston Hall in 1631 and completed the building in 1635.

Of all the Holtes whose portraits hang at Aston Sir Thomas is the dominant figure, and nowhere more than in the kitchen with its splendid spit and unwieldy box mangle, for it was in his previous kitchen at Duddeston Manor that Sir Thomas was said in 1606 to have split his cook's head with a cleaver, so that one half fell on his left shoulder and one on his right. Though Sir Thomas won a libel suit concerning this, when he added the badge of baronetcy, the Red Hand of Ulster, to his coat-of-arms, there were those who said it represented his own hand, bloody from the deed.

In 1624 Sir Thomas violently opposed the marriage of his heir, Edward, to Elizabeth King, daughter of the Bishop of London, and, though Charles I intervened on the side of the couple, Sir Thomas was still opposed to his son when Edward died in 1643 at the siege of Oxford. December of that year brought Aston Hall's most exciting episode when Birmingham Cromwellians attacked it for three days before Sir Thomas and his Royalist garrison gave in. He was heavily fined and imprisoned by the Commonwealth party, twelve of the defenders were killed in the fight, and damage from cannon balls to the balustrade of the great staircase is today a visual reminder of the engagement.

Sir Thomas had fifteen children by his first wife, Grace Bradbourne—Grace abounding—and none by his second, Anne Littleton of Pillaton, near Penkridge. The story is only legendary that Anne disliked one of her step-daughters and persuaded Sir

Thomas to lock her up until she went mad. Mr. Ronald Healey, supervisor of Aston Hall, told me: "This daughter is supposed to be our ghost, the White Lady. I have been here thirty years, but I have never seen her. My outstanding memory is of the grace and beauty added to the Long Gallery by Princess Alexandra when she had tea there in 1958."

Princess Alexandra is not the only royalty to have visited Aston Hall. Charles I slept there two nights in 1642 just before the Battle of Edgehill, and today King Charles's Room with his bed is directly off the Great Drawing Room. Queen Victoria declared the hall and grounds open to the public by the Aston Hall and Park Company in 1858, and she was not amused when, in 1863, a 'female Blondin' fell to her death there from a tightrope during a money-raising fête. The Queen's disapproval, and her shock that the place she had inaugurated was not yet paid for, jerked Birmingham Corporation into paying off the remaining £19,000 in 1864.

A frieze of animals in the entrance hall at Aston includes a prominent elephant, the crest of the family of James Watt, inventor of the steam engine, whose son, the younger James, leased Aston Hall in 1818. For all its visual charm and faithful reproduction of periods in its history, Aston Hall comes most alive through the people who have lived there—plus one who merely hangs on the wall of the Great Drawing Room, the intriguing Elizabeth, Lady Monson, daughter of Sir George Reresby. A verse in gold incorporated in the frame of her portrait begins:

> Did not a certain lady whip,
> Of late her husband's own lordship?

Seemingly she "Ty'd him naked to a bedpost", and "clawed him with fundamental blows"—an exhibition having much in common with modern films, but arising, I understand, from a conflict of political loyalties.

One way and another, poor William, Viscount Monson, had a rough passage—and maybe he deserved it, being partly instrumental in the execution of Charles I. He was stripped of his honours at the Restoration, and drawn on a sledge by ropes round his neck from the Tower to Tyburn and back before being imprisoned in the Tower for life.

Sir Thomas Holte died in 1654. Because his estranged eldest son, Edward, and all his other sons had pre-deceased him, he was succeeded by his grandson, Robert, who became an M.P.—and a prisoner in the Fleet debtor's prison. Nevertheless, the first of his two marriages, to Jane Brereton of Brereton Hall, Cheshire, brought this property to the Holtes in 1722. Meantime, the third baronet, Sir Charles, had restored the family fortunes, while his daughter, Mary, was stitching the famous hangings and the carpet bearing the Holte arms.

The fourth baronet, Sir Cloberry Holte, married a Barbara Lister, of whom he later wrote: "She is seldom at home, or satisfied when she is there." So he left her only £10. She married again, and Sir Cloberry's mother thought her a bad influence, allowing her to spend only two weeks each year with her sons at Aston. Despite three marriages, the elder of these sons, Sir Lister Holte, remained childless, and the succession passed to his brother Charles, the sixth and last baronet, who never lived at Aston Hall, as his wife and Lister's widow, Sarah, were always at logger-heads.

Sir Charles had only one daughter, Mary Elizabeth, and no sons, so the direct Holte line died. Mary married Abraham Bracebridge of Atherstone, and on a bedside table in the Victoria Room at Aston Hall—with its tantalising glimpse of a corner of the playing pitch at Villa Park—is a copy of Washington Irving's *Bracebridge Hall*. The American writer often stayed in Birmingham with his relatives, the Van Warts, and *Bracebridge Hall* is partly inspired by Aston Hall. The break-up of the Holte estates is a complicated business, arising from Abraham Bracebridge's failure in the soap trade and a partition of the estates in several counties to satisfy his creditors and Sir Lister's legatees, including the Legge family—the Earls of Dartmouth—and the Digbys of Meriden.

In 1818 a Warwick banking firm, Messrs. Greenway, Greaves, and Whitehead, bought Aston Hall and leased it to James Watt, who lived there until he died in 1848. In that year most of the 300 acres of surrounding parkland was sold for building, and the remainder of a herd of deer dispersed. Afterwards Birmingham Corporation began to take an interest in the hall and what was left of the park. So the Holte line has ended, and today their mansion re-echoes to the hurrying feet of schoolchildren pursuing social studies. But I believe the Holte crest has lived on and become widely known in the Midlands, though none suspect its origin. This is the squirrel trademark of Ansell's Brewery—a more recent Aston landmark than the hall—acquired in 1934 by Ansell's along with Holt's Brewery of Aston, who used it on their seal as long ago as 1896, though they were not related to the Holtes.

The parish of Yardley, previously a rural district of Worcestershire, but acquired under the Greater Birmingham Act of 1911, brought to the city at least three old buildings of outstanding interest which survive to this day. Yardley Parish Church, dedicated to the Saxon princess St. Edburgha, standing where some unremembered missionary preached to a Saxon community in a clearing of the Forest of Arden, incorporates work of the thirteenth, fourteenth, and fifteenth centuries, during the last of which its western tower was added with a tall spire visible from far out in Warwickshire. In the exterior spandrels above the north aisle door are carved a Tudor rose and a pomegranate, testifying to a sad but eminent lady, Katherine of Aragon, who once held the Manor of Yardley. It was given to her in 1533 by King Henry VIII, who had discarded her as a wife in favour of Anne Boleyn. The rose is his emblem, the pomegranate that of the Spanish city of Granada, whence Katherine came to England to marry Henry's elder brother, Arthur, Prince of Wales. In the north aisle is a window to the Rev. William Sutherns, last of the Yardley Trust schoolmasters who taught down the centuries in the schoolroom depicted in the window, which still stands south of the churchyard, retaining its original fifteenth-century roof with massive trusses.

Memorials to the Hays and the Ests in the Gilbey Chapel of Yardley Church introduce us to three families who lived nearly two miles distant at Hay Hall beside the River Cole, in what is now the Tyseley industrial area. Come there, to the works of Reynolds Tube Co. Ltd. Every day you see, without realising it, some of the company's butted frame tubes, forks, and stays on countless bicycles. Every time you pass under the electricity grid cables you can look up and see the short transverse cable spacers, made by this firm. One of their products you are not likely to

encounter is the oxygen bottle that went to the summit of Everest
with Hillary and Tensing, and still lies on that mountain. Ships'
masts and jackstaffs, office furniture, road shelter frames, hurdles,
refrigerating components, flagpoles, de-icing devices out on the
nose of aircraft—Reynolds tubes are used in them all. Squirrel
poles for destroying the nests of the grey squirrel, balancing poles
for circus performers; these are among the less expected of their
products. Cars, aircraft, and marine engineering; guided missiles;
the latest industrial and scientific development looks to the firm
for components.

Yet, preserved in the modern Tyseley factory is an old manor
house, Hay Hall, probably built by one Robert de la Hay around
1300. Its oak roof-trusses and other structural features bear close
resemblance to other Warwickshire buildings of the period,
notably the Guild Hall at Henley-in-Arden. In early Tudor days
Hay Hall was re-shaped to an 'H' design, and the other major
addition, around 1790, was a Georgian frontage, now tastefully
decorated with flowers in season and with sufficient trees to constitute a green oasis in an industrial desert. The interior originally
had the Great Hall of its day, and though this is now divided into
a number of rooms, the mullioned windows, huge open fireplace,
and roof-trusses enable us to envisage that medieval hall. Though
a modern wooden staircase has been installed in what was the
original entrance hall, there are still low corridors and lintels to
interior doors, and, as part of Hay Hall is used as a kitchen, the
appetising odours evoke pictures of the hall as once it was. On a
first-floor landing a modern showcase and an ancient museum
collection make incongruous neighbours, the museum containing
relics unearthed in Hay Hall. From the fabric come wattle sticks
of hazel and a portion of stained window glass of Tudor times.
Still showing signs of its 1939–45 black-out paint, this bears the
initials A.E. linked by a tasselled cord design.

It is likely that this glass commemorated the wedding of Anne
Gibbons and Edward Est, to whose family Hay Hall was transferred with the last of the de la Hays, Marion, in 1423, when she
married Thomas Est, Governor of Kenilworth Castle. Anne and
Edward became man and wife about 1538, and the design which
entwines their initials is identical with one binding the W.S. on
a signet ring of Shakespeare's. Among other exhibits in the

museum case are a glass bottle 300 years old, hand-made nails and chains and old knife blades, while beside them is the showcase of modern aluminium alloy products.

Three of Yardley's bells send us on a shorter journey of only a quarter of a mile from the church to an Elizabethan black-and-white timbered house, Blakesley Hall, built by Richard Small-brooke, whose family is remembered in the name of Smallbrook Ringway in the city centre. The bells were given in 1638 by Aylmer Folliott, who lived in the hall—he also bequeathed his "best hatt" to the vicar. In 1935 Blakesley Hall was restored by Birmingham Corporation and opened as a museum, with special emphasis on archaeology and local history. One now defunct industry that originated in Birmingham is recalled in exhibits of objects made from the papier mâché for which Henry Clay took out a patent in 1772, his first step to a fortune from the new process. The long eighteenth-century barn houses the collection of ancient fire-fighting appliances—the Tozer collection, after the dynasty of Birmingham fire chiefs.

Continuing clockwise from Yardley round the ancient manors on the outer perimeter of Birmingham we come to King's Norton, where the king was lord of the manor, thus giving a name to Kingswood, a district on the Alcester Road mentioned in the Subsidy Rolls of 1275. Soon after this date Roger Mortimer, Earl of March, enclosed an area there with a dyke and charged some landowners with trespass when they destroyed it. King Edward III subsequently supported them against Mortimer. In 1633 when the Manor of King's Norton had reverted to the Queen, Henrietta Maria the wife of Charles I, she met violent opposition from the tenants as she tried to enclose 669 acres on common land. Kingswood, offered them as compensation, was, they said, so full of trees as to be useless. Today Kingswood has given its name to a tower block of flats on the Druids Heath Estate.

Westward of this new municipal estate, which will fall into place in a later chapter, we come to King's Norton 'village'—with a much more authentic village atmosphere than Acocks Green, Selly Oak, Moseley, and Erdington, which still retain the term for their central points. The Rea valley gives King's Norton an identity of its own, dividing it sharply from Cotteridge so that the lofty fifteenth-century spire forms a focal point for everything on its own bank of the insignificant river. A triangular village green with lime trees, the black-and-white 'Bull's Head', and the sign of an earlier 'Saracen's Head' still preserved on the verger's house, all picturesque in themselves, are enhanced immeasurably as a group by St. Nicolas Church and the heavenward aspiration of its spire.

Even more charming off the north-east corner of the church is the former grammar school with its timbered upper section. The building defies accurate dating, though the school probably originated in 1344, when Edward III signed letters patent licensing one William Paas to bestow a house and lands on a chantry of the Virgin Mary. In the reign of Henry VIII Henry Saunders was paid an annual stipend of £10 as schoolmaster, and with the help of John Peart, as usher at £5 a year, he taught 120 pupils. Numbered among them was probably the village Dick Whittington —a son of a nailer, Robert Avenon or Avenant—who walked to London, prospered, and became Lord Mayor, being eventually knighted by Queen Elizabeth.

During the Stuart period King's Norton Church and School had a notable Puritan divine as minister and master, the Rev. Thomas Hall. His scholars came from distant regions, many going on to university. The student hooliganism of the 1960s is not entirely new, and Thomas Hall suffered regularly from the traditional barring-out of schoolmasters by pupils, having his teeth broken in one fracas. He would have found other targets for his pamphleteering today, for in addition to tilting against maypoles he attacked "the loathsomeness of long hair" in men, as worn by the Royalists.

The school continued as such with varying degrees of fortune, until the formation of school boards under the Education Act of 1870 brought education into the sphere of local government, and King's Norton School closed in 1875, the endowment being used for the benefit of boys attending the public elementary school. A gift from the Pilgrim Trust enabled the thorough restoration of the old building in 1951, and it is now an ancient monument, a museum of sorts, and the meeting place of various societies.

Over the centuries the boys of King's Norton School witnessed some turbulent occasions. From 1616 to 1623 the minister at the church was one Nathaniel Bradshaw, a sturdy opponent of ale-drinking during hours set aside for worship, so that he reported certain publicans and their customers to the Worcester Diocesan Ecclesiastical Court. By way of reprisal he was attacked and his house sacked. One of his principal assailants, George Middlemore, a local landowner, also molested Bradshaw's successor, Tobias Gyles, who was schoolmaster as well as minister. Gyles was something of an absentee, often in London, and discipline among his pupils suffered in consequence. So one October morning in 1625 Middlemore and others broke into the school, wielding staves and cudgels, intending to evict Gyles—but he was absent. Thus began a feud against the reverend schoolmaster which Middlemore prosecuted for four years, even unsuccessfully petitioning the Lord Treasurer to suspend his stipend, and swearing, "I will spend £500, but I will weary him out."

Gyles did eventually lose his job in the school, though he remained curate, until, having composed his quarrel with Middlemore, he married that gentleman's son, Robert, clandestinely at midnight in Hazelwell Hall to Eleanor Fox, a Moseley heiress, and was duly suspended from his curacy.

King's Norton always had something of a toping tradition, particularly on May Day in the seventeenth century. A framed poem entitled "The New Bell Wake" hangs in the church and celebrates the hanging of a new treble bell in 1783 or 1826. One verse runs:

> They drank, too, at a furious rate
> And nearly spent their store;
> Twopence was all left on the plate
> And they could raise no more.
> The warden coming, just in time,
> Behaved them fair and well,
> They gave a shout when he turned out
> Two shillings for each bell.

The village green was the venue for an annual mop fair which, in the 1880s, was described as "the King's Norton Saturnalia" by a newspaper, which reported:

> Hardly a man or woman with any pretensions to self-respect could be seen at the Mop last Monday, and the thousands were composed of

shouting hobbledehoys, screaming girls, drunken men, and shouting women. They swarmed from the station in hundreds during the day, and as night drew on the crushing, the swearing, created indescribable confusion. . . . The public houses were packed and customers had to fight their way in and out, treading on floors wet with slopped beer. Some disgraceful scenes took place in one part or another of the vicinity during the day and night. The general proceedings offered a spectacle of debauchery, drunkenness, noise, and blasphemy.

Several personal and place-names well known in Birmingham appear on monuments in King's Norton Church. After the date, in July 1588, of the death of Humphrey Littleton's wife had been inscribed on her tomb a space was left for his ultimate date. It remains blank, for on his death in 1624 Humphrey was buried at Naunton Beauchamp, near Pershore. The Littletons lived at Grovely, which has given its name to Grovely Lane running down from West Heath to the Austin Works.

The recumbent effigies of Sir Richard and Dame Anne Greves of Moseley Hall lie on an altar tomb at the base of the tower. High Sheriff of Worcester in 1609, and at his death in 1632 Deputy Lieutenant to James I in Wales, Sir Richard owned a large area of south Birmingham. By the end of the eighteenth century the family had met with disaster, its last representative, a labourer in a gravel pit, being carried to a pauper's grave from a house he rented for 1s. 3d. a week in Edgbaston Street.

Above the baptistry the Ests of Yardley occur again in the memorial to Sarah Est, who died in 1725, "second wife of the late Henry Est of Slade Pool, who was buried among a great number of his ancestors at Yardley in 1721".

Industry came to agricultural King's Norton with the Worcester and Birmingham Canal, and by 1881 the population of the parish exceeded 34,000, spread about 40 square miles from Balsall Heath to Wythall. In 1911 King's Norton was annexed to Birmingham and became part of Warwickshire along with Northfield, with which and Beoley parish it had been constituted an urban district in 1898.

In and around Birmingham are several boulders brought down by glacial action from the Arenig region of North Wales. Cannon Hill Park has one, another gave its name to Gilbertstone Avenue, Yardley; there is one in Olton Park, and one on the roadside at Bell Heath, just south of Romsley Hill in Worcester-shire. A fifth gives its name to the Great Stone Inn at Northfield, for it is preserved in the village pound adjacent to the pub. Across the road in this intriguing little backwater is St. Laurence's Church. This was the centre of old Northfield, but a secondary settlement sprang up on the Bristol Road, and by 1840 was larger than the original village. Bournville, Bartley Green, and Weoley Castle were all part of Northfield, and large council estates have blanketed the agricultural land of Allen's Cross running up towards the prominent clump of Frankley Beeches.

A Domesday reference to a priest ministering to the Saxon inhabitants of "Nordfeld" is not paralleled by any record of a church at that date, and St. Laurence's was built in the thirteenth and fourteenth centuries in the Early English and Decorated styles of the period, though the base of the tower is probably Norman.

Birmingham is a down-to-earth place. So many of its wealthy families have had such recent and close connection with industry that they tend towards ostentation rather than old-fashioned snobbery. One of the few snobbish manifestations in the city is the pronunciation of 'Edg-bar-ston' for 'Edg-bass-ton' in the name of the modish suburb of bygone days. It began in Domesday Book as Celboldestone and progressed as Edgboldeston (1160), Egboldston (1184), and Eggesbaston (1503). The first comprehens-ible link with the Birmingham of today was the marriage of Isabel, last of her line and heiress of Sir Richard de Edgbaston, to Thomas Middlemore, with whose descendants the manor was to remain for 300 years. Legend has it that during the absence of Sir Richard at the Scottish Wars of the fourteenth century Middle-more rode to Edgbaston to pay court to Isabel, arriving in the nick of time to save her from robbers who were attacking her in the woods around Edgbaston Hall. E. Marston Rudland tells the story in his *Ballads of Old Birmingham*, finishing with the wedding of Thomas and Isabel:

> And the goodly fief of Edgbaston
> With the fief of the Middlemore's is one.

In 1500 Richard Middlemore added a north aisle to the small chapel known to have stood near Edgbaston Hall in 1340, and his widow Margerie added the tower. Their son, Humphrey, a Carthusian monk, suffered martyrdom in 1535, a victim of the anti-Romish zeal of Bluebeard Henry VIII. A window in the south aisle depicts the building of the tower and Humphrey being led to execution.

During the Civil War the Richard Middlemore of the day was a Royalist and papist, so Edgbaston Hall was sequestrated in 1644 and occupied by Colonel John Fox, a tinker from Walsall, who marched in with sixteen men, soon to be reinforced by 200 Birmingham metal workers. They stripped the roof from the church to fortify the hall and melted down the lead for bullets. After the Restoration of the Stuarts the Middlemores were again in favour, and in 1683 Royal Patents were granted for collecting money throughout the Midland counties for the rebuilding of Edgbaston Church. But with the end of the Stuarts, and amid the rejoicing at the coming of William of Orange in 1688, the Birmingham mob burned down Edgbaston Hall lest it become a sanctuary for Roman Catholics. Mary Middlemore, granddaughter of Richard, had married Sir John Gage, and one of their two daughters, Bridget, married Thomas Belasyse, Viscount Fauconberg. In 1717 they sold the Manor of Edgbaston to Sir Richard Gough, who rebuilt Edgbaston Hall and later put the church in perfect repair. His descendants became the Calthorpes, who remained Lords of Edgbaston, though from 1786 to 1791 the new hall was the home of Dr. William Withering, a founder of the General Hospital in Birmingham. Sir James Smith, the first Lord Mayor of Birmingham, lived at Edgbaston Hall from 1908 to 1932, it subsequently becoming the club house of Edgbaston Golf Club.

Edgbaston Church, dedicated to St. Bartholemew, who appears gaunt beneath his fig tree in a new west window, continued to undergo alterations after the 1725 restoration by Sir Richard Gough, and in 1885 descendants of the former lords of the manor, the brothers William, Richard, and James Middlemore, built the present chancel.

Alongside several memorials to the Goughs and the Calthorpes is one to Dr. Gabriel de Lys, exiled from France as a child, and founder of Birmingham Deaf and Dumb Institution; and another to Henry Porter, whose widow, Sarah, married Dr.

Samuel Johnson, the lexicographer. Near a yew tree in the western end of the churchyard lies Joseph Henry Shorthouse (1834–1903), the Birmingham author of the famous historical novel *John Inglesant*. Edgbaston Church has its mystery—the seeming 777 carved in an oval above the north entrance presumably in the post-Civil War restoration. Conjecture associates this with a capital M for Middlemore, either there badly worn before Fox's desecration and copied blindly by the restoring masons, or an M carved there by them, of which only the deep strokes have remained.

III

SECOND CITY

In the middle of the eighteenth century Aaron Atkin, a sawmaker, set out from Sheffield to walk to Birmingham. Accompanying him, each carrying the tools of his trade, were his three sons: Alfred Amos, also a sawmaker; Edwin, a joiner's toolmaker; and George, a planemaker. Reaching Birmingham, the Atkins set up as sawmakers, acquired a rival's premises in Ludgate Hill, and prospered. Though the workshop moved several times, there was always an Atkin in the business until 1949, when it was bought by Arthur Woodward Bayley, though the original name still adorns the present Bradford Street façade—"Atkin, Sawmaker, Est. 1760."

One other Birmingham firm in December 1969 claimed on its frontage, where Charlotte Street runs out of St. Paul's Square, to have been established in 1760—the refinery of John Betts and Sons Ltd. The founder of the firm, Alexander Betts, also came from Sheffield, and in 1969, when a move was contemplated from the original site, Mr. John Betts, the seventh generation from the founder, was chairman and managing director, while his sons, Christopher and Stephen, make an eighth generation in the refinery.

John Betts and Sons Ltd. is the oldest firm in Birmingham still in the hands of the founding family. Alexander Betts came to Birmingham just as the jewellery trade was assuming importance, and he and his son John, who became an alderman on Birmingham's first town council, built up their business on dust—the sweepings from the floors of countless jewellers' workshops, from which the refinery recovered any particle of precious metal,

48

together with the 'lemels' or fine filings of gold and silver—from the French 'limer', to file. This is now a mere 10 per cent of Betts's business, most of the remainder being the recovery of silver from photographic paper, X-ray plates, and photographers' solutions.

Aaron Atkin and John Betts were not the only immigrants into this boom town of the mid-eighteenth century. The Mecca of ambitious men from far and wide, Birmingham was becoming self-conscious, taking stock of itself in frequent surveys, maps, and plans. In 1720 the population was only 11,400, living in 1,900 houses. When Bradford made his survey in 1750 there were 4,058 houses and 23,688 people. At the time of Hanson's "Plan of Birmingham" in 1778, 42,250 people lived in 7,200 houses, and by 1785 the first 50,000 was passed—52,250 in 9,500 houses. The Census of 1801 showed 15,630 domiciles with a population of 73,630 stepping confidently into the nineteenth century. This was not entirely a natural increase. It owed something to the Atkins and the Betts, incomers from several parts of England during a century when Birmingham was aptly described as "a haven of economic freedom", and if there was a large proportion of incomers among the ultimately successful men it is surely because those who would seek a new environment in days when travel was so difficult were obviously more ambitious and determined than most.

Samuel Timmins summed up the appeal of Birmingham in a "Report on the Industrial History of Birmingham" arising from the meeting of the British Association in the town in 1865:

During the 17th and 18th centuries the progress of Birmingham manufactures was simply marvellous. Our town seemed to have the power of attracting within its boundaries artisans of every trade and every degree of skill. Although not situated on any of the great highways of the land, it was near enough to be easily accessible. It awarded almost perfect freedom to all who chose to come. Dissenters and Quakers and heretics of all sorts were welcomed and undisturbed so far as their religious observances were concerned. No trade unions, no trade gilds, no companies existed, and every man was free to come and go, to found or to follow or to leave a trade just as he chose. The system of apprenticeship was only partially known, and Birmingham became emphatically the town of 'free trade', where

D

Saturday afternoon in Handsworth Park
Saturday afternoon at Cadbury's, Bournville

practically no restrictions, commercial or municipal, were known. Coal and iron were easily obtainable from the growing mines and iron works of Staffordshire, and every facility was afforded by such proximities, and by the numerous water mills and the central position of the town, for the rapid extension of the hardware trades.

Two "Plans of Birmingham", W. Westley's in 1731 and Hanson's in 1778, span a trebling of the population. Both maps show almost identical ribbon development down Digbeth and Deritend, with Park Street still the limit of building eastward from the town centre, and Edgbaston Street and Smallbrook Street the southward boundaries west of St. Martin's; but Hanson's map shows the development of Hill Street, Princes Street, Navigation Street, and Swallow Street to Paradise Row west of the line of Dudley Street and Pinfold Street on the 1731 map. It also shows the beginnings of Bradford Street, named after Henry Bradford, where in 1767 land was offered gratis to anyone desirous of establishing trade there, those who could not afford a stone building being allowed to have a wooden shed or a single room for up to 2s. a week.

The major development, however, was downhill from Colmore Row towards St. Paul's Church, though stopping short at Lionel Street, but continuing across Snow Hill between Bath Street and Steelhouse Lane where Slaney Street and Weaman Street, laid out by 1731, were built up by 1778. In Steelhouse Lane Samuel Garbett was refining metals with the aid of sulphuric acid, while iron from Sweden came in as the raw material for Kettle's Steel Houses, from which the thoroughfare was named. These occupied the site where the General Hospital was later to rise, a monument to Dr. John Ash, whose estate was developed as the fashionable Ashted after he left Birmingham in 1788.

Upper Priory ran down from Steelhouse Lane to the site of the thirteenth-century priory, developed in the eighteenth century as Old Square by John Pemberton, the wealthy ironmonger who was descended from Roger Pemberton, a Birmingham goldsmith of the sixteenth century. Among the occupants of the sixteen select residences surrounding a central garden in the square were Henry Bradford, Edmund Hector the bookseller, friend of Dr.

Samuel Johnson, and Sampson Lloyd, the banker—third of that name.

In a warehouse in Upper Priory the unlucky genius John Wyatt was perfecting around 1750 an invention which sent him often to the pawnshop and eventually to a debtor's prison, though it earned a fortune and a knighthood for Richard Arkwright—the spinning machine. Born in 1700 at Weeford, near Lichfield, the eldest of eight brothers, Wyatt grew up a carpenter; but around 1730 he attracted attention outside Weeford when trying to develop a machine for cutting files. A Birmingham gunsmith, Richard Heeley, advanced money against ownership of the completed machine, but lost his rights when unable to continue financing the inventor.

Wyatt's next collaborator was a Lewis Paul of London, but within a year the machine had reverted again to Wyatt when finances dried up, and he dropped the idea. Next came his ill-fated spinning machine. In a shed near Sutton Coldfield Wyatt spun the first thread of cotton yarn produced by mechanical means, and around 1744 he set his spinning engine to work under the motive power of two or more donkeys walking round an axis in the Upper Priory warehouse. Unfortunately the patent for the spinning machine was in the name of Wyatt's old partner, Lewis Paul, who had again become his backer, and, having no financial interest in it, Wyatt took employment with Matthew Boulton.

Lightning conductors and lathes were among the fruits of Wyatt's inventive genius. In 1749–50 he made four 'fire extinguishing' machines for Birmingham, but his particular contribution was his compound-lever weighbridge. Arising from the need to weigh iron as well as the wood used in smelting it, his plans were already forming while he was in prison for debts incurred with his spinning machine. At the Birmingham Department of Weights and Measures they have a model of his original weighbridge in Snow Hill—the 'Town Machine', as it was known, installed by the Overseers of the Parish of Birmingham. By drawing a cart on to a platform it transformed the weighing of heavy loads from the cumbersome steelyard method, which necessitated lifting cart and contents in chains. Installed in 1741 outside Birmingham Workhouse it brought Snow Hill a 'first' in the

world, to which was added forty years later another 'first', when
Richard Ketley, proprietor of the Golden Cross Inn just below
Bath Street, founded the first known building society in Britain.

Wyatt's weighbridges were installed far and wide, and Avery's
still continue to make weighbridges at the Soho Foundry, 60
feet and more in length, and with up to 400 tons capacity, as
against the 10 feet and 6 tons capacity of the Snow Hill original,
though the first significant departure from Wyatt's principles
was Avery's modern system of recording the weights electronic-
ally.

If Arkwright got the knighthood really earned by Wyatt's
spinning machine, two knighthoods were bestowed on descendants of Wyatt's seven brothers, one of whom, Jeffrey Wyatt,
architect to George IV, transformed Windsor Castle from a
medieval fortress into the grand country house we know today.

John Wyatt died on 29th November 1766 and was buried in
the graveyard of Birmingham's new church, St. Philip's, in the
shadow of the newly built Blue Coat School, now Regent House,
where his headstone can still be seen.

Westley's "East Prospect of Birmingham", dated 1732, shows
St. Philip's as the dominant one of a trio of outstanding structures
—St. Martin's spire, and the tower of the Free Grammar School in
New Street, while his "South-West Prospect" throws into
prominence, to the right of St. Philip's, the tall stately buildings
of Temple Row, which got its name from a pigeon loft known
as the Temple near the top of Needless Alley. To the left of the
new church stands the Colmore mansion, New Hall.

With St. Martin's the only Established Church for a population of 15,000, an additional church became necessary at the
beginning of the eighteenth century. Four acres of "Mr. Phillips'
barley close", sometimes known as Horse Close, were conveyed
to the Church Commissioners, and between 1711 and 1715 one
William Shakespeare built a church to the design of Thomas
Archer of Umberslade Hall, Hockley Heath, near Birmingham.
Dedicated to St. Philip after the donor of the land, Robert
Phillips of Newton Regis in the north of Warwickshire, the
church nowhere commemorates the saint in glass, stone, woodwork, or embroidery. Originally built of non-durable sandstone
from Rowington, the church had to be refaced with harder

sandstone from Hollington, Staffordshire, in the 1860s. Birmingham people, apologetic for so uninteresting a cathedral—it can be 'done' in fifteen minutes—take comfort in St. Philip's having been built not as a cathedral but as a parish church, though St. Nicholas, Leicester, also a parish church become cathedral, kept me for six solid hours packed with interest on my first visit.

When William Hutton, the Birmingham historian, first saw the assembly shown on Wesley's "Prospects" he said: "I was delighted with its appearance and thought it the pride of the place. If we assemble the beauties of the edifice; the spacious area of the churchyard ornamented with walks in great perfection, shaded with trees in double and treble ranks, and surrounded with buildings in elegant taste, perhaps its equal cannot be found in the British dominions." Alas, St. Philips' idyllic environment is no more. The cathedral stands today on an island of guano, its trees frosted at all seasons with the droppings of the starlings and pigeons, and reeking to high heaven, particularly after rain, when the noisome pathways become slippery and hazardous in the extreme.

The tower of St. Philip's was still under construction after the consecration, and in 1723, at the suggestion of Sir Richard Gough of Edgbaston, George I gave £600 towards the completion of the fabric. For his good offices the boar's head crest of the Goughs is featured on the weather vane instead of a cock. The church being completed, we may as well follow its subsequent fortunes here.

Birmingham was in the diocese of Coventry and Lichfield until 1836, when St. Philip's parish was transferred to Worcester diocese, but in 1888 the Bishop of Worcester suggested that Birmingham become a separate ecclesiastical entity. Though this did not mature, a suffragen bishopric of Coventry was created with special responsibility for Birmingham. With the preferment of Dr. Charles Gore to Worcester in 1902 the possibility of Birmingham becoming a separate diocese was again discussed, and in a letter to *The Times* Canon Freer, a considerable property owner in the town, offered £10,000 towards this. Gore matched the gesture with his own offer of £10,000 plus £800 annually from his stipend at Worcester. In 1904 Joseph Chamberlain sponsored the Birmingham Bishopric Bill on the undertaking that Gore was appointed bishop. The Bill became law, Gore was appointed and enthroned in St. Philip's on St. Chad's Day, 1905. Under him the new bishopric prospered, and when he was translated to Oxford in 1912 he had the rare experience of seeing a statue raised in his own lifetime outside the west door of St. Philip's.

One of the few items of interest in St. Philip's is the State Flag of Maryland, U.S.A., presented to Bishop Hamilton Baines, Rector of Birmingham, in 1922. In 1696 Dr. Thomas Bray, Rector of Sheldon—now within the city—was assigned to assist the young church in Maryland, and to help in this work he founded the Society for the Propagation of Christian Knowledge in 1698. Two years later he came back to England convinced that a further society was essential to supply missionaries for overseas, and, with the sympathy of William and Mary, then on the throne, the Society for the Propagation of the Gospel was founded. It is inevitable that some typical Burne-Jones consumptives should be incorporated in St. Philip's, in the east window. The artist, Sir Edward Burne-Jones, was born barely 100 yards distant in Bennetts Hill and christened in the church.

When Leland entered Birmingham in 1538 he found cutlers, nailers, smiths, and lorimers in the town of Tudor days. Three hundred years later, in 1845, another traveller entering Birmingham for the first time, Hugh Miller, the Scottish geologist, wrote:

> The sun had set ere I entered Birmingham through a long low suburb, in which all the houses seemed to have been built during the last twenty years. Particularly tame-looking houses they are; and I had begun to lower my expectations to the level of a flat, mediocre, three-mile city of brick, a sort of manufactory in general, with offices attached, when the coach drove up through New Street, and I caught a glimpse of the Town Hall, a noble building of Anglesea marble, of which Athens in its best days might not have been ashamed. The whole street is a fine one. I saw the lamps lighting up under a stately new edifice, the Grammar School of King Edward the Sixth, which . . . bears the mediaeval stamp: still farther on I could descry, through the darkening twilight, a Roman looking building that rises over the market place; and so I inferred that the humble brick of Birmingham represents merely the business necessities of the place: and that, when on any occasion its taste comes to be displayed, it comes to be a not worse taste than that shown by its neighbours.

Thus Miller appraised King Edward's School, designed by Charles Barry, completed in 1833, and demolished in 1936; our noble town hall, part copy of the Temple of Jupiter Stator in Rome, completed by John Hansom in 1833, the year before he registered his idea of the Patent Safety Cab; and the Market Hall with its imposing Doric columns, opened in 1835 and destroyed by German bombs in 1940.

It was a noise that particularly intrigued Miller:

> what seemed to be somewhat irregular platoon firing, volley after volley, with the most persistent deliberation. The sounds came, I was told, from the proofing-house—an iron-lined building in which the gunsmith tests his musket barrels . . . Birmingham produces on the average a musket per minute, night and day . . . it besides furnishes the army with swords, the navy with its cutlasses and pistols, and the busy writers of the day with their steel pens by the hundredweight and the ton, and thus it labours to deserve its name of the Great Toy Shop of Britain by fashioning toys in abundance for the two most serious games of the day, the game of war, and the game of opinion making.

In the latter part of the eighteenth century Edmund Burke had described Birmingham as "the toy-shop of Europe". A toy has come today to have special reference to a child's plaything, but in the past it had the wider significance of something of an amusing or trifling kind even for an adult. Birmingham's toy trade anticipated its jewellery trade and embraced such showy items as brooches, watch-chains, bracelets, and even the buckles which were so staple a product of Birmingham manufacture.

Leland's lorimers had moved to Walsall, his nailers to Dudley, Stourbridge, and the Bromsgrove area, and his cutlers to Sheffield. Even the last of the smiths had gone from Digbeth, John Roberts, a considerable character who had three wives and twenty-eight children, the last three by his third wife whom he married when he was nearly 80. Digbeth Institute now occupies the site of his forge.

In place of these skills, Birmingham had developed the skills of its gunsmiths into a major industry. The story is told that when William III bemoaned his having to depend on Holland for the Army's supply of guns, Sir Richard Newdigate, the M.P. for Warwickshire, told him: "Sire, there are men in my constituency who can meet Your Majesty's requirements." Soon the Birmingham gunmakers were the Government's leading suppliers of muskets, and in 1767 Sketchley's Directory of Birmingham listed sixty-two workshops engaged in making guns and analogous trades. The gunmaking area was Steelhouse Lane, Whittall Street, St. Mary's Row, and Weaman Street, where Samuel Galton had a proof-house for barrel testing in his own works. On 16th March 1814 Birmingham Proof House was opened in Banbury Street at a time when the local gun trade was booming through the Napoleonic Wars to such an extent that Birmingham was known as 'the small arms arsenal of the world'.

In the Proof House Birmingham now had the equivalent in the gun trade of what the Birmingham Assay Office had been to the precious metal trades since its inception in Little Cannon Street in 1773. Matthew Boulton was the first manufacturer to use it, and the seventy varieties of ware hallmarked for him in the initial list are evidence of the vast range of operations at Soho Foundry. The Assay Office took up its present quarters in Newhall Street in 1893. Its hallmark is an anchor, and it is by far the largest of the six assay offices in Britain.

The expression 'a Brummagem button' to describe a native sprang from one of the town's major manufactures. In 1755 John Taylor's button factory was second only in size to the Soho Foundry among local works, employing 500 in producing buttons to the value of £800 a week. Taylor rose from being an artisan to become High Sheriff of Warwickshire. Not only did he give the world the gilt button; in partnership with Sampson Lloyd II, he also founded Birmingham's first bank. Taylor's gilt button made a timely appearance just as the shoe buckle was giving way to laces, thus keeping up the rate of employment.

Boom town conditions meant considerable changes in the pattern of Birmingham life. More workshops were being built; existing ones expanded, and the increasing army of artisans had to be housed. So the old spacious estates were broken up, among them the Colmore Estate, to make way for the workaday streets between Colmore Row and the jewellery quarter, and bounded west and east by Easy Row and Livery Street, which when it was constructed in 1745 was the longest street in Birmingham, thus giving rise to a local saying which has endured over 200 years: "A face as long as Livery Street".

The Colmores originated at Tournai in France, and acquired some of their New Hall Estate and other property in Birmingham as a land speculation on the dissolution of the Priory or Hospital of St. Thomas of Canterbury in 1536. In Tudor times a William Colmore, a governor of the Free School who also created a dole for the poor of Birmingham, was a mercer with business premises at 1 High Street on the corner of Molle Street, as Moor Street was then known. From there their land extended to Tanter Fields, otherwise The Butts, where the yeomen practised archery—nowadays Stafford Street. The family crest of a moor's head was a rebus, a heraldic pun. The moor obviously referred to 'more', while the 'col' came from the moor's neck (French 'col'). So it is not impossible that Moor Street got its name from the crest of the family in the corner house.

Colmore Row, one of Birmingham's major thoroughfares, takes its name from the family, as does Colmore Street on the family's Bell Barn Estate, but an excursion into the history of the Colmores reveals the origin of a much less obvious group of street names. William Colmore, the mercer, had two sons, Ambrose and William, who added considerable areas to the family possessions. Either William junior or his son built New Hall, north of Colmore Row as we know it, from which a fine avenue of elms led down the route of what is now Newhall Street to the house. The parkland of the New Hall Estate stretched from our present Sand Pits to Livery Street and was bounded on the north by the Carver family estate, hence Carver Street, Hockley, while Water Street is on the site of a large pool which drained both estates.

A third William Colmore became a colonel in the Parliamentary forces during the Civil War, when he was prominent in the defence of Coventry. A directory of 1781 listed several Colmores in Birmingham—Henry, painter and pawnbroker in Digbeth; Stephen, grocer in Digbeth; Joseph, gardener in Deritend; and, of the old family, Thomas, merchant of Edgbaston Street; Samuel, plater of Digbeth; and John, at 1 High Street, now a hosier and hatter.

The succession of William Colmores continued with two more at Warwick, where they are buried in St. Mary's, with the family arms of three golden crescents on their gravestones. The second

of these had four sons, Thomas, Charles, George, and Edmund.
Thomas, born in 1689, married in 1717 the young widow of
Isaac Milner, a wealthy London merchant, and became himself a
wealthy London merchant. Charles, the second son, settled in
London, and two years after his brother's wedding with Milner's
widow he married her daughter, also Ann Milner. Meanwhile
Thomas and his wife had possessed themselves of £13,000
belonging to the children of Isaac Milner. Ann the younger thus
began a suit for its recovery, as a result of which Thomas had to
relinquish to his young sister-in-law his entire interest in the
Colmore Estate, retaining only an annuity for himself and his
wife.

After they had had three children—William, who died young,
Charles, and Richard—Charles senior died before Ann, but she
was an able representative of the family. In 1747 a private Act of
Parliament gave her the right to cut up her estates and to grant
building leases. In the development that followed, the thoroughfare which had been Bull Lane, Mount Pleasant, and New Hall
Lane, was renamed Ann Street (from the modern Newhall
Street westward) and Colmore Row. Edmund Street (from
Broad Street corner only as far as Newhall Street) was named
after the Rev. Dr. Edmund Colmore, Ann's brother-in-law,
the youngest of her husband's brothers. Great Charles Street,
named after Ann's heir, had earlier been called Great George
Street after another of her brothers-in-law. Her husband was
commemorated in Little Charles Street, now no more, which ran
slightly north of the line of the ultimate extension of Edmund
Street to Livery Street.

Charles Colmore succeeded to the estates while his mother,
Ann, was alive, and she retired to Bath on an annuity. In 1764
there was trouble when an attempt was made to close a footpath
through the grounds of New Hall, the 'rougher element' breaking
down the gate, though law-abiding citizens offered a reward of
five guineas for the discovery of those responsible. This trouble
apart, the Colmore estates were always developed in conformity
with the needs of the people of Birmingham. Charles gave the
site of St. Paul's churchyard and a vicarage in 1768, plus £1,000
towards the building of the church. Later a site was given for
St. Thomas Church in Bath Row.

The man who gave his name to Great Charles Street died in 1794 and lies buried at Hendon, Middlesex. He and his wife, Mary Gulston, had four children, all of whom died unmarried, three being remembered in street names in Birmingham's jewellery quarter: Lionel Street, Mary Ann Street, and Caroline Street.

His eldest son, Charles, having died in 1785, and Mary Ann dying in April 1794, Charles Colmore added a codicil to his will stipulating that should Lionel and Caroline die without issue, his estates were to go to his "dear friend", Francis, Lord Hertford, of Ragley Hall, Alcester, or his son, Lord Yarmouth. With Lionel's death in March 1807, Caroline inherited the entire estate, and in 1825 when it appeared unlikely she would marry, she applied for aid from the Court of Chancery to realise large sums of money. In 1829 the remainder of the estate was divided between her and Francis Charles, the third Marquess of Hertford, the grandson of her father's "dear friend". Caroline Colmore lived at Cheltenham, where she died in 1837, aged 70, to be buried at Charlton Kings on the outskirts of the Gloucestershire spa. She had settled her estate on her friend Frind Cregoe on the understanding, usual in such cases, that he adopted the name of Colmore. Cregoe came of an old Cornish family and lent his name to Cregoe Street on the Colmore's Bell Barn Estate—now the newly planned Lea Bank.

Frind Cregoe-Colmore lived only two years longer than his benefactress, and like her he is buried at Charlton Kings with his wife Elizabeth and their son and heir Colmore Frind Cregoe-Colmore. This son married twice and had four children. His heir, William Barwick Cregoe-Colmore, was born in 1860, and Barwick Street behind the Grand Hotel, which closed in 1969, is named after him. It is pronounced Barrick.

In 1857 the site of the present Council House in Victoria Square was sold by his father for £33,000. When in the 1890s an extension to the Council House became necessary, terms were arranged for a 99-year lease, but the Colmore Estate generously gave a 999-year lease instead. Meanwhile, in 1889, the estate gave a quarter of an acre near the Council House for the School of Art, following this with £1,000 for the extension of the school. Cornwall Street and Margaret Street enclose the School of Art, the one named after the Cregoe family's county of origin, the other after Mrs. Margaret Alice Radcliffe, a daughter of Colmore Frind Cregoe-Colmore. William Barwick Cregoe-Colmore died in 1918 and, to meet the death duties, much of the property on the Bell Barn and Oozells estates was sold on terms favourable to the tenants.

William was a bachelor, and his estate, property, and investments were divided in equal thirds between his sisters, Mrs Margaret Radcliffe, a Mrs. Roche, and a Mrs. Adams. Today the income from these estates so intimately associated with the growth of Birmingham goes far afield. The Roche share goes to their successors, the Eustace-Duckett family in Ireland; the Radcliffe share to a Colonel Radcliffe in Rhodesia; and the Adams share to the Trevor family in Argentina.

Suffolk Street, to the west of the Colmore city centre estate, and Norfolk Road in Edgbaston are two street names which show how far flung were the estates of Birmingham's landed gentry. When, in 1788, Sir Henry Gough of Edgbaston Hall inherited the estates of his uncle, Sir Henry Calthorpe, he did the decent thing and tacked the avuncular surname on to his own, becoming Gough-Calthorpe. Eight years later he was ennobled as Baron Calthorpe of Calthorpe in the County of Norfolk. In due course the county name was bestowed on the Edgbaston road. The Calthorpes lapped over into Suffolk, Ampton Road and Pakenham Road in Edgbaston being named after villages on their land north of Bury St. Edmunds, and Suffolk Street after the county. Elvetham Road, Edgbaston, takes its name from another of their seats, Elvetham Hall at Elvetham in the north of Hampshire.

Another great family brought Suffolk names to parts of Edgbaston which they owned. The Gooch family seat, Benacre Hall, and the village where it stands, Wrentham, south of Lowestoft, have given names to Benacre Street and Wrentham Street off Bristol Street, while Gooch Street runs close to them. The street map of Edgbaston has been said to resemble the genealogical tree of the Gough-Calthorpes. The first of the family in Birmingham was Sir Henry Gough, who bought Perry Hall in 1669, and whose forefathers back through Tudor times were wealthy wool merchants in Wolverhampton, and lords of the manor of Old-fallings.

Sir Henry had sixteen children. He also had a younger brother, Richard, an eminent East India merchant who was knighted by George I and who in 1717 bought for £25,000 the lordship of Edgbaston from Bridget, Lady Fauconberg, co-heiress of the Middlemore Estate. Four times Sir Richard Gough made the journey to China and India, taking as his secretary on one of the voyages 11-year-old Harry, sixth son of Sir Henry. This infant prodigy stayed in the East and prospered to such good effect that when his uncle bought the Edgbaston lordship he was able himself to pay £13,600 for the remainder of the Middlemore Estate, including land in Ladywood and a 25-acre farm where Gough Street now runs into Suffolk Street near the new Holloway Circus.

On his part of the Middlemore Estate Sir Richard rebuilt Edgbaston Hall in 1717–18. Edgbaston parish then consisted of some sixty scattered houses and farms, and, as was so often the case, the farmers left their names in the new roads when their land was developed. Such names in the Edgbaston area are Harrison's Road, Wheeley's Road, and Pritchatt's Road. Sir Richard was succeeded by his son Henry, who was created a baronet, and took as his second wife Barbara Calthorpe, only daughter of Reynolds Calthorpe of Elvetham. It was their son, Henry, who inherited his uncle's estates in 1788, and became the first Lord Calthorpe. Both he and his father preserved the residential quality of Edgbaston by refusing to allow the building of factories along the Worcester–Birmingham Canal through their territory.

Henry, Lord Calthorpe, married Frances Carpenter, daughter and co-heiress to General Benjamin Carpenter—hence Carpenter Road, Edgbaston, where Sir Harry's Road already commemorated Lord Calthorpe's father. After their marriage Henry and Frances left Edgbaston Hall and the family never lived there again, though their names began to appear in the new roads of the neighbourhood. By 1835 George Road, running near Calthorpe Road off Islington Row, was named in honour of the third Lord Calthorpe, who carried the Gold Spurs at the Coronation of George IV. His brother, Frederick, gives his name to Frederick Road, parallel with the other two. He married, in 1823, Lady

Charlotte Somerset, eldest daughter of the sixth Duke of Beaufort, so after Frederick became the fourth Lord Calthorpe in 1851, Edgbaston came by Charlotte Road and Beaufort Road in 1855, with Duchess Road in honour of Charlotte's mother. It was from the Beaufort marriage that the Calthorpes got the Fitzroy which has figured ever since in the names of one branch of the family, and which is now perpetuated in Fitzroy Avenue, Harborne, where Hamilton Avenue comes from the same branch, and Balden Road is named after Mr. E. H. Balden, the Calthorpe Estate agent until the mid-1920s. Blakeney Avenue is a place-name from the Calthorpe's Norfolk estate.

Frederick and Charlotte had six daughters and four sons, through three of whom the title descended. We are indebted to the sixth baron for giving his Christian name, Augustus, to a road in Edgbaston, and even more indebted for his withholding his other name, Cholmondeley. John Somerset, the seventh Baron Calthorpe, gave his name to Somerset Road. In 1845 he obtained a royal licence to discontinue for himself alone the surname and arms of Calthorpe and to be known only as Gough. Arthur Road, leading from Edgbaston Hall to Wheeley's Road, was named after George Arthur, second son of Frederick and Charlotte, who died aged 16 and was the only one of their four sons not to hold the title.

While these members of the nobility were giving their names to Edgbaston's aristocratic thoroughfares, the Gooch family names were being bestowed in and around St. Luke's parish on streets destined to house the poorer working classes. The family traces its Suffolk lineage back to the sixteenth century, the baronetcy commencing in 1746 with William Gooch, a bonny fighter in Queen Anne's wars, who became Governor of Virginia in 1727. He was succeeded by his brother, Thomas, Bishop of Ely, who married three times, his first wife being Mary Sherlock, daughter of a Dean of St. Paul's and sister of Thomas Sherlock, Bishop of London.

By way of a land speculation in 1730 Bishop Sherlock bought a large tract in Birmingham from the Marrow family, so when his nephew, Sir Thomas Gooch, the third baronet, began developing the area he had inherited he showed his gratitude by naming two of the streets off Gooch Street, Sherlock Street and Bishop

Street, with Thomas Street near by. This development needed a private Act of Parliament, passed in 1766. It is suggested that all the Christian names given to streets in the Highgate area subsequently came from members of the Gooch family, but a search has failed to reveal any Angelina, Charles Edward, William Henry, or Leopold among the Gooches. The sixth baronet, Sir Edward Sherlock Gooch, however, married in 1839 as his second wife Harriet Hope Vere, of Craigie, Linlithgow, and Hope Street now intersects Vere Street in this Gooch territory.

The origin of street names is often obvious. It is well known in Birmingham that Adderley is the family name of the Lords Norton, now of Fillongley Hall, near Coventry. So the origin of Adderley Road, Washwood Heath, is clear enough. Wives' surnames, however, are less easy to trace, though in noble circles a name from the distaff side is often adopted as an additional forename. Throughout the Adderley family tree one finds not only several Ralphs, Edmunds, and Reginalds—one or other of whom has given his name to three roads off St. Saviour's Road, Saltley— but Arden, Bowyer, Hartopp, and Leigh. These four surnames of ladies who married into the Adderley family have all left street names in the Saltley–Washwood Heath area. As long ago as 1636 Sir Charles Adderley, equerry to Charles I, married Anne Arden, daughter of Sir Henry Arden of Park Hall, Warwickshire. In 1703 another Charles Adderley married Mary Bowyer, eldest daughter of a Sir William Bowyer. Hartopp Road commemorates Anna Maria, who in 1811 became the wife of Charles Clement Adderley, father of the first Lord Norton. She was the eldest daughter of Sir Edmund Cradock-Hartopp, Bart., the descendant of a famous Leicestershire Cromwellian. Then when, in 1842, the first Lord Norton married Julia Anne Eliza Leigh, daughter of Lord Leigh of Stoneleigh, he passed on her name to his son and heir, and today we have Leigh Road in the Adderley territory.

Hams Road, off Adderley Road, hides the most interesting story in the Adderley saga. In 1760 the Adderley of that time completed building a fine residence which he called Hams Hall at Lea Marston, Warwickshire, where the power station now rears its cooling towers. After the First World War Hams Hall stood vacant. It was brought to the attention of Mr. Oswald Harrison, a shipping magnate, who had spent some time unsuccessfully seeking a home in the Vale of White Horse Country in Gloucestershire, from which he could hunt with Earl Bathurst's hounds. Harrison bought Hams Hall and had it transported, lock, stock, and barrel, to the village of Coates, near Cirencester, where he rebuilt it. He did not live long to enjoy it, but Hams Hall still stands some 70 miles from its original site, known today as Bledisloe Lodge and used as a students' hostel by the Royal Agricultural College, Cirencester.

Hams Hall Power Station and little Hams Road, Saltley, are the reminders it has left in Warwickshire.

Venetia Road. It has an exotic sound, smacking somehow of the blue Mediterranean. It is, in fact, an insignificant cul-de-sac off Garrison Lane, Small Heath, in the greyer regions of Birmingham, where Camp Street, Artillery Street, and Arsenal Street tell of the military barracks once there. Venetia Road, however, has an aristocratic pedigree, for, being joined in matrimony with Kenelm Road, barely half a mile away, it has an association with the Digby peerages of Sherborne in Dorset, and of Geashill in what was King's County, Ireland. Venetia herself was a beautiful lady. Her father, Sir Edward Stanley of Tong Castle, Shropshire, was a patron of Shakespeare, and her paternal grandparents were Sir Thomas Stanley and Margaret Vernon of Haddon Hall, Derbyshire, from whose wedding celebrations the bride's sister, Dorothy, is said to have eloped with John Manners in England's classic love story. She married Kenelm, son of Sir Everard Digby, who was executed for complicity in the Gunpowder Plot, but after ten years of wedded bliss Venetia died in 1633 from the effects of 'viper wine' administered by Kenelm to preserve her flawless complexion. She was buried at Christ Church, Newgate, where Kenelm was laid beside her after his death on 11th June 1665. During a privateering venture in the Mediterranean he had defeated a French and Venetian fleet at Scanderoon, and his epitaph declares:

> Under this tomb the matchless Digby lies,
> Digby the great, the valiant, and the wise:
> Born on the day he died, th'11th of June,

Colmore Circus becomes a beer garden during a City Centre Festival

On which he bravely fought at Scanderoon;
'Tis rare that one and the same day should be
His day of birth, of death, and victory.

There is only one Venetia in the Digby saga, but there are
many Kenelms, and I cannot say to which Kenelm Road, Small
Heath, is dedicated. The family had a seat at Tilton in Leicestershire, which gives its name to Tilton Road, near Venetia Road.

The Digbys were eventually ennobled, and in 1718 a certain
Martyn Baldwin left Meriden Hall, between Birmingham and
Coventry, to the fifth Lord Digby's son, the Hon. Wriothesley
Digby, and it is his descendants who have held the Small Heath
property and given Digby names to its streets. A Deed of Coven-
ant in Birmingham Reference Library, dated 12th November
1875, concerns the opening of roads on Garrison Farm Estate,
Bordesley, and mentions John Floyer of West Stafford, Dorset;
George Pleydell Mansel of Langton Lodge, Dorset; and Wynn
Albert Bankes of Westminster. It is surely more than coincidence
that we have a Floyer Road and a Bankes Road parallel to Kenelm
Road, and a Mansel Road running across them and bordering
Digby Park. Further burrowing in *Burke's Peerage* reveals a
Charles Wriothesley Digby marrying in 1831 Elizabeth, only
daughter of the Rev. William Floyer, and in 1856, as his third
wife, Adelaide, daughter of the Rt. Hon. George Bankes.

The father of this much-married man was the Rev. Charles
Digby, Canon of Windsor, who in 1775 married Mary, daughter
of the Hon. Hugh Somerville. Does this account for Somerville
Road, Small Heath, and Hugh Road, off Kenelm Road? And is
there not significance in the fact that another Charles Wriothesley
Digby of Meriden Hall married in 1881 Dora Adelaide Fether-
stonhaugh-Frampton? This would have given prominence to the
names Charles and Dora at the time when Charles Road and Dora
Road, Small Heath, were being developed.

Next along Coventry Road from Charles Road, Muntz Street
is named after a notable family of Umberslade Hall, Hockley
Heath, prominent in politics and industry in Birmingham. They
came originally from the Palatinate of Minsk in Poland and
founded the firm ultimately known as Muntz Metals of French
Walls—the Muntz metal being an invention for making bolts,
nails, and ships' sheathing. One of their earliest representatives in

E

Perrott's Folly, established as Edgbaston Observatory in 1884

Birmingham was Philip Henry Muntz, in 1839–41 the town's second mayor, who entered Parliament in 1868. He was preceded at Westminster by George Frederick Muntz, Birmingham's sole representative there from 1840 to 1857. George had inherited the metal business of Muntz and Purden at the age of 17, and it soon gave him a fortune. He was responsible for our postage stamps being perforated, and he insisted that the Government give an adequate reward to the man who perfected perforation.

Off Muntz Street, where Small Heath Alliance, the forerunners of Birmingham City Football Club, once had their ground, runs Wright Street, named after John Skirrow Wright, social reformer, civic leader, and industrialist, born in 1822, who died in Birmingham Council House on 15th April 1880 while attending a committee meeting.

There is a Wright Road in Washwood Heath, off Alum Rock Road. This is named after Joseph Wright, who came to Saltley in 1844 with his two sons and founded a year later the Metropolitan-Cammell Carriage and Wagon Company. A coach-builder who owned many stage-coaches, he realised that the railway age was superseding the earlier method of travel. He soon found himself employing 900 men, turning out rolling stock for almost the entire world. He died in 1859. Wright was a Nonconformist, but with a fine impartiality he contributed £500 towards the building of St. Saviour's Church, Saltley.

Three more of the 'incomers' to Birmingham prospered here and have left their names in the streets and roads—John Jennens from Yorkshire, Joseph Gillott, also a Yorkshireman from Sheffield, and Francis William Daniels, a schoolmaster from Gloucestershire.

John Jennens founded an ironmongery business, but on his death in 1651 his son, Humphrey, turned to iron-making with furnaces at Bromford, near his home, Erdington Hall; at Aston, where you can still find Furnace Lane; at Furnace End beyond Shustoke, and elsewhere. Humphrey Jennens' town house was a Queen Anne mansion in High Street, now the site of Birmingham Co-operative Society, and he had large investments in real estate in Birmingham. His son, Charles, was the rich eccentric of the family. Known as Solyman the Magnificent, he normally

travelled in a coach and four with four footmen. He built Gopsall
Hall, an ostentatious place near Twycross on the Warwickshire–
Leicestershire border, where he spent £80,000 on the grounds
alone. There his protégé, Handel, wrote part of *Messiah*. Charles
Jennens was a close friend of the Young Pretender. He was god-
father, too, to Charles Finch, a son of Heneage, third Earl of
Aylesford, and left him £5,000 when he died a bachelor on
22nd November 1773 aged 75, to be buried in his native village
of Nether Whitacre.

All his magnificence is commemorated in Jennens Row, a
tatty little street beside St. Bartholemew's car park; his noble
association dignifies Heneage Street near by, and "the largest and
finest house in west Leicestershire" gives its name to unpretentious
Gopsall Street. This was not the end of the vicarious splendour
bestowed by its Jennens associations on darker Birmingham.
Charles's niece, Lady Sophia Howe, eldest daughter of Admiral
Howe, married Penn Assheton Curzon, who inherited most of
the Jennens estate. Thus we have, all in that vicinity, Penn Street,
Howe Street, and Curzon Street.

Joseph Gillott was born at Sheffield in 1799 and apprenticed to
a scissors grinder. The post-war slump after the Battle of Waterloo
sent him to seek work in Birmingham, which he found with a
firm making metal buckles for shoes, belts, and other things.
These buckles were produced by a new process, being stamped
out on presses. Young Gillott also found a girl friend, Maria
Mitchell, whose brothers, William and John, were manufacturers
of steel pens. The layman, not the trade, invented the word 'nib'.
Originally nib and holder were made in a single piece known as a
'pen', which was fitted on to a wooden stem. The layman's nib
came later, known to the manufacturer as a 'slip pen', to be fitted
into the metal 'tip' on a wooden 'pen stick'. This was normally of
beech, more expensively of cedar, and most rarely of amboyna or
ginger wood.

As Joseph Gillott watched his brothers-in-law making each pen
individually, for sale at around 2s., his active mind saw the possibility of adapting the buckle press to the pen trade, so in his attic
in Bread Street, now Cornwall Street, he set about the adaptation.
Soon he was in production, though initially he had to temper his
pens in a frying-pan over the fire. He was able to cut the Mitchells'

price by half, and the virtue of his pens was the consistency in their thickness of writing compared with the variation in individually made pens.

On the morning of 15th September 1823 the industrious Joseph rose early and made a gross of pens. Then, changing from his working clothes, he went and married Miss Mitchell, but took his pens with him and sold them at a shilling each to the wedding guests.

"Questionable taste, but good business," said his great-great-grandson, Mr. Nicholas Gillott, to me recently.

Such was Joseph's business acumen that he opened accounts in all of Birmingham's banks as his trade expanded. Around 1828 he moved to Church Street, and in 1833 he had premises for the first time resembling a factory in Newhall Street. Then, between 1838 and 1840, he built a big new works on the corner of Graham Street and Frederick Street, Hockley, just in time to cash in on Sir Rowland Hill's penny post. The steel-pen trade and the penny post were complementary. Each flourished because of the other, with widening education to cause them to prosper still further. The 1860s saw the apex of the pen trade's fortunes, and of Joseph Gillott's. The young scissors grinder became a millionaire.

Graham Street, which saw Joseph Gillott's rise, gets its name from one of Wellington's Peninsular War generals who fought at the Battle of Vittoria, commemorated in Vittoria Street. Six years after this battle, in 1819, a story was published which attained, and maintains, world-wide fame. It was written in the house on the Graham Street–Frederick Street corner which in those days belonged to Alderman Henry van Wart, whose wife, Sarah, was the sister of the American writer, Washington Irving. While staying with the van Warts in 1816 inspiration overtook Irving, who sat up throughout one entire night and, by candle-light, wrote *Rip Van Winkle*, which he read to the van Wart children at breakfast.

Thus it was in an encouraging literary atmosphere that Joseph Gillott produced the pens from which so much more literature was to flow all over the world. As his business grew so did his family, numbering ten in all. Montague Road, Edgbaston, was named after the ninth of these. One of Joseph Gillott's property deals was concluded in 1853, when he bought part of Ladywood

for £90,000. This, with his Rotton Park Estate, made his boundaries generally along Hagley Road from Stirling Road to City
Road, and Dudley Road to the north. Today his name is perpetuated in Gillott Road.

After his death in 1872 Joseph Gillott's art collection realised
£164,530 at Christies, and his collection of musical instruments
included six Stradivarius violins. Precious stones also fascinated
him, he would produce costly gems casually from his pockets.
Shrubs, too, interested him, and he was able to indulge this
interest in the grounds of 'The Grove', Great Stanmore, Middlesex, where he lived after his retirement. This move accounts for
the name of Stanmore Road, parallel with Gillott Road. His
property he left to his twelve grandchildren. Of these six were the
offspring of his second son, Joseph II, who inherited the business
and built as his residence Berry Hall beside the River Blythe at
Solihull. Joseph II was succeeded in the business by his second son,
Joseph III, though his eldest son, Algernon Sydney, is remembered
in Algernon Road. Algernon's only son, Bernard, became the
last of the Gillotts to have his own road—Bernard Road, off
City Road.

Bernard Gillott was over 40 when he entered the pen business,
of which he became chairman and managing director. Today his
son, Nicholas, is managing director of a firm which the founder
would not recognise, though he would applaud the adaptability
which has brought it safely through the competition of the telephone, the typewriter, the fountain pen, and the ball pen. As
newer writing implements appeared Gillotts took to making
clips for them, where previously they had made nibs. Today the
firm's main output is in furniture castings.

In 1878 George Holloway, M.P. for Mid-Gloucestershire,
wrote an essay on old-age pensions and superannuation describing the working of the Stroud Holloway Original Benefit
Society, which he had founded in 1874. Appalled by the fears of
his employees at the prospect of illness and old age in days long
before the welfare state, Holloway set up a society in which for a
penny-a-day contribution members would receive 10s. a week
sick benefit, a sum of money at death, or an annuity after 65.

A young schoolmaster at Ebley, near Stroud, was so enthusiastic about Holloway's ideas that after sixteen years' teaching he came to Birmingham in 1891 as district manager for the Sceptre Life Association in the Midlands. His name was Francis William Daniels, and he might have come to Birmingham when he was only 14, for an uncle wanted him in his pin-manufacturing business. When he eventually came Daniels proposed to rectify the one weakness in Holloway's society. It should not, Daniels thought, be restricted to a predominantly country area. It would operate best among industrial workers in a large town. So he presented his plans for a Birmingham mutual sick benefit and old-age society to Alderman William Kenrick of Edgbaston, who was prominent in politics and business, and so impressed him that he undertook to become president of the society if his actuary reported favourably. This the actuary did and Alderman Kenrick was president for twenty years, a period later exceeded by his son, Alderman Wilfred Byng Kenrick.

In 1906 the society took the name of the Ideal Benefit Society, and by now it had divisional headquarters in London, Nottingham, Derby, Leicester, and in Yorkshire. Its Birmingham office was now at Coleridge Chambers, which, greatly daring, it built in Corporation Street. As early as 1893 the society had given notice that its funds would be "lent on freehold and leasehold security, preference being given to members, who will be encouraged to buy or build their dwelling houses, and to pay off their mortgages out of their profits in the society". This foreshadowed the society's first venture into estate building and development at Bordesley Green, Birmingham, where, in 1910, a start was made on the Ideal Village.

Thus the Ideal Benefit Society enters our realm of street names. Daniels Road obviously commemorates the founder, while Finnemore Road is named after one of the earliest chairmen of the executive committee, Mr. William Finnemore, father of Sir Donald Finnemore, the former High Court judge. Ideal names also proliferate in the Cherry Orchard Estate at Handsworth Wood, and in estates at Olton, Knowle, and Shirley. When Coleridge Chambers became inadequate for the flourishing society a site was bought in Steelhouse Lane, but this was sold at a profit of £11,000 before building began. The executive then acquired the home of the late Sir John Holder in the sylvan surroundings of Pitmaston, between Moseley and Selly Park, where Holder's Lane and Sir John's Road still commemorate the baronet brewer. The old house was demolished and the present distinguished and delightful offices built and declared open in 1931.

One of the most mysterious street names in Birmingham is A.B. Row, Aston. It gets its strange name because it formed the boundary between the borough of Aston Manor and Birmingham before the Greater Birmingham Act of 1911. In 1885 a Redistribution of Seats Act had increased the parliamentary though not the municipal area of Birmingham. Subsequent Greater Birmingham schemes saw only the incorporation of Balsall Heath, Harborne, Saltley, and Little Bromwich in 1891, adding 4,000 acres to the city and raising the strength of the council to seventy-two. Then in 1911 came the incorporation of King's Norton, Northfield, Erdington, Handsworth, Aston Manor, and Yardley.

Thus a chapter beginning around the year 1769, when the Lamp Act established Street Commissioners as the chief governing body of Birmingham, ends with a city council increased to 120 members controlling 40,000 acres with a population of 850,000.

Birmingham had become the 'second city'.

IV

COALS BY CANAL

On 6th November 1769 the first coal boats arrived in Birmingham by canal, and the price of coal at once fell from 13s. a ton to 7s. On Saturday, 1st November 1969 a dozen boats belonging to members of the Birmingham Canal Navigation Society chugged out from Birmingham in a bi-centenary cruise to retrace, where possible, the intricate loops of the canal to Swan Village, Wednesbury, whence the original boats came 200 years earlier.

The celebration cruise was significant; so was the fact that the boats left from Brindley Walk, a newly constructed roadway leading to a delightful revival of the canal age. The City of Birmingham Architect's Department is to be congratulated on what Mr. Alan Maudsley, the City Architect, has described in *The Birmingham Post* as a project "to inject into the central area a colour and gaiety so lacking in a city without a river". Begun in 1967 with two blocks of flats above undulating lawns alongside the canal behind Baskerville House, it aims to produce a waterside vista from Summer Row to Kingston Row.

The amenities provided [wrote Mr. Maudsley in June 1969] will include a canalside public house and coffee bar, grouped around restored 18th and 19th Century cottages at Kingston Row; a leisure amenity to be enjoyed by office workers as well as boatmen and canal steerers. Birmingham's most ambitious waterside scheme has become known as the 'Plus 20' and involves extensive decks and piazzas, with housing, churches, and schools, pleasantly orientated towards the Birmingham Canal as it turns towards Wolverhampton.

In July 1969 Birmingham was the venue chosen by the Inland Waterways Association for its annual national Rally of Boats, at which a pillar was unveiled beside the Brindley Walk lawns. It bears a plaque which gives a plan of the Birmingham Canal Navigations over the 200 years from 1769 to 1969.

Birmingham has become remarkably canal conscious during the past decade, this rally being the culmination, and bringing to Gas Street Basin, another pleasant survival in the city centre, several hundred boats in the biggest boating spectacle the country has ever experienced. It was a splendid compliment to Birmingham canal enthusiasts that in April 1968 Alderman Sir Frank Price was appointed Chairman of the British Waterways Board. Lord Mayor in 1964-5, Sir Frank, born and reared in a city slum and educated at local council and art schools, has often been dubbed 'Mr. Birmingham'. Leader of the Labour Party on the city council for several years, Chairman of the Public Works Committee during much of the reconstruction of the city, and incumbent of countless national and civic offices, he has brought his abounding energy to the task of reviving canals where revival has any justification. They seem to have quite a degree of this for pleasure purposes, though the several attempts by private individuals and groups to open the Midland canals to commerce again have met with little success. Nevertheless, Sir Frank was telling the truth when he wrote in July 1969: "It is a fact that Birmingham was launched into the powerful industrial position it now enjoys by the decision made 200 years ago to extend the canal system from the Black Country right into the heart of the city."

In the mid-eighteenth century access to Birmingham was by stage-coach and horse-drawn wagon along 'holloways' worn deep across the countryside by the constant passage of wheels and hoofs. Holloway Head in Birmingham recalls them, while Drew's Holloway, on the Stourbridge road just beyond Halesowen, gives some indication of the steep banks enclosing these primitive roads. Sir William Dugdale's diary tells us that he did a journey from London to Banbury by the Birmingham stage in 1679. William Hutton, the writer, has recorded that a traveller would make his will before committing himself to the stage-coach from Birmingham to London. The route around Banbury was infested by highwaymen, none more notorious than Sansbury, and as late as 1822 a reward of £1,000 was offered for the recovery of two parcels containing 794 £5 notes and 32 £1 notes, the property of Taylor and Lloyd, the Birmingham bankers, stolen from the Balloon Post Chaise in London.

Birmingham's principal coaching inn was 'The Swan', near the New Street corner of High Street. Its name survived in Swan Passage, with Chapman's famous bird shop on the corner, until the Bull Ring development after the Second World War. On 24th May 1731 the Birmingham Stage Coach started a two and a half days service to London via Warwick, Banbury, and Aylesbury, at a cost per passenger of 21s. and one penny per pound on luggage over 14 pounds. At the same time the Weekly Wagon did the London run, setting out from 'The Nag's Head', Digbeth. By 1742 the Flying Coach was doing the journey in two days. Another route was in operation a few years later, via Henley-in-Arden, Chipping Norton, and Oxford; and about this time the three days on which a post-chaise set out from Birmingham to London were increased to six.

The winter of 1766–7 was exceptionally severe, and deep snow in the holloways practically cut off Birmingham from contact with the outer world. Some of the more progressive townsfolk, casting about for alternative means of transport, met at 'The Swan' in January 1767, when distress from lack of coal and food was at its worst, and proposed the cutting of a canal between Wolverhampton and Birmingham, with facilities for carrying coal from Black Country pits. On 15th July 1767 a notice appeared in the *Gazette* stating that James Brindley, the illiterate engineering genius who had recently constructed England's first canals in Lancashire, had made a survey for the Birmingham Navigation, that the cost would not exceed £50,000, and that £35,000 had already been subscribed. A Parliamentary Bill was promoted, and when, on 26th July 1768, the Royal Assent was given, there was general rejoicing, with the ringing of church bells throughout the town.

By the autumn of 1769 Samuel Simcox, supervised by Brindley, whose health was failing, had completed a canal 22 miles long at a cost of £70,000. The £140 shares were restricted to a maximum of ten per shareholder, one of whom, the poet John Freeth, broke into verse—to be quoted by every subsequent Birmingham historian—on the arrival of those first coal boats.

> Then revel in gladness, let harmony flow,
> From the district of Bordesley to Paradise Row;
> For true feeling joy in each breast must be wrought,
> When coals under fivepence per hundred are bought.

He continued—in less-quoted lines—to foretell the industrial progress of Birmingham now that it had an "easy intercourse" with a wider world.

> And Birmingham, for every curious art
> Her sons invent, be Europe's greatest mart;
> In every Kingdom, ever stand enroll'd,
> The great Mechanic Warehouse of the World.

The canal wharf in Birmingham ran almost up to Paradise Row, as Paradise Street was then called, and it was not closed until 1926.

Around 1825 Thomas Telford was called in to improve Brindley's winding canal. He straightened it, avoiding eight miles of loops, and cut down the Smethwick summit to remove the locks so that a 40-foot-wide waterway extended from Birmingham to Wolverhampton, with a new reservoir at Rotton Park as a water supply. Continuing down the locks to the Staffordshire and Worcestershire Canal at Aldersley Junction, the Birmingham Canal's entire length was now reduced from Brindley's twenty-two miles to Telford's fourteen.

The £140 shares having already risen to £400 by 1782, a Bill was put before Parliament for another canal from Wednesbury to Birmingham, with plans to continue to a junction at Fazeley with the Coventry Canal, and for a terminus in Birmingham at Fazeley Street, Digbeth. A scheme was then mooted for the Birmingham–Fazeley company and the Trent and Mersey company to combine in constructing eleven miles of canal from Fazeley to Fradley Junction on the Trent and Mersey Canal. This would reduce by eighteen miles the distance to Birmingham from the Rivert Trent via Great Haywood, the Staffordshire and Worcestershire Canal, and thence from Aldersley along the existing Birmingham–Wolverhampton waterway. Shareholders in the original Birmingham Canal were indignant, and violent argument ensued, Parliament eventually resolving the difficulty by passing a Bill which gave the original company the option to construct the Fazeley Canal. The eleven miles from Fazeley to Fradley were completed by 1786, and, with the Coventry Canal south of Fazeley running through the Warwickshire coalfield and joining the Oxford Canal at Hawkesbury, followed by the eventual construction of the Birmingham and Warwick Canal with its extension to the Oxford Canal at Napton Junction, the pattern was formed of Birmingham's commercial canal connections with London, which ran down only in the 1950s.

Pairs of narrow boats—never barges—70 feet long by 7 feet wide to fit Midland canal locks, carrying between them 50 tons or so, would bring food produce or raw materials from London docks to the wharfs at Tyseley and Bordesley, continue empty on the 'Bottom Road', hated by the boatmen, through Camp Hill and Saltley Locks to Salford Bridge, and round by Fazeley to the coalpits of the Nuneaton and Coventry area, where they would load up with coal for the canalside warehouses and paper mills around Watford. Goods from Hull, Manchester, and Liverpool were now flowing into Birmingham by way of Fradley and Fazeley, while grain came by canal from Oxfordshire.

No infatuation with canals can render the 'Bottom Road' to Salford Bridge anything but filthy, environed as it is with engine sheds and sidings, with odorous gasworks, with arch after purplish arch carrying Birmingham's teeming traffic, and with locks whose sides are thick and ebony-coloured with slime and oil. But beauty blossoms even here when oil-bursts erupt on the murky surface of the canal into kaleidoscopic changes of hue, deep glowing red, purple, violet, emerald, silver; ever-widening circles until a lock below is opened and the circles become first a broken mosaic, and then rainbow streaks as the water gathers momentum towards the sluices.

When in February 1791 a Bill was passed for the construction of the Worcester and Birmingham Canal, there were fears that the Black Country coal supplies would run out if they were distributed down the Severn and widely over the West Country, but the promoters assured the public that there was coal for 700 years waiting to be mined alongside the Birmingham–Wolverhampton Canal. Even so, the Birmingham Canal Company saw the Worcester Canal as an instrument which would deprive it of traffic to the Severn via Aldersley and the Staffordshire and Worcestershire Canal to Stourport. So they managed to get a clause in the Worcester Canal Act denying the new company physical access to the existing Birmingham Canal. Thus, though the Worcester Canal came up through King's Norton, Selly Oak, and Edgbaston to Gas Street Basin, it made no water connection there, the Worcester Bar separating it from the existing canal. The bar has since been breached, and there is a through way.

The Worcester Bar put ideas into the heads of the proprietors of the Dudley Canal. By continuing their canal to the Worcester Canal at Selly Oak by way of Halesowen and a new Lappal Tunnel, which, at 3,975 yards long, became the fourth longest in Britain, they could carry coal from the Netherton pits to the Severn without it coming to Birmingham. Cadbury's Bournville works are alongside the Worcester Canal, and, with George Cadbury a great believer in inland waterways transport, the firm made considerable use of the canal. As recently as 1967 I left Bournville Wharf aboard one of a flotilla of five pairs of narrow boats bound for London with 200 tons of R.X. cocoa, which was to be transhipped in London docks and taken to Holland, where they have a chemical process for extracting the last 10 per cent of cocoa butter. This done, the cocoa butter was returned to Bournville via Hull and road transport—a roundabout method used while Cadbury's were installing plant to do the job in their new Chirk factory. The ten narrow boats travelled twelve miles along the northern section of the Stratford Canal to its junction with the Birmingham and Warwick section of the Grand Union Canal at Kingswood, and thence to London.

The Stratford Canal Act was granted in 1793, and work began at King's Norton, the northern end. With so many new junctions being effected, canal proprietors were jealous of their water, and 200 yards from the confluence with the Worcester Canal a guillotine lock was constructed to prevent the flow of water from the Stratford to the Worcester. It consisted of two guillotines, a boat's length apart, which were raised and lowered in slots by winches. Normally they were kept lowered. On the approach of a boat the nearer guillotine was raised, to be lowered again when the boat had passed beneath. The far guillotine was then raised, the boat passed out, and the guillotine was lowered behind it. Thus neither side lost water. Unused since nationalisation brought the waterways under one management, the guillotine lock still remains, open but in good condition, and, as Lifford Lane bridge spans the canal between the two guillotines, with the lockhouse standing by, and a canal signpost, bridge, and toll house only 200 yards distant at the junction, Birmingham is still blessed with a most impressive assembly of canal architecture in an area which a private individual proposes developing as a 'Little Venice' marina.

Charles Hadfield sums up the ultimate extent of the Birmingham canal system in *British Canals* (Phoenix House, 1950):

> The Birmingham system of canals continued to grow and to throw out branches, till in 1898 the waterways then included in the group had a length of 159 miles. The system lies on a plateau at three main levels, the Wolverhampton, 54 miles of canal at 473 feet; the Birmingham, 33 miles at 453 feet; and the Walsall, 20 miles at 408 feet. These levels are connected to each other and to the lower levels that join the waterways running from the plateau by flights of narrow locks. These connecting waterways have all to climb to the plateau by further flights of locks, for instance, the thirty locks at Tardebigge which lift the Worcester and Birmingham Canal 217 feet. The Birmingham system has 216 locks in its 159 miles, all of which are narrow, and it forms the centre of the canal system of England.

There were around 550 private canal basins into Birmingham and district factories in the waterways' heyday, bringing in fuel and raw material and taking away the finished products. Gradually, with the advent of railways, the short haul became more practicable than long journeys by canal, and in 1905, of the 7,546,000 tons of goods carried on the Birmingham Canal Navigations, only 1,376,000 tons were moved outside the area.

Commercial canal traffic has practically ceased in Birmingham today, but as the experience of travelling on working boats even seventeen years ago was to go back a century almost unchanged, perhaps I may record a short journey I made myself in April 1952 —one of many which have taken me over much of the English inland waterways system. It was on *Towy*, with *Kubina* a pair of tar boats belonging to Thomas Clayton (Oldbury) Ltd., a canal carrying company founded in 1842 by William Clayton, great grandfather of Mr. A. H. Clayton, the manager and director in 1952, when hauls between local gasworks and Oldbury tar distillery formed the bulk of the work by Clayton's ninety boats—150,000 tons of tar and tar products having been carried by them in 1951.

A tiny candle-illumined cabin was the only light in the deep murk below the canal bridge at Oldbury as I stumbled down a bricked slope to the towpath. It was not yet four o'clock on a dark morning.

"*Towy*, ahoy," I bawled, wondering if that was the correct canalese. A dog barked and an answering voice came from an unexpected direction. Gleaming lights and clouds of smoke and vapour high on the tar distillery only accentuated the gloom at my feet, but with vague watery noises an even blacker shape materialised as *Towy* slid her stern across the canal to provide a bridge, and I went aboard to meet Skipper Leslie Berridge. A taciturn man of 35, he had some schooling, but went on the boats at the age of 14 and is married to a boat girl. He banged on the side of the cabin.

"Get up, you two," he shouted to his daughters, Annie, 13, and Gertie, 12, and we edged along the narrow gunwale to the engine room, for'ard of the cabin. There, after a fearful pyrotechnic display, the 15-horse-power diesel engine sputtered into life and fumes belched from its exhaust which rises above the engine room and adds its discomfort to the smuts which fly from the cabin chimney within a few feet of the helmsman's eyes.

Towy was lying alongside its butty *Kubina*; the two narrowboats housing the Berridge family. Mrs. Berridge was confined aboard *Kubina* with her new sixth-born. Johnnie, aged five, and Tommy, three, were also sleeping there, and Annie joined them, leaving Gertie as sole crew of *Towy*. Eight-year-old Leslie, having already fallen in the cut fifteen times, was deemed safer at Wood End Hall, the Erdington hostel of the Birmingham Education Committee which gratuitously accommodates up to twenty-nine canal children during term and sends them to school.

At 4 a.m. we were off, empty, for Nechells Gasworks. A smell compounded of oil, tar, and canal enveloped us, and a darkness, which Leslie's eyes could penetrate though mine could not. With consummate helmsmanship he sorted out water from land even when light from factories fell across the canal, making confusion worse confounded. In such patches the angles of buildings were reflected faithfully in the motionless water ahead, to break into grotesque dances in our disturbed wake. Past Accles and Pollocks, past Simplex, and up to Spon Lane and Chance's glass works we puttered. Travelling overhead cranes were lit by the beams from furnaces. Entrances to factory canal basins loomed like black caverns, but one revealed momentarily a beautiful industrial diorama of blue radiance and red flame, while a glass-sided work-shop floated past like a green aquarium. Then a cutting, with pollarded willows above, a tracery against a sky already hinting at dawn. Gertie made her appearance as we went down the three locks at Smethwick, nonchalantly steering while drinking a cup of tea.

"Watch her put it straight into the lock," said the skipper proudly as *Towy* crossed a short pound from one lock to another we had just opened. It entered flawlessly.

Tangyes, Avery's Scales—Midlands industry passed in review. When we reached the long straight beside the railway through Winson Green I could see well enough to take the tiller. A bombed mill where once flour boats congregated was passed on our left, and we came up to our first, unaccustomed, slant on the city centre—a back view of Wales Cots in Oozells Street, with netball stands on its flat roof, and the television contraption atop Telephone House.

Gertie ran ahead at Tindal Bridge with a kettle for water from a towpath tap. The Worcester Canal branched from our right, tunnelling beneath the Church of the Messiah in Broad Street, and at the Crescent arm we began our descent of the thirteen Farmer's Locks. Gertie, a windlass in her belt, took me to the first lock. It was empty. Deftly she raised the nearside paddle with her windlass and rushed to the bottom gate to close it. Charging back again to the top gate, she raised the centre paddle and crossed the gate to raise the far one. The lock filled in a minute. Then, pressing our combined weight on the arm, we ponderously opened the top gate. Normally Gertie manages this alone.

Behind us Leslie brought *Towy* into the lock, closed the top

The Cathedral of St. Chad above the murals in Kennedy Gardens

gate and paddles, released the water through the paddles of the bottom gate, and, when *Towy* had sunk to the level of the next pound, opened it and chugged out. Steadily Gertie and I shoved and turned our way downstream, under Summer Row at Saturday Bridge; beneath the Science Museum and Newhall Street; through the massive railway arch at Snow Hill; to the foot of the lock staircase and an unusual view of St. Chad's Roman Catholic Cathedral.

"Them locks is Brummagem," Gertie informed me, and "Mom had her teeth out there," pointing to the Dental Hospital. This bright-eyed little girl, to whom Brummagem is thirteen locks and a dental hospital, has had no schooling and cannot read or write. She has never slept in a house nor seen the sea, though she regularly does the round trip with *Towy* and *Kubina* to Ellesmere Port, whence the family returns with 44 tons of fuel oil, earning £11 on the trip.

Birmingham was waking. Peeping through warehouse windows I saw men packing crates; lathes were whirring; fans ejected dust, hot air, and industrial odours on to the canal side. Here was a strange beauty, more angular, less colourful than trees and fields, but as fascinating. Shafts of sunlight striking through arches, the changing shapes of smoke wreaths; enough to distract a writer's attention from low bridges which threatened to decapitate him, bridges where the lower brickwork of the arches is deeply incised by the friction of two centuries of tow ropes. To the boatmen there are no bridges—just bridge 'oles.

The 'Aston Eleven' or the 'Lousy Eleven' might equally refer to the Aston Villa Football Club according to the loyalties of the man in the street or the current form of the team. To the man on the canal they refer to eleven back-breaking locks. Lock-keeper Parker, who ticks off passing boats on a slate, showed me that a dozen or so boats descend and climb the stair daily, but as many as seventy-seven each way were recorded on 4th February 1928.

Windsor Street Gasworks receded astern. Thimble Mill Lane bridge, a surprisingly graceful curve of the many-storeyed building of New World Gas Cookers rising cliff-like from the canal, Cuckoo Bridge, and, at Salford Bridge, a glimpse of the outside world so easily forgotten in the deep gorges of the canal. From here the canal came to life. Off a boat-building yard we encoun-

F

The Great Hall and the Chamberlain Tower of the University of Selly Oak

tered a Clayton 'black boat' laden with creosote for the General
Electric Company. From a hatch on the houseboat *Corn in Egypt*
a head enquired of Leslie as to the health of Bill, who was, apparently, still "on the box". Then her father called to Gertie
below, "Here's your Auntie Ivy," and as our boats passed he told
his relatives, who ply from Camp Hill Wharf, "We've got a
babby now." Following Auntie Ivy was narrow boat *Gipping*, a
dog in his kennel amidships, and Mrs. Jinks shaking a mat over
the stern.

So to the gasworks. Our hatches were opened, and within
fifteen minutes 22 tons of crude tar, at 90 degrees Fahrenheit,
poured from the feeder into our holds. Surely *Towy*'s timbers
will never rot.

A mallard drake was swimming around at Nechells as we
began our return journey, as gay and exotic as it was unexpected
among power stations and railway sidings. Speed was reduced
along the wharf while we trawled for coal from the canal bottom,
the most profitable five minutes fishing I have ever seen. The outward journey had taken four and a half hours, reaching a maximum speed of 5 miles per hour. Our return, working the twenty-
seven locks in reverse direction, was to take an hour longer.
Fleeting vistas from bus tops are the extent of the townsman's
familiarity with Birmingham's canals. The canalside view of a
bus is of a momentary red or yellow switchback appearance
across hump-backed bridges, up, down, and gone. Otherwise,
with few exceptions, this trench through the city, this 'cut', is a
world apart and, one fears, a dying world.

One boat only passed us on our homeward way, an open boat
with wire coils horse-drawn from Hockley to Power's of Saltley.
But continually we passed through a graveyard of boats; water-
logged, their timbers decayed, their skeletons rusting. Gold to
the scrap merchant, dross to the canal carrier. Back at Junction
Wharf, Oldbury, while *Towy* disgorged her tar, I warmed my
chilled body at a Viking funeral, a leaping fire of narrow-boat
timbers and the mast of a butty.

But around me, in and on a dozen boats, was prolific life like
that of a fair-ground. Laundry blew merrily, toddlers frightened
my parental heart with their waterside gymnastics, heirs to a
separate race which has intermarried and gone its way for nigh on

200 years unchanged. Before you apply ordinary standards to its conditions and upbringing, remember Leslie Berridge's father-in-law who wants to return to the boats from his new house because it is too draughty.

By 1845 a railway mania was setting in, spelling the ultimate doom of the canals. In 1824, when application was made to Parliament for powers to construct a railway from Birkenhead to Birmingham, the canal proprietors were able to prevent it. But 6th May 1833 saw the passing of the Bill, providing for a railway from Birmingham to Newton-le-Willows, Lancashire, where it would link with the Liverpool and Manchester Railway. From a temporary terminus at Vauxhall the first train left Birmingham on 4th July 1837, hauled by the engine Wildfire. A few hours later the first train from Liverpool pulled in to Vauxhall. By the next year the line had been extended from Vauxhall to Curzon Street, and Birmingham had its first permanent station, with the London to Birmingham Railway also running into it in 1838, though that line was still trying to build Kilsby Tunnel, and passengers had to be transported by stage-coach between Denbigh Hall, south of the tunnel, and Rugby, to resume their journey by train. In 1840 the Birmingham and Gloucester Railway moved in to Curzon Street from its previous terminus at Camp Hill.

Curzon Street Station shared the same architect and date with Euston Station—Philip Hardwick, 1838. He gave Curzon Street an imposing façade with four Ionic columns, described in Pevsner's *Warwickshire* (Penguin Books) as of "austerely elegant design". Hardwick's Doric arch at Euston has gone, so, says Pevsner, "As the Euston Arch was wantonly destroyed, the Curzon Street Goods Station must be preserved at all costs." With the Kilsby Tunnel finished in September 1838, the London and Birmingham Railway was completed. First-class trains did the journey in five hours, and mixed trains in five and a half. As the green-liveried engine with its black funnel drew into Curzon Street, the third-class passengers must have alighted bleary-eyed from their open carriages despite the gauze spectacles they were advised to wear in the tunnels.

Like all new-fangled things, the railway had its critics. Writing in the *Birmingham Journal* of 8th September 1838, "An Enemy of

Imposition" from Handsworth, said that the London and Birmingham Railway quoted him 1s. 4d. to convey a 3-pound basket from Birmingham to Coventry, "just 100% more than conveyance by coach". "I therefore transmitted it from the Castle coach office," he concluded, "the charge for which was only 8d. So much for the boasted economy of the London and Birmingham Railway."

Nevertheless, the line was so successful that other companies wanted running powers on it to London. The Midland Counties Railway was making provision for this by constructing a line from Leicester to join the London and Birmingham at Rugby, while the North Midland Railway proposed doing it by a line from Derby, through Tamworth to Whitacre, and a Stonebridge Branch to continue from Whitacre to a junction with the London and Birmingham at Hampton-in-Arden. This Derby-to-Hampton line of 38½ miles was opened to traffic on 12th August 1839, thus getting nearly a year's start over the Midland Counties Leicester-to-Rugby line, which began operations on 1st July 1840. Competition for passengers to London became furious until a second-class passenger was charged only 1s. and a first-class passenger 2s. over the Derby–Hampton section instead of the correct local fare of 6s. and 8s. This competition was one of the reasons which brought about the incorporation of the North Midland, the Midland Counties, and the Birmingham and Derby Junction railways into the Midland Railway on 10th May 1844.

This amalgamation spurred the London and Birmingham, the Grand Junction, and the Manchester and Birmingham railways into amalgamation themselves as the London and North Western Railway on 16th June 1846, thus avoiding the need to change trains at Curzon Street between the north and London. To facilitate matters even more the London and North Western Railway built a new station, known first as Navigation Street, later as New Street. This necessitated Birmingham's first slum clearance, as a number of streets were obliterated, including Peck Lane, King Street, and The Froggary, a Jewish quarter. Three places of worship were demolished, Lady Huntingdon's Church, The Chapel, and the Welsh Chapel. Showing more concern for pedestrians than modern administrations, the Government insisted that, because the new station cut off one part of the town from another, a footbridge with right of way be provided. With the late 1960s' reconstruction of New Street Station it is a major mountaineering feat to cross the footbridge.

When New Street Station was opened without any ceremony on 1st June 1854, Aris's *Birmingham Gazette* declared "the vast structure merits the distinction of being the finest railway station in the world". It had taken seven years to build at a cost of £500,000, and its arched roof, 840 feet long, covered four through platform lines and four transverse turntable roads in an arched span of 212 feet, the largest single-span roof in the world. Adjacent to the station was the Queen's Hotel, initially with sixty bed, sitting, and dressing rooms, though later enlarged several times before its ultimate closure in 1965.

In 1847 Isambard Brunel began constructing another line from London to Birmingham, and on 1st October 1852, two years before New Street Station was in use, the first public train entered Snow Hill Station, then a temporary wooden structure, having steamed from Paddington via Oxford and Banbury, a route of $129\frac{1}{4}$ miles as against the $112\frac{3}{4}$ from Euston. The previous day had seen a débâcle when a train of ten coaches drawn by a locomotive called Lord of the Isles had left Paddington for Snow Hill with directors and officials aboard in festive mood to celebrate the new line. At Aynho, south of Banbury, it collided with the rear of a local train and the Lord of the Isles was derailed. A substitute engine pulled the distinguished but crestfallen party to Leamington Spa for dinner.

This route, which was to capture the affection of Brummies as the Great Western Railway in a way that the Midland and the London and North Western Railway failed to do, came into Birmingham over a 150-foot iron bridge across Sandy Lane and a viaduct of fifty-eight brick arches at Bordesley, and finally through a tunnel constructed as an open cutting, but covered to comply with an Act of 1846. Twice rebuilt since 1852, Snow Hill Station assumed its final form in 1914, and in 1910 the Great Western route from Birmingham to London was shortened to $110\frac{3}{4}$ miles.

'Beneath the clock at Snow Hill' was for many years a place of rendezvous for friends in Birmingham. Open to the skies across the lines, Snow Hill Station was a pleasant place where sunshafts struck down through the smoke, a sight implanted in the mind's eye of many thousands, and mourned, for it is no more. In 1964, the year when it was decided to rebuild New Street Station, it was also resolved to do away with Snow Hill, and by the beginning of 1970 the dignified booking hall was roofless and rosebay was growing between the metals, though grants had just been announced by the Ministry of Transport which would keep unremunerative services from Wolverhampton Low Level and Langley Green running into Snow Hill for a further two years. Moor Street Station, opened in 1909 but built permanently in 1914, has replaced Snow Hill as the terminus for trains coming into the city from Warwickshire.

Though New Street Station enjoyed a spell around the 1890s when it attracted crowds on Sundays to see the arrival of great actors and actresses appearing during the following week at Birmingham theatres, it was more generally execrated by the people of Birmingham, and in 1944 no less a personality than Emmanuel Shinwell described it as "an abortion". Yet it has been chosen to remain, and despite the shops above it, and the Stephenson Tower block of flats rising slenderly into the clouds, the new New Street retains that dark, claustrophobic character of its platforms, rendered even worse than in the days of steam by the frightening reek of diesel fumes.

Railway enthusiasts are as virulent and well organised in Birmingham as elsewhere, with the Birmingham Locomotive Club, the Birmingham Society of Model Engineers, the West Midland Area of the Electric Railway Society, the Light Railway Transport League, the Railway and Canal Historical Society, the Stephenson Locomotive Society, the Tramway and Light Railway Society, and the local branches of the Festiniog Railway Society and the Talyllyn Railway Preservation Society. Various of these groups promote frequent nostalgic journeys over long-silent sleepers, and there are regular steam jamborees at the Tyseley locomotive sheds which attract phenomenal attendances.

A Birmingham journalist might get away with the wrong name of the Foreign Secretary, but woe betide him if he makes the minutest error in any railway matter. So to appease these connoisseurs, mention must be made of the Birmingham West Suburban Railway, opened in 1876 from Granville Street to a junction with the Gloucester line at King's Norton, via Church Road and Somerset Road stations in Edgbaston, Selly Oak, and Stirchley. The Granville Street terminus was replaced by Five Ways Station when the line was extended to New Street in 1885.

Finally, in deference to all Brummies of riper years, we must include that local institution which vied with Wigan Pier as a music-hall joke—the Harborne Express. To the native, Birmingham's most famous stretch of railway was the two and a quarter miles of the Harborne Branch of the London and North Western Railway, with its stations at Monument Lane, Rotton Park, and Hagley Road, and the terminus at Harborne. Open to passengers on 10th August 1874, it closed to them on 24th November 1934, but remained open to freight until a Beeching closure in 1963.

V

THE TUMULT AND THE SHOUTING

BIRMINGHAM has had its share of fighting and civil commotion, one of its major episodes being commemorated by an inscription on the Ship Inn, Camp Hill, not a mile from the Deritend crossing of the Rea. "Prince Rupert's Headquarters, 1643" is the legend blazoned in gilt letters above the door. Near the inn are a Rupert Terrace and a Cromwell Terrace, and to make more sure that the Battle of Birmingham is not forgotten, it forms the subject of an impressionist mosaic in the sunken walls of Colmore Circus.

During the Great Civil War most industrial towns were sympathetic to Parliament, Birmingham among them. From its infant gun trade—said to have begun in 1603—and its many older-established blade mills and cutlers' workshops, the Parliament forces obtained many of their weapons, which were contemptuously denied to King Charles I when he tried to buy them. In 1642, on his way to the Battle of Edgehill, Charles slept two nights at Aston Hall, and addressed recruits to his banner from a spot which has given the name, Kingstanding, to a large municipal estate in Birmingham. As his troops moved south, however, Birmingham citizens attacked and robbed the King's baggage train and took its guards prisoner, sending them to Cromwellian gaols. This led to Clarendon describing Birmingham as "a town generally wicked ... declaring a more peremptory malice to His Majesty than any other place". So, early in 1643, Prince Rupert marched from Oxford with a twofold objective—a punitive assault on the disloyal Birmingham bladesmiths, and to restore Royalist authority in Lichfield, where in March of that year Lord Brooke had defeated the Royalist garrison.

It was on Easter Monday, 3rd April, that Rupert's Cavaliers, consisting of 1,200 horse and 700 foot, opened the attack early in the afternoon. They came in from the Stratford and Alcester roads, and were twice beaten off by 140 musketeers aided by townsmen with any weapon to hand, who manned hastily raised barricades. When the Cavaliers outflanked these defences they were fired on from the houses; street fighting developed, and many dwellings were set on fire. In Deritend the smiths, cutlers, and nailers fought on the thresholds of their homes and workshops before they were put to the sword and their property destroyed. The Royalists lost one of their leaders when the Earl of Denbigh was shot dead in his saddle—he is not to be confused with his son, who was a well-known Parliamentary commander, a circumstance which makes our Denbigh Street yet another example of impartiality in nomenclature.

Pamphleteers subsequently spread themselves on the 'Birmingham Butcheries'. One wrote:

> The Cavaliers rode up into the Towne like so many Furies or Bedlams ... they shot at every door and window where they could espie any looking out, they hacked, hewed, or pistolled all they met with, blaspheming, cursing, threatening, and terrifying the poore women most terribly, setting naked Swords and Pistols to their breasts, they fell to plundering all the town before them, as well Malignants as others, picking purses and pockets, searching in holes and corners, Tiles of Houses, Wells, Pooles, Vaults, Gardens, and every other place they could suspect for money.... That night few or none went to bed, but sate up revelling, robbing, and tyrannising over the poore affrighted women and prisoners, drinking drunke, healthing upon their knees, yea, drinking Health to Prince Rupert's Dog.

Next day the Royalists continued to burn and pillage before moving on to Lichfield. The Birmingham Parliamentarians got something of a revenge in December 1643 when they attacked Sir Thomas Holte and his Royalist garrison at Aston Hall, and after three days compelled its surrender. Sir Thomas was heavily fined and imprisoned. One could wish equally heavy punishment of football rioters from Aston Villa's ground at Villa Park, who have on occasion in recent years wrecked the 'Holte Arms', across the road from Aston Hall.

As an outcome of the Declaration of Indulgence in 1672, Nonconformists became entitled to worship publicly in chapels of their own, while Roman Catholics were allowed to celebrate Mass in private houses. Birmingham soon had two Nonconformist chapels: the Old Meeting House, as it came to be known, on the present Dudley Street side of New Street Station; and another in Digbeth. In 1715 the Old Meeting House was set on fire and destroyed by a High Church mob, which would have also wrecked the Digbeth building had the owner not placated them with drink and a promise to discontinue services there.

The 1715 rumpus was but a curtain-raiser for the much more serious Priestley Riots in 1791, when the French Revolution across the Channel was causing 'loyalists' in Britain to find 'revolutionaries' and 'Jacobins' behind every bush—and particularly in every Nonconformist chapel. A New Meeting House had been built in Birmingham in 1732 in Moor Street, and to it the Rev. Dr. Joseph Priestley was appointed as pastor in 1780. An experimental chemist, he set up his laboratory at his home, Fair Hill, in Sparkbrook, and over the next decade he became the focus of Tory hatred, which eventually bubbled over in the riots named after him. Let me introduce these troublous days into the story of one whose property suffered at the hands of the rioters, William Hutton, Birmingham's first historian.

One day in 1741 a youth of 18 limped into Birmingham's Bull Ring. He had walked a good distance over the past few days —from Nottingham, where he was apprenticed to his uncle, a weaver. He had 'played the wag' from work to visit Nottingham Races, and his uncle's displeasure had been displayed so forcibly that he had run away. Now here he was in Birmingham, tired and friendless.

"I sat to rest," he was to write later, "on the north side of the Old Cross, near Philip Street, the poorest of the poor belonging to that great parish of which, 27 years after, I should be Overseer." Two men in aprons stood him a pint with bread and cheese at 'The Bell' in Philip Street before finding him a night's lodging for three-halfpence.

The young man was William Hutton, who was to fill other important posts in Birmingham in addition to being an Overseer, but who is best remembered as a local historian. He died on 20th

September 1815, is buried in Aston Parish Church, and has a memorial in St. Margaret's, Ward End. On his first runaway visit young William stayed in Birmingham only a few days, but long enough to say of the inhabitants: "They possessed a vivacity I had never beheld. . . . I saw men awake: their very step along the street shewed alacrity. Hospitality seemed to claim this happy people for her own."

Yet it took nine years before he returned to live among such paragons, setting up as a bookseller in High Street on the site of the old Tolbooth, or Leather Hall, at £8 a year rent. His premises comprised a 'half-shop' with a modest stock of second-hand volumes, but at once, in 1751, he opened the first circulating library in Birmingham, and in 1756 the first paper warehouse. He later wrote of another innovation: "I was also the first to introduce the barrow with two wheels; there are now more than 100."

The young bookseller quickly established himself in the town of his adoption. Married to Sarah Cock on 23rd June 1755, in St. Philip's Church, which—unlike many of us today—he thought "the credit of the place", he had a daughter, Catherine, in 1756, and a son, Thomas, a year later.

When a Court of Requests was set up in Birmingham for the recovery of debts under £2, Hutton was one of seventy-two commissioners appointed, and he delivered his judgements from the chamber over the Old Cross near where he once sat as a penniless wanderer. Local politics in Birmingham in the 1760s was concerned with the Lamp Act, passed ultimately on 21st April 1769. This aimed at improving anti-social conditions in the town brought about by private development. As Hutton wrote in 1765: "When land is appropriated for a street the builders are under no control . . . hence arise evils without a cure, such as narrowness which scarcely admits light." Yet when two of his houses which formed a gateway to New Street were endangered by the Bill, Hutton, in an outburst of blatant self-interest, opposed it.

He was now feeling the urge of all successful men—to build a home out of town. On his frequent visits to Derby and Nottingham he passed through Saltley and was always impressed by a half-acre of land known as Bennetts Hill on the road to Washwood Heath. In 1769 he bought it; building began at once, and

Hutton observed with surprise that the workman cutting the first turf "engaged in prayer" before doing so. Red Hill House, as Hutton called his new home, was completed and occupied before 1769 ended. The house stood on the left of Washwood Heath Road leaving Birmingham, and his son was to build a house opposite known as Bennetts Hill House. Today Bennetts Road, Hutton Road, and Hutton Street are reminders in the area of the connection, while Herrick Road recalls a Councillor Herrick who acquired Bennetts Hill House from the Huttons around 1900 and lived there until it was demolished in the 1930s. At Red Hill House there were effigies of Hammond and Pitmore, hanged in 1781 at Washwood Heath for murder and highway robbery. Hanging continued there until 1832, and on 19th April 1802 a crowd of 10,000 gathered to watch the execution of eight prisoners for forgery, sheep-stealing, and burglary.

In 1825 Hutton's daughter, Catherine, herself the authoress of three novels, addressed a letter from "Bennetts Hill, near Birmingham", and wrote: "I say 'near' because an upstart of a street has arisen in Birmingham which has assumed the name of Bennetts Hill." Yet the vicinity of the street, in the city centre, had been known as Bennetts Hill for quite as long as the Saltley site.

While at Red Hill House Hutton tried his hand at farming. Buying a farm at Stechford, he visited it four or five times a week on foot for several hours' work before breakfast. He wrote: "I have been in Yardley Field making hay when the clock struck nine in the evening and again the next morning when striking four."

It was 1780 when Hutton set about his famous *History of Birmingham*. His intentions to publish were made known on 31st January 1781, when he "supped with a large company at the Bull and Gate. Rollason my printer was there." Publication came on 22nd March 1782 of a volume containing nearly 300 pages, 24 plates, and some drawings which are the only representations remaining of buildings long since gone. In thirteen years the history went through three editions, and there have been others since. William was elected a Fellow of the Antiquarian Society of Scotland. A picture of him around this time shows him in knee-breeches and a frock coat with a white waistcoat and white stockings, a balding man with silvery sideboards, his right hand balancing a book on a table, a spotted dog beside him, and a cornucopia and a beehive immediately behind him.

Life at Red Hill House was pleasant and dignified but for the fearful episode in July 1791, when Birmingham's historian was himself involved in history. Hutton numbered among his friends the new Unitarian minister of the New Meeting House, Dr. Joseph Priestley, who was becoming regarded more and more as an enemy of the State and an emissary of the Devil, preparing, through his chemistry experiments, to blow up churches. "To dispute with the Doctor," wrote Hutton, "was deemed the road to preferment—he has already made two bishops." Dropping in casually to tea one day at Red Hill House, Priestley invited Hutton to a dinner at Dadley's Hotel, Temple Row, on 14th July 1791, to celebrate the anniversary of the storming of the Bastille by the Jacobins during the French Revolution. Said Hutton: "I wish well to liberty everywhere, but public dinners are out of my way."

As the eighty-one diners dispersed after the function they were greeted with cries of "Church and King for ever" from a mob of anti-Jacobins—men, Hutton wrote, "who would have sold their King for a jug of ale and demolished the Church for a bottle of gin". Strangely, Priestley was not at the dinner, but the mob rushed to burn down the New Meeting House, and moved on yelling and waving torches to Fair Hill, Sparkbrook, to set fire to his house and laboratory, possibly the best equipped in England. Priestley himself, unrecognised, moved about the fringe of the mob as it wrecked his home, flooded his cellars, and got drunk on his wine. Shortly after the riots he went to America and never returned to Britain.

Among other places attacked by the rioters was Hutton's shop in High Street, because, although not a Unitarian, he had, as a Commissioner, made enemies among those sued for small debts. Chanting his formula, "Thee pay sixpence and come again next Friday," the mob flung Hutton's bales of paper and choice prints in the mud and trampled them underfoot. All this despite appeasement with a barrel of ale and 329 gallons drunk at Hutton's expense at a nearby inn. The rioters then moved on to Red Hill House, but William and his son beat them to it, and, in the early

hours of 16th June, removed themselves, Mrs. Hutton, and
Catherine in a post-chaise to Sutton Coldfield, where they found
accommodation at the 'Three Tuns'. Catherine took it all so
philosophically that she wrote: "I went out to purchase muslin
for a nightcap, otherwise my pocket handkerchief must have
been the substitute as it had been the night before."

In the occupants' absence the mob wrecked Red Hill House, as
it had previously done Baskerville House, the home of John
Ryland; Bordesley Hall, where the manufacturer, John Taylor,
lived; Showell Green, home of the Russells; the house of a Mr.
Humphreys at Sparkbrook; Thomas Hawkes's home at Wake
Green, Moseley; and Moseley Hall, then tenanted by the Dowager
Countess of Carhampton. Throughout the proceedings the
rioters were urged on by two leaders on horseback. Robert K.
Dent, in *The Making of Birmingham*, writes that

> the third day of the riots struck terror into the hearts of the law-
> abiding inhabitants. The pretty stretch of country visible from the
> top of the Bull Ring was dotted over with blazing or smoking home-
> steads. Lawlessness prevailed everywhere. The bankers took the
> precaution to lodge all their convertible property in places of safety.
> The inhabitants feared to stir abroad, and if they did so, they were
> made to vociferate the war cry of the party, "Church and King for
> ever." The dungeon in Peck Lane was broken open and lost its
> prisoners . . . and hundreds of drunken ruffians lay in the streets in a
> stupified state.

Across the town Matthew Boulton and James Watt armed their
workers to defend the Soho Factory, but the rioters did not range
that far. Despite appeals in the churches for a resumption of law
and order, the mob went on Sunday morning to Warstock,
where it burned down the house of a Mr. Cox, a place occasionally used as a Dissenters' Meeting House. Then it turned its
attentions to Edgbaston Hall, the home of Dr. William Withering, but interruption came in the news that the military were
approaching Birmingham, and the rioters broke and went into
hiding. Two troops of the 15th Regiment of Dragoons made a
forced march from Nottingham, and were greeted by the
magistrates and thousands of residents, overjoyed that the short
reign of terror was at an end.

As to the Huttons, after some days they returned to rooms at an inn in Vauxhall Gardens, and ultimately William was allowed £5,390 compensation against the £6,736 he claimed from the town for damage to his property.

Obviously the authorities were late in taking a strong line with the Priestley rioters. When, in 1792, a 'Church and King' mob tried to repeat in Manchester what the anti-Jacobins did in Birmingham their first intended victim, a wealthy merchant and ex-Borough Reeve, gathered his friends, and when they fired over the heads of the mob it dispersed at once.

To say that Thomas Attwood "was once the most popular man in all England" is to make such a claim that the source must be revealed. It is the guide book to the village of Hanley Castle, Worcestershire, where Attwood was buried in the church-yard after his death at Malvern on 6th March 1856. His obituary in the *Birmingham Journal* is even more extravagant: "Twenty-five years ago there was no more popular man in the British Empire."

The British Empire is dead, and in 1924 Thomas Attwood was sent to his present resting place in the oblivion of Calthorpe Park, wither they moved his statue from Stephenson Place, where it had faced up Corporation Street since its erection in 1859. How many citizens of Birmingham today could say who Attwood was? Yet he was largely responsible for some of the most stirring scenes in the history of Birmingham in a peaceful agitation which culminated in his becoming the town's first Member of Parliament. Again to quote his obituary: "He was the leader of the most formidable confederacy that the kingdom ever saw; with no weapons but the will of the people, he used that power with wisdom, temperance, and firmness, and brought the nation safely through a crisis as perilous as that which was consummated at Runnymede or Edgehill."

This crisis was the agitation that led to the passing of the Reform Bill in 1832, mainly due to pressure from the Radical Political Union fathered by Attwood. Parliamentary representation in the early nineteenth century was as astonishing as it was corrupt. Seats in Parliament were sold openly by auction. Of Gatton, Surrey—still only a hamlet with 180 population—the auctioneer claimed that there were "no torturing claims of insolent electors to evade, no tinkers' wives to kiss, no impossible promises to make" and that "the honours of the State await the purchaser's plucking, and with its emoluments his purse will overflow". It was the time of the rotten boroughs. New Romney, Kent, with eight voters, had two M.P.s; the notorious Old Sarum, nothing but a thornbush on a Wiltshire hill, supported seven Members. Meanwhile, thriving towns like Birmingham, Leeds, and Manchester were not represented in Parliament. The third son born on 6th October 1783, to Matthias Attwood, at Hawne House, Halesowen, Worcestershire, was to change all that.

Matthias Attwood was a prominent iron-founder and property owner. Thomas, his son, had his early education at Halesowen Grammar School, and, barely attained to manhood, he became a partner in Spooner, Attwood, and Co. Ltd., bankers. In October 1811, aged only 28, he was elected High Bailiff of Birmingham, the town's highest office. Thomas Attwood's first interventions in national politics were aimed at safeguarding Birmingham's growing commerce. He spoke and wrote against the monopoly exercised by the East India Company, and in 1812 he headed a Birmingham delegation before a Commons committee to oppose the system of government by Order in Council. It was some of these Orders opposed to American trade interests that brought the United States' declaration of war against Britain in 1812. Attwood helped to get the Orders revoked, but news of their repeal crossed the American declaration of war in mid-Atlantic. For Attwood's efforts the people of Birmingham subscribed £300 for a massive silver cup designed by a local artist, Samuel Lines. It was presented to Attwood on his 30th birthday to the cheers of thousands—a sound to become familiar to him in future years.

In 1815 he began twenty-five years of writing on currency reform, and ten years later, during the depression following the Napoleonic Wars, it was written that "through his exertions the Bank of England and the credit of the country were saved from irretrievable ruin". He had urged the Prime Minister, Lord Liverpool, to print a large supply of £1 notes so that when a run on the banks started in December 1825 with the Bank of England holding barely one million pounds in gold, only the speedy issue of these £1 notes saved Britain's credit. Not that Thomas Attwood yet had any standing in Parliamentary politics, though

The Victorian 'Bull's Head', Bishopsgate Street, in marked contrast to Cumberland House, Broad Street

this was soon to be remedied. Convinced that there was little hope of permanent improvement within the existing system, Attwood planned his Political Union to reform it. In 1827 an attempt was made to get the vacant Parliamentary seat for East Retford, Nottinghamshire, transferred to Birmingham. It failed, but the idea of representation was afoot, and it was raised again on 11th May 1829 by Attwood at a town meeting "to consider the distressed state of the country".

On 14th December 1829 Attwood and fifteen other Birmingham men met at the Royal Hotel, New Street, and founded The Political Union for the Protection of Public Rights. Its objects, mainly for Parliamentary reform and tax reduction through Peace, Order, Unity, and Legality, were put to a meeting of 15,000 in Beardsworth's Repository in Cheapside on 25th January 1830. Huge meetings continued to be held, with banners, processions, and an 'I'm Backing Britain' motif in a Union Jack badge. At a Political Union dinner on 18th October 1830 to commemorate the French Revolution, 3,600 attended, each person being restricted to one pint of ale at, and one after, the dinner. Two months later the Union sent Grey's new Liberal Government a petition which closely anticipated the Chartists' Six Points of 1837, including pleas for paid M.P.s, secret ballots, no property qualification, triennial parliaments, and votes for all taxpayers.

In February 1831 an attempt was made to disenfranchise Evesham in favour of Birmingham, but in August this seemed unnecessary when Commons passed the Reform Bill. Lords rejected it, however. Britain was on the brink of a bloody revolution, and all Attwood's conciliation was needed to prevent riots in Birmingham, where for a week the Scots Greys were in barracks, booted, saddled, and loaded with ball cartridge. But Attwood's peaceful persuasion was more striking than violence, for on 7th May 1832 he addressed the biggest meeting Birmingham has ever known when 200,000 from all over the Midlands gathered on six acres of land at Newhall Hill to petition the Lords to pass the Bill. A thousand banners waved and 1,000 musical instruments thrilled the multitude as they sang the Union's "Liberty Hymn". Nine days later 50,000 were back at Newhall Hill celebrating Grey's recall to office after Wellington's

G

The Art Gallery tower with 'Big Brum', the Council House dome, and the Chamberlain fountain

failure to form a government. Travelling to London with a deputation to wait on the Prime Minister, Attwood was made a Freeman of the capital. On 7th June 1832 the Reform Bill received the Royal Assent. Birmingham was enfranchised, and on 12th December 1832 it returned unopposed its two first M.P.s—Attwood, and the Vice-Chairman of the Birmingham Political Union, Joshua Scholefield.

Birmingham's first contested election took place on 7th January 1835, in the new town hall, where the front of the great gallery collapsed under the strain, throwing many voters on to those beneath them. Attwood and Scholefield were this time opposed by Attwood's partner in the bank, Richard Spooner, a Conservative, who on a show of hands polled 915 votes against their 1,718 and 1,660 respectively. Birmingham was obviously a Liberal stronghold, and in 1837 the Hon. A. G. Stapleton, the next Tory to oppose the sitting members, had a lively reception. On polling day a mob outside Conservative headquarters in the Royal Hotel broke windows and stoned or belaboured anyone suspected of being a Conservative. Besieged in the hotel, the Conservatives barricaded the doors, and some went to the roof and pelted the mob with tiles. The police drove the crowd into St. Philip's Churchyard, but, reinforced, it returned to keep up the siege all night. Help came to the beleagured Tories in the morning with a troop of the Worcestershire Yeomanry from West Bromwich and a party of Lancers from Coventry.

Attwood resigned his seat through ill-health in December 1839, never having made the mark in Parliament that he had made outside. He died at Malvern on 6th March 1856, his marble statue being erected in Birmingham three years later.

Six years after Attwood's monster meeting another multitude assembled in Newhall Hill on 6th August 1838 for the inauguration of the Chartist Movement. The Six Points of its formal Bill, called the People's Charter, were universal male suffrage, equal electoral districts, annual Parliaments, payment of members, secret ballots, and no property qualification for M.P.s. These had largely been anticipated in 1830 by Attwood's Political Union, so it is not surprising that he was among those present at Newhall Hill in August 1838.

Though all was, apparently, harmony among the many varying groups on this occasion, there was soon considerable conflict between the militants and the moderates, Birmingham opinion generally leaning to the latter, and looking to moral force to implement the Charter.

Later in August a meeting of 100,000 in Holloway Head, Birmingham, adopted the National Petition embodying the Six Points, and by May 1839 this had collected 2,283,000 signatures throughout Britain. It was taken to Attwood's home, as he was to present it to Parliament. A Convention of fifty-three delegates had been elected by the various Chartist bodies, and on 13th May 1839 this Convention moved to Birmingham, where it felt the atmosphere would be safer and more congenial than in London. Supporting a motion to make this move, Bronterre O'Brien, one of the Chartist leaders, said: "If we remain in London I am satisfied other arrests will take place, but if we remove to Birmingham I have no hesitation in saying the arrests will be at an end. There we shall have half a million of men ripe and ready, men accustomed to make guns and to wield the hammer, and in the midst of men of this description no government will dare to molest us."

With the arrival of the Convention the meetings already being held nightly in the Bull Ring and at Holloway Head were intensified. By the removal, under the Commissioner's Act of 1801, of the shambles, the roundabout houses, and other tightly packed buildings, a fine open space had been cleared in the Bull Ring uphill of St. Martin's, and there, in 1809, Nelson's statue was erected by public subscription.

When the speakers began to exhort their hearers to violence the Birmingham magistrates proscribed the meetings, but little notice was taken of the prohibition. The situation was becoming ugly. Hundreds of special constables were hurriedly sworn in and occasional arrests made, or speakers were escorted from the town by a force of Dragoons. On 1st July the fiery Chartist leader, Feargus O'Connor, addressed a large gathering at Gosta Green, but the evening mob was soon back in force in the Bull Ring, with daytime processions through the town cheering and jeering, and waving banners proclaiming their demands, much like any long-haired 'protest' mob of 1969. In this dangerous situation the magistrates imported sixty policemen from London, but on 5th July these newly arrived guardians of law and order took such a drubbing from the rioters that a troop of the 4th Royal Irish and a company of the Rifle Brigade were called out. They pushed the mob from the Bull Ring to Holloway Head, but there railings were uprooted, and, brandishing the wooden posts as offensive weapons, the mob streamed back towards the Bull Ring. Police who had taken refuge in the Market Hall Tavern and the Grand Turk Inn were rescued with difficulty by the soldiers. The *Birmingham Journal* reported:

> Two of the policemen who had been stabbed, one in the abdomen, the other about the groin, were carried into Mr. Wainwright's where surgical assistance was rendered although little hopes were entertained of their recovery. Such of the police who were only slightly or not at all hurt continued to patrol the Bull Ring along with the troops, and soon succeeded in taking into custody ten or twelve men, some of whom were armed with deadly weapons, while some had their pockets filled with stones.

In a way that is sickeningly familiar today the leaders of these lawless hoodlums published resolutions condemning the "blood-thirsty and unconstitutional force" used against them. Authority struck back by arresting two of the Chartist leaders responsible for this publication, and on 15th July they were committed for trial by the magistrates. When it was known that they had been allowed bail the crowd outside the Public Offices in Moor Street dispersed. But, in R. K. Dent's words: "Some organisation had evidently been at work preparing for a demonstration of the power of the mob, and that night was enacted another of those lawless scenes for which Birmingham had gained an unenviable notoriety." The Bull Ring Riots were about to break.

By 8 p.m., although Bull Ring shopkeepers had closed earlier than usual, the large crowd was orderly enough, but this was changed when 500 rioters came up Digbeth and attacked the prison in Moor Street. From this they extended their wrecking activities to a grocer's premises and to the shop of an upholsterer, breaking windows and doors, and hurling the contents out to the street. These two shops were then set on fire with bed-ticking from the upholsterer's. By this time the mere sightseers had made themselves scarce, but the rioters turned their attention to a pork-butcher's, followed by a jeweller's, two chemists, a biscuit maker, and a couple of cheese factors. The Nelson Hotel was then attacked, its windows and shutters being smashed, while a silver-smith's stock was pillaged, stolen, or just trodden underfoot. All this devastation was wreaked in about ninety minutes, and with the arrival of the police and military the mob fled, while fire engines from the Birmingham, the District, and the Norwich Union insurance offices, escorted by the 4th Dragoons, arrived on the scene and managed to confine the fires to the first two shops attacked.

Meanwhile many inhabitants of the Bull Ring had decamped with anything of value they could move to safer surroundings. So many arrests were made that Moor Street prison was full. Throughout 16th July special constables and troops patrolled the town, and when, in the evening, the Chartists began massing again in Holloway Head, the Riot Act was read by a magistrate. A number of manufacturers took their own precautions, arming their workers, who stood guard as night fell. Shops were closed and riflemen stationed at strategic points. Two troops of Dragoons with a piece of ordnance were despatched post haste to Holloway Head, and 400 Chartists promptly scattered. A search was made in the neighbourhood and prisoners were taken. Yeomanry detachments were deployed in the suburbs. The town seemed under siege, with all honest householders staying indoors. The precautions succeeded, and the night passed without trouble.

At Warwick Summer Assizes sentences of transportation and terms of imprisonment were passed on some of the leading rioters, while the Hundred of Hemlingford bore the cost of compensation to those whose property had been damaged—an amount in excess of £15,000. Behind his palisade of mock boarding pikes and twisted ship's cable, Nelson settled down to a more peaceful existence, though the Bull Ring remained the Speakers' Corner of Birmingham until it was obliterated recently. One of its regulars was Ernest McCulloch, impeccably dressed like a top civil servant in dark suit and black homburg, but with a voice resonant with 'Brum', who tapped his audiences for over £75,000 in a lifetime of good works. One of the favourite tricks of the

'Prince of Beggars', as Ernie was called, was to find a poorly clothed boy in the between-wars depression, put him up for 'auction' in the Bull Ring, and with the proceeds take the child and buy him clothes and shoes.

Another favourite Bull Ring orator of the 1920s was Alderman W. E. Lovsey, a homespun Conservative with a splendid turn of repartee. One day in the late 1920s a heckler shouted at him, "You keep telling us the same old story, Alderman; Nelson must be sick to death of it." Like lightning came Alderman Lovsey's reply: "If he is, my friend, he's too much of a gentleman to interrupt."

The Birmingham mob has been nothing if not impartial. Seventy years after its loyal cries for Church and King against the Nonconformists it was out in force attacking the High Church party, which was setting up a remarkable Anglo-Catholic tradition in the Bordesley Rural Deanery in parishes on the inner ring south-east of the city centre.

The slump following the Napoleonic wars was ending when Holy Trinity Church was built on Camp Hill. Copied from King's College Chapel, Cambridge, and marking a change from classical architecture to the Gothic, it commanded a vista down Bradford Street to a skyline not yet dominated by the Council House dome and the Art Gallery tower. Bordesley was housing an expanding population, but a memorial at the west end of the church to John Simcox, who died in March 1837, could still describe him as "a native of this hamlet".

The first vicar, inducted in 1823, was succeeded in 1841 by Dr. Joseph Oldknow, Birmingham's first ritualist. Twenty years later a young priest, the Rev. James Pollock, took a curacy at St. Paul's, Ludgate Hill, and suggested a 'mission' church. This came to nought, but when Dr. Oldknow decided to build a mission in the Leopold Street area he offered the district to Father Pollock, who was duly licensed and opened the chapel of St. Alban on 14th September 1865. His younger brother, Father Tom, who wrote the hymn "We are soldiers of Christ Who is mighty to save", came to help for a fortnight and stayed twenty-five years.

For nine months in 1867–8 the brothers endured physical

hazard and obloquy from a mob because of their 'high' practices; their services were interrupted, and they were regularly besieged in the church from morning service until after Evensong and escorted home by as many as thirty policemen, harassed by a riotous crowd. These were the days when Birmingham had its own Ian Paisley, a fanatical Protestant Electoral Association rabble-rouser, William Murphy, who exhorted the mob to attack ritualism of any kind. Murphy himself had been the target of mob rioting during a lecture in Carr's Lane on 17th June 1867, when the rioters pillaged Park Street, damaged the exterior of St. Martin's, and pelted the police and military with tiles and brickbats. But generally he had the Low Church mob behind him against the doctrines of the Oxford Movement, created by Newman, Pusey, and Keble, which asserted clerical authority and insisted that Anglican teaching and Catholic doctrine were not incompatible.

As adherents to the Oxford Movement, the Pollock brothers bravely stood their ground, and eventually two beautiful churches rose in Highgate, monuments to their steadfastness. St. Alban's, Conybere Street, opened in 1881; and St. Patrick's, Frank Street, first a 'mission' of St. Alban's and then a parish church, was dedicated on 18th November 1896. James Pollock died in December 1895, Tom a year later, having followed his brother as Vicar of St. Alban's for ten months.

Twelve years after the St. Alban's 'bother' Holy Trinity became the storm centre. In August 1879 the vicar, the Rev. R. W. Enraght, who had succeeded Dr. Oldknow in 1874, was admonished by the Bishop of Worcester for his ritualism, including the wearing of alb, chasuble, and biretta, the elevation of the Host, church processions, lighted candles, and making the sign of the Cross at absolution and benediction. On 14th March 1880 an inhibition was served on Enraght, who had ignored the admonition. The subsequent Easter Vestry in the church saw the overwhelming defeat of the chief complainant against the vicar in his bid to become people's warden. With Enraght standing firm, the next move, on 20th November 1880, was his committal, by Lord Penzance, Dean of Arches, as "contumacious and in contempt". Father Enraght was arrested and taken to Warwick Gaol on 27th November, having previously addressed a crowd in

Camp Hill which sang the Doxology. Protest meetings followed, continuing until the vicar's release early in 1881, but the worst scenes were to come in March 1883, at the appearance of the Rev. A. H. Watts, appointed by the Bishop of Worcester to succeed Enraght.

A score of police attended the morning service on 11th March, with a large force in reserve in Ravenhurst Street. The church-wardens greeted the new vicar coldly with a written 'protest', and the service became a bedlam with coughing, catcalls, and some fisticuffs as the High Church partisans expressed their displeasure. Crowds followed Mr. Watts to Christ Church vicarage, Sparkbrook, after the service. At Evensong a plain-clothed police officer sat in the choir stalls alongside the new vicar.

On the next Sunday eighty police and a crowd of 6,000 gathered outside Holy Trinity, but with the presence of the mayor order was maintained. Father Enraght struck his last blow in the Easter Vestry on 26th March—a hectic affair held in the church. He proposed as people's warden a Dr. Taylor, who on his election immediately rose with a resolution that "the parishioners refuse to accept the Rev. A. H. Watts". Again there was physical violence, but in the outcome Mr. Watts was accepted and remained, and Holy Trinity is the only one of these Anglo-Catholic churches which went 'Low'. By October 1969 it was closed and decaying, with the white cross from Dr. Oldknow's grave broken off and lying in the rubble.

Another of Bordesley's controversial 'High' churches is St. Aidan's, Small Heath, created a conventional district in 1891 under the Rev. James Agar-Ellis, who lived in a gardener's cottage transformed into a clergy house while the church was being built. It was dedicated in 1896. Like the Pollocks, who were landowners in the Isle of Man, Agar-Ellis came of influential parents, being the son of the Hon. George Welbore Agar-Ellis of the Diplomatic Service. These priests chose to sacrifice their patrimony to toil in darker Birmingham. In *The Age of Reform*, E. L. Woodward wrote of the leaders of the Oxford Movement at the universities: "They belong to the comfortable and well-provided classes; their most ascetic practices were carried out against a background of comfort. They had no anxieties about their own livelihood."

Bordesley was in Worcester diocese, and St. Aidan's was soon in trouble with an unsympathetic bishop for using incense; but with the creation of the Diocese of Birmingham in 1905 the first bishop, Charles Gore, allowed its use.

St. Agatha's, Sparkbrook, is a very small parish with a massive tower rising above Stratford Road in one of Birmingham's coloured quarters, but the church had a ready-made congregation at its consecration in 1901, for it was built to replace Christ Church, which stood at the New Street–Colmore Row corner. The foundation stone and the font from Christ Church were moved to St. Agatha's baptistry, while the clock and bell also came from the original church. Because the noisy Stratford Road runs at the geographical east end, St. Agatha's was constructed with its chancel at the geographical west end—a chancel completely destroyed by German bombs in the Second World War.

Last of the great Anglo-Catholics of Bordesley was the Rev. G. D. Rosenthal, Vicar of St. Agatha's from 1918 to 1938. The church has no high tradition save what was built round his powerful personality. In his book, *So-Called Rebels*, written with Canon Belton of St. Patrick's, Father Rosenthal takes up the story of the Anglo-Catholic struggle with Dr. Barnes after his enthronement as Bishop in October 1924. Rosenthal, who came to St. Alban's as curate in 1906, had ministered in St. Gregory's 'Mission' with the Rev. Lewis Blood from 1913 to 1918 while the church was being built. The new parish of St. Gregory's was constituted on 14th October 1924, but the Bishop refused to license the Rev. Cyril Brown as vicar because he insisted on reserving the Sacrament—and only after five months was a licence granted.

A similar case occurred in 1929 when the Bishop refused a licence to the Rev. G. D. Simmonds at St. Aidan's. An Action in Chancery ensued, the Judge ordering the licensing of Father Simmonds, and the Bishop paying the costs.

St. Oswald's has never known storm and stress, but in the Rev. Hubert Sands, de Crespigny Thelwall, and Edward Leach, it had three vicars spanning some fifty years who were doughty Anglo-Catholics. I have a boyhood memory of a sermon in which Father Thelwall justified the carrying of the Cross in procession, the alternative, he said, would be to amend the famous processional hymn to

> Onward Christian soldiers,
> Marching as to war;
> With the Cross of Jesus
> Left behind the door.

On the night of 18th December 1901 sixteen policemen filed into Ratcliff Place from Door L of Birmingham Town Hall, and marched up Broad Street to Ladywood Police Station. If one of their number was slighter than his comrades this passed unnoticed by the milling crowds. They were too busy looking for David Lloyd George. Little did they realise that he was among the men in blue, masquerading in the uniform of Police Constable Stonier to escape the fury of Birmingham's imperialists and Tories, who had just prevented his speaking in the Town Hall.

At the time Joseph Chamberlain was the darling of Birmingham, and as Colonial Secretary he was more closely identified with Britain's participation in the South African War than any of his government colleagues. Lloyd George, on the other hand, was a pro-Boer and the arch-tweaker of the Chamberlain tail, so when he was billed to speak at a Liberal Association Rally in the Town Hall the Tories swore they would prevent it. Advance tickets were distributed to the Liberal faithful, but they were of such simple design that they were easily copied. So they were replaced by more elaborate tickets with a watermark. Nevertheless, one of the first people into the Town Hall on 18th December was Joseph Pentland, an Ulster Tory, known to be pledged to shout Lloyd George down—and he had a ticket. So, too, had many hundreds of other Chamberlainites—forgeries all, produced by Pentland, who was a printer in Moat Row.

The appearance of Lloyd George with the chairman brought a storm of booing. Not a word of the chairman's introductory speech was audible, but when Lloyd George rose the clamour was terrific—yelling, stamping, the shrilling of whistles, and the blowing of a bugle, with the waving of flags. The object of all this execration stood coolly waiting for a lull in the uproar. It came only when stones began to crash through the high windows, showering glass indiscriminately on pro-Boers and anti-Boers;

all of whom sought what protection they could find. With a momentary cessation of the stone barrage the crowd in the hall piled into the gangways and rushed the platform. They were held back by squads of police, and after some minutes of battle the lights were lowered. The tumult ceased as though by magic. Pentland and his supporters left the hall, and from the base of a statue outside he read a telegram he proposed sending to Chamberlain telling him that Lloyd George had been refused a hearing.

The crowd continued to surge around the Town Hall, cat-calling and singing;

> We'll throw Lloyd George in the fountain
> And he won't come to Brum any more.

There is no doubt that the Liberal leader's life was in danger when the Chief Constable (later Sir Charles Rafter) had his brainwave to recruit Lloyd George into his force and thus provide a getaway which was quite successful. Meanwhile baton charges by the police and counter charges by the mob continued. At one point a scaffold pole was used as a battering ram against the Town Hall doors on Victoria Square. The police repelled this assault, and, shoulder to shoulder, wielding their batons, they forced the crowd back along Colmore Row, one young man being killed.

By 11 p.m. it was realised that Lloyd George had escaped, and the demonstrators dispersed. The uniform which was the Welsh Wizard's salvation was never worn again—not out of P.C. Stonier's reverence for Lloyd George, nor because he disapproved of him, but because next day the constable was transferred to the plain-clothes department of the C.I.D.

VI

THE INTELLECTUAL LUNATICS

BIRMINGHAM has long wanted to move its civic centre from
Victoria Square to a site at the city end of Broad Street, and
various layout design competitions have been fostered over the
past thirty years. The irregular octagonal Hall of Memory had
been built there in 1923-4. Nikolaus Pevsner's volume on
Warwickshire, in his Buildings of England series, dismisses it as
"insipid". Away across the lawns and fountain a loggia was added
in 1925. Pevsner says it looks "very lost". The east wing of two
large administrative blocks proposed in a civic-centre scheme of
1934 was built in 1938-9. Pevsner considers it "pompous and
arid".

To me, early in 1970, it adds up to the one pleasing group of
Birmingham's twentieth-century architecture, though an open-
top car park with a seaside roller-coaster effect outflanks the group
from one angle. The "pompous and arid" block is called Baskerville House—and thereby hangs Birmingham's most macabre
story, together with an introduction to a modest eighteenth-
century gathering of Birmingham men which loses none of its
glamour as the years roll on.

The respectable gentleman walking down New Street one day
in 1829 would have passed not only Christ Church Passage but
Christ Church itself, which stood where today Victoria Square
turns into New Street. A few more paces and the Royal Society
of Arts building was already there, but in those days it had a
portico extending across the pavement. Passing beneath this, our
respectable gentleman—a master plumber and glazier named Job
Marston—knocked on the door of his friend, George Barker, a

leading solicitor and a churchwarden at Christ Church. Of the servant who appeared, Marston asked: "Is Mr. Barker at home?"

Then things took a strange turn. Answering a brief, "No, sir," the servant walked away, leaving the door open. Marston entered, saw a key on the table, slipped it in his pocket, and returned to his shop in Monmouth Street, as the Snow Hill end of Colmore Row was then called. Shortly afterwards he was to be seen accompanying one of his workmen pushing a barrow on which a heavy object was covered with a green baize cloth. They stopped at Christ Church, where, with the key he had purloined, Marston opened the door of the catacombs. There, into vault 521, he helped his workman manhandle the burden revealed when the baize was removed—a leaden coffin.

The body of John Baskerville had come to the second of its three resting places, and George Barker, churchwarden and solicitor, had to square his conscience that, while he would not open up the catacombs for Marston, he had mentioned to him that the key would be on his hall table at a specified time.

In life John Baskerville was a notable figure. Born at Wolverley, near Kidderminster, in 1706, he came to Birmingham in 1725, was a writing-master and a stone-cutter, and later set up in business as a japanner in 1738. In 1747 he moved from Moor Street and built a house and workshops at Easy Hill, where the Hall of Memory and Baskerville House now stand. He became Overseer and Surveyor of the Highways, and, in 1761, High Bailiff of the Manor of Birmingham. But it was as a printer and a type-founder that Baskerville achieved his greatest fame and worldwide recognition. We, however, are more concerned with his death—and what happened afterwards.

In Baskerville's garden at Easy Hill stood the conical base of a disused windmill. This the printer adapted as his own mausoleum, even going so far as to write the epitaph which adorned it after his death on 8th January 1775. "Stranger," this ran, "Beneath this Cone in Unconsecrated Ground, a Friend to the Liberties of Mankind Directed his Body to be Inhum'd. May his Example contribute to Emancipate the Mind from the Idle Fears of Superstition and the Wicked Arts of Priesthood."

So the atheist Baskerville was interred—and that should have been the end of the matter. Sarah, his widow, died on 21st March

1788, and her tombstone can still be seen in St. Philip's church-yard. The house at Easy Hill became the home of John Ryland, and was burned down during the Priestley Riots of 1791. Later the old windmill base was demolished when Thomas Gibson, a Cambridge Street iron merchant, built canal wharves on the spot. Not until these were extended in December 1820 was Basker-ville's coffin exposed. Five months later it was opened in Gibson's warehouse when Aris's *Birmingham Gazette* of 28th May 1821 described the body as being "in a singular state of preservation . . . wrapped in a linen shroud very perfect and white. The skin on the face was dry and perfect . . . eyes gone . . . but eyebrows, eyelashes, lips, and teeth remained." Because the body gave out "an exceedingly offensive and oppressive effluvia strongly re-sembling decayed cheese", the coffin was quickly sealed, but it lay about Gibson's warehouse until August 1829, when it was removed to Job Marston's shop in Monmouth Street.

A suggestion that Baskerville became a public peepshow at a shilling a time seems unlikely, but one Thomas Underwood sketched the remains—now badly decomposed—and recorded that several people saw them. "A surgeon in Newhall Street," he wrote, "tore a piece from the shroud, which he incautiously put into his coat pocket, and died in a few days." Pieces of Baskerville's shroud are still extant, and I have seen one attached to a copy of William West's *History of Warwickshire*.

Up to September 1829 the saga of Baskerville's bones, though strange, had been straightforward. Now mystery crept in. The *Birmingham Journal* of 5th September 1829 included a short note: "Baskerville. The remains of this singular but celebrated man (after an exhumation of seven years) have been buried once more, in a piece of ground adjoining Cradley Chapel, the property of a branch of Baskerville's family." How this story originated is not known, but two others were bandied around—that the Baskerville coffin was in a vault beneath St. Philip's Church, Birmingham, or that it had been secretly interred in Mrs. Basker-ville's grave. The coffin had certainly become an embarrassment to Job Marston, though another fifty years were to elapse before, on 22nd November 1879, a letter from W. J. Scofield of Ham-stead in the *Birmingham Weekly Post* gave a true account of what did happen in 1829 as told to him by Marston's widow. It was that, when the rector refused Marston permission to bury the coffin at St. Philip's because of Baskerville's atheism, a bookseller named Knott or Nott offered the hospitality of his vault—No. 521 —in Christ Church catacombs. Thus it was that churchwarden Barker connived with Marston and the interment took place.

Corroboration of this came on 12th April 1893, when interest having been aroused once more by a lecture on Baskerville from the author Talbot Baines Reed to Birmingham Archaeological Society, a churchwarden, Albert Taylor, inspected the register of burials in the catacombs. He discovered that one fewer burial was recorded than there were vaults, and that Vault 521 was without a name of the occupant. So the vicar, Canon Wilcox, opened the mystery vault on 12th April 1893, before an invited audience which included the mayor, pressmen, and other local worthies. And there, revealed yet again to human gaze, was the leaden coffin. It bore the name John Baskerville in separate letters of printer's type soldered to the coffin. In chalk beneath had been written "Removed 1829", while in faint 'pinpricks' was the legend "Died 1775".

Once again the coffin lid was prised off. Baskerville's remains had deteriorated considerably since 1829 and presented to the chilled onlookers "no more than the osseous framework, covered only with brownish integument, upon which patches of white mould were growing. The head was bound with linen, much discoloured, and here and there we saw portions of what appeared to be a shroud."

When the solemn group had gazed their fill the lid was replaced, the coffin soldered up, and the vault resealed. Canon Wilcox had solved a mystery. He had also committed an offence by disturbing the coffin without permission from the Home Office. On 14th April a question was asked in Commons, and Asquith, the Home Secretary, admitted that this was the first he had heard of the affair. Three days later he gave a considered reply in which he seemed to find some extenuation in the nature of the mystery which the exhumation sought to solve, and concluded: "Although the vicar and churchwardens acted without legal authority, I do not think that the public interest requires that I should take any steps."

Baskerville was accorded belated recognition as a result of the exhumation. Outside the north wall of Christ Church a tablet was placed by public subscription inscribed: "In these catacombs rest the remains of John Baskerville, the Famous Printer," and signed by the mayor and others present at the exhumation. So Baskerville was left in peace at last—but only for five years. Already the movement of people from the centre of Birmingham was rendering Christ Church redundant, and an Act of 1897 authorised its demolition. The catacombs had first to be emptied, and as no one claimed Baskerville's battered coffin it was re-interred with most of the others at Warstone Lane Cemetery, Birmingham, in a vault beneath the chapel. The tablet from Christ Church was placed there with it with the date of Baskerville's last journey added—26th February 1898.

He must have turned in his grave when the chapel was demolished in 1953, but the catacombs beneath were undisturbed. So the atheist of Easy Hill continues to lie in ground consecrated by the Church of England. The fame of the printer lives on and, under the direction of the Birmingham School of Printing, several books on him have been produced recently—in 14-point Baskerville type.

Baskerville was a member of Birmingham's famous Lunar Society, that gathering of scientists, philosophers, and eccentrics who met monthly for luncheon on the Monday nearest full moon, and so protracted their post-prandial discussions that they needed its light on their homeward way at a time when public lighting was negligible. The Lunar Society was spontaneously generated somewhere around 1766, and met at the homes of its members. It could have begun in Lichfield at the home of Dr. Erasmus Darwin, grandfather of Charles Darwin, author of *The Origin of Species*. Perhaps its origin must be sought at Soho House, the Handsworth home of Matthew Boulton, pompous, almost regal, who inherited a small buckle factory from his father and transformed it to the renowned Soho Works, where, through the development of James Watt's steam power, he engaged in many new projects in mass manufacture in addition to his products of dignity and beauty, his gold and silver candelabra, urns, and 'Sheffield' plate.

Boulton was Birmingham-born, in Snow Hill, one of the city's

"The Blind Girl" by Sir John Millais

greatest sons. Sir Arthur Bryant has said that he looms through the eighteenth century like a Titan in the mist. He not only financed Watt's steam engine, he suggested many of the improvements that made it a practical proposition. Discouraged by authority, Boulton established his own mint and saved England from the continued curse of false coinage. Later he designed and built the Royal Mint in London. His more local achievements were to have helped in founding the General Hospital, been an instigator of the Botanical Gardens and of the musical festivals which, in 1846, brought Mendelssohn to the Town Hall to conduct the first performance of *Elijah*, to have founded the Assay Office, and to have won the licence for the Theatre Royal.

Matthew Boulton, James Watt, and William Murdock are commemorated in Broad Street, poring over plans in a gilt group, 9 feet tall, completed by the Birmingham sculptor, William Bloye, in 1952. Murdock, an Ayrshire Scot who altered the spelling of his name from Murdoch in England because of the inability of an English throat to give it the true guttural value, was the inventor of coal-gas lighting. For fifty-three years, from 1777 to 1830, Murdock was associated with the Soho Works, for some time looking after the firm's pumping machines in Cornwall. He also made improvements to the steam engine.

Boulton's physician, Dr. William Small, a man who was interested in metallurgy, chemistry, and engineering, was also a friend of Erasmus Darwin, and a note has been preserved in which Boulton offers Small a lift to Lichfield to a "philosophical feast"—obviously a Lunar Society meeting. James Watt, inviting his fellow members to a gathering at his home, Heathfield House, Handsworth—long since demolished—set out something of an agenda: "For your encouragement there is a new book to cut up, and it is to be determined whether or not heat is a compound of phlogiston and empyreal air, and whether a mirror can reflect the heat of the fire. . . . Perhaps you may be told what light is made of, and the theory proved both by synthesis and analysis."

Erasmus Darwin wrote of the gatherings: "Lord, what invention, what wit, what rhetoric, metaphysical, mechanical, and pyrotechnical, will be on the wing, bandied like a shuttlecock from one to another of your troop of philosophers." Small wonder it has been written of the Lunar Society that it was "a

H

Digbeth Police Station, St. Martin's Church, and the Rotunda

clearing house of ideas that widely influenced the course of the Industrial Revolution".

Joseph Priestley was a member of the Lunar Society, and Priestley Road, Sparkbrook, was named after him. There he lived, and a plaque above numbers 19 and 20 marked his home until the bulldozers took over in the late 1960s, wreaking much more havoc than the Priestley rioters of 1791. Backing on to the site, in Main Street, was Oxygen Place, a reminder that the doctor 'discovered' the properties of oxygen when he realised that a candle burned more brightly and a mouse lived longer in it. Priestley experimented with nitrogen, ammonia, sulphurous acid, and other gases, and to him we are indebted for soda water, for he perfected a method of "impregnating water with fixed air". We possibly owe this debt for soda water to the Lunar Society generally, for its members subsidised Priestley by £100 a year to help his scientific experiments.

Just as Priestley and Erasmus Darwin often sat side by side at Lunar Society meetings, so their roads run cheek by jowl in Sparkbrook. Next to Priestley Road, Erasmus Road testifies that the Darwin family once had a residence in the vicinity, actually in Highgate, where there is a Darwin Street. The Darwins were a Shropshire family, an association that doubtless gives its name to little Salop Street off Darwin Street.

Erasmus would travel to Lunar Society gatherings in a small carriage with food, books, and all the necessaries for writing, for he did much of his work while travelling. Like so many of his fellow-members, he was an inventor of sorts, and perpetrated a speaking machine which would say "Mama" and "Papa", a rotary pump, and a manifold writer.

Sparkbrook has another street name which introduces an eminent member of the society, Larches Street, off Ladypool Road, which is named after 'The Larches', once the home of Dr. William Withering, who earlier lived at Edgbaston Hall. He died in 1799 and is buried at Edgbaston Old Church, where a foxglove is carved on his memorial. This commemorates Withering's greatest contribution to medicine, the discovery of digitalis in foxgloves. This drug, widely used in cardiac and circulatory troubles, he is said to have run to earth after months of searching for a Shropshire gipsy who had used an infusion of foxglove leaves to cure a patient whose case Withering thought hopeless. In addition to being one of the leading botanists of his day, Withering at one time was supposed to have the largest practice of any physician outside London.

Galton House, Steelhouse Lane, and Barr Hall at Great Barr were two of the most frequent venues of Lunar Society meetings. They were the homes of the Galtons, a Quaker family who made a fortune manufacturing guns and later turned to banking. Samuel Galton, sen., born at Bristol in 1719, married into the Birmingham gun trade. The Gaumont Cinema now stands where once he lived in Steelhouse Lane, bringing Birmingham the distinction of the "largest screen in Europe". For long the cinema paid tribute to the Lunar Society with a beautiful ceiling depicting the star-spangled heavens, with a central moon, and the signs of the Zodiac surrounding it. Leaving Steelhouse Lane, Galton bought a country seat, Duddeston Hall, "amid scenes of perfect and luxuriant solitude", where today Galton Street runs down to Duddeston Mill Road alongside the railway marshalling yards. Here, in Samuel's day, was a four-acre lake, and when the old man blew a whistle flocks of assorted and exotic water fowl came to feed.

His son, Samuel Galton, jun.—who attended the Society of Friends meetings in Birmingham for forty years, despite being under expulsion because of his un-Quaker-like gun-making—lived at Barr Hall, now St. Margaret's Hospital, and it is on record that it was his butler who first referred to the Lunar Society members as "the lunatics". Samuel jun. married Lucy Barclay of the London banking family, a young woman preposterously said to be the daughter of George III and Hannah Lightfoot, known as 'the fair Quakeress'. Samuel bought the Warley Estate for £7,300 and employed the famous Humphrey Repton as landscape gardener. His son, Hubert Galton, built a Gothic mansion, Warley Abbey, which was demolished by Birmingham Corporation in 1957—a building famous for the ghost of a grey lady once sketched by Harry Furniss, a *Punch* artist, and reproduced. This Galton occupancy of Warley has left around Lightwoods Park a Galton Road, a Barclay Road—after Lucy—and a Hadzor Road, after Hadzor House, just east of Droitwich, which became the seat of this branch of the family in 1821.

Samuel Galton jun.'s son, Samuel Tertius Galton (1783–1844), married Violetta, eldest daughter of Erasmus Darwin, and bought Claverdon Leys Estate, near Warwick, where they are buried at Claverdon Church. With them lies their youngest son, Sir Francis (1822–1911), most eminent of the Galtons. Francis left King Edward's School, Birmingham, because his bent was towards science and the school's towards classics. Wealthy enough to live as a gentleman, he travelled widely and explored almost unknown tracts of South-west Africa. In 1863 he published a work on mapping of weather in which he coined the now universal term 'anti-cyclone' for a fine-weather system. The influence of heredity fascinated him, and he built a laboratory in London for work on the subject, in the course of which he became interested in fingerprints. His conclusions led to the use of fingerprints by the police in criminal detection.

The Galtons were a brilliant family. Sir Douglas Galton, a cousin of Sir Francis, was born at Hadzor House, Worcestershire, also in 1822. At the Royal Military Academy, Woolwich, he created an examination record by coming first in every subject. Commissioned in the Royal Engineers, he used an electric spark for the first time to detonate gunpowder while blowing up the wreck of the *Royal George* at Spithead in 1842. After service abroad, including work on the fortification of Gibraltar and Malta, he came home to investigate bridge building in iron, railway construction, London drainage, the Thames Embankment, and other projects. One of his great interests was in improving sanitary conditions in hospitals, and it was ironical that he should die, in 1899, of blood poisoning.

Near Sir Francis Galton's grave in Claverdon churchyard is a cross to Tertius Galton Moilliet (1843–95) with two female Moilliets. So we are led to two streets in Winson Green—Moilliet Street, and, running off it, Abberley Street. A Jean Louis Moilliet came from Geneva at the age of 16 and in 1801 married Amelia Keir, daughter of James Keir of Hill Top, West Bromwich, a member of the Lunar Society, a chemical manufacturer at Tipton, and father of the heavy chemical industry in Britain. After leaving the Army Keir set up a glassworks at Stourbridge. Later he took sole charge of the Boulton and Watt engineering works at Soho, but declined a partnership. In 1779 he invented and patented a metal which could be forged or wrought either red-hot or cold, and in the following year he set up his chemical works and soap factory at Tipton.

Dr. Jonathan Stoke, Josiah Wedgwood, Sir William Herschel, the astronomer, and Sir Joseph Banks, the naturalist, were also members or regular guests of the Lunar Society. Two others of the Lichfield contingent were Thomas Day, a minor author, and Richard Lovell Edgeworth, the novelist, who invented a velocipede and a pedometer. They were concerned in one of the most amusing sequences of the society. In pursuance of his ideas on education, Day brought up an orphan girl and later a foundling girl with the intention of moulding them into the perfect wife, but neither would marry him. He then proposed, in turn, to two sisters, but they also rejected him and married instead, the one after the other's death, his friend Edgeworth.

Jean Louis Moilliet was described as "a foreign merchant of New Hall Street" before his marriage, but after this he was naturalised and referred to as John Lewis Moilliet. In 1815 he joined the Birmingham and Warwickshire Bank, founded in the 1770s by Robert Coales, merchant and sword-cutler of Bartholemew Street. In due course the bank became known as Moilliet and Sons, and in 1865 it merged with Lloyds, when James Keir Moilliet, a grandson of Jean Louis, became a member of the provisional committee and then a director of Lloyds Banking Company, retiring in 1877. The Moilliets bought Abberley Lodge, Great Witley, in Worcestershire in 1836, and rebuilt it in Italian style at great expense—hence Abberley Street.

Banks having entered this chapter, it seems as good a place as any to include one of the soundest and most respectable institutions Birmingham has given to the world. The Lunar Society is popularly supposed to have come into being in 1766. During the spring of the previous year, on 3rd June 1765, Lloyd's Bank originated at premises in Dale End, being known as the Taylor and Lloyd Bank, with a capital of £6,000 subscribed equally by John Taylor and John Taylor Junior, button manufacturers, and Sampson Lloyd II with his son, Sampson III. At a division of the profits after six years each of the quartet received £2,629. In the first hundred years of the bank's activities the population of Birmingham increased from 25,000 to 320,000, and it is said that quite one-half of the town was in debt to the bank at various times. When a lack of small change caused difficulties, bank-notes for 5s. 3d. and 7s. negotiable for guineas on demand were issued by Taylor and Lloyd. Normally the bank issued notes of its own for £5, five guineas, and even £100.

The Lloyd family sprang from romantic beginnings in Wales— from one Celynin, a descendant of Aleth, King of Dyfed, South Wales. At the dawn of the fourteenth century Celynin settled at a house in Llwydiarth, Montgomeryshire, known as Dolobran, which eventually descended to his great-great-great grandson, who assumed the surname of Lloyd of Llwydiarth. He was an ancestor of John Lloyd, father of Charles Lloyd, whose eldest son, Charles II, really sparked off the Lloyd saga. On New Year's Day 1661 Charles II married a daughter of a Pembrokeshire man, Sampson Lort, whose Christian name was to be handed down through several generations of Lloyds, and came eventually to grace Sampson Road, in the Birmingham suburb of Spark-brook, alongside the Lloyd residence, 'Farm', while Dolobran Road and Montgomery Street perpetuate the Lloyd's Welsh origin.

Becoming a Quaker at an injudicious time, the second Charles Lloyd suffered ten years imprisonment in Welshpool, though his wife was allowed to live with him and bore him two sons in gaol, Charles III in 1662, and Sampson I two years later. There was also a daughter who married a Birmingham man, and while staying with them in 1698 Charles II died. Buried in Bull Lane, Birmingham, he was exhumed in 1851 during the upheaval that took the Great Western Railway into Snow Hill Station, and his descendant, George Braithwaite Lloyd, preserved the skull until it was reinterred in the graveyard of the Friends' Meeting House in Bull Street. In the same year that his father died Sampson Lloyd moved to Birmingham to avoid persecution as a Quaker in Wales, establishing a successful iron merchant's business in Edgbaston Street. Then with his son, Sampson II, he built a slitting mill in Digbeth on the River Rea. On 28th April 1742 Sampson II bought 'Farm' and moved from Park Street in the city centre to this fine Georgian residence some two miles out.

This second Sampson died in 1779 with the bank a sound concern and the management in the hands of Sampson III and Charles

IV—his sons by different wives. Charles, who had learned banking in Barclay's counting house, was a man of considerable culture, a pacifist as befitted his Quaker principles, active in slave emancipation, and able to repeat several books of the Bible from memory. His home was Bingley House, demolished in 1850 to give place to Bingley Hall of exhibition fame—and there he frequently entertained the Lunar Society. At his death in 1828 Taylor and Lloyd's was still standing foursquare, though the slump after the Napoleonic Wars had caused the failure of many banks. The Taylor interest ceased with the death of James Taylor in 1852, and the bank was known as Lloyds and Company until 1st May 1865, when its name was changed to Lloyds Banking Co. Ltd. Other banks were taken over, Stafford Old Bank, Wednesbury Old Bank, Coates, Moilliet and Sons—and the first annual report recorded a paid-up capital of £143,415, a reserve fund of £27,750, and current and deposit accounts of £1,166,000.

Charles IV's third son, Robert, forsook the faith and simple costume of the Quakers, and his mother rebuked him in a letter: 'I was grieved to hear of thy appearing in those fantastical trousers in London." Meanwhile, from Sampson III, had sprung a line which continued to live at 'Farm'. In 1791 the first Samuel Lloyd brought two more road names to Sparkbrook, Kendal Road and Braithwaite Road, when he married Rachel Braithwaite of Kendal. The marriage of his eldest son, George Braithwaite Lloyd, to Mary Dearman brought her surname to Dearman Road along 'Farm's' eastern boundary. A third Samuel Lloyd was the last of the family at 'Farm', which was given to the City of Birmingham by his second cousin, Alderman John Henry Lloyd, Lord Mayor in 1901-2. Alderman Lloyd was a director of Lloyd's Bank, and when it took over a run-down steel firm as a bad debt he and his cousin, another Sampson Lloyd, were put in to revive it. That firm is today Stewarts and Lloyds Ltd.

Despite their Welsh origin, the Lloyds symbolise the stolid English virtues, and E. V. Lucas, the essayist, sums them up admirably as "a family pacific not only by nature but by religion, law-abiding, sagacious, and prosperous, lacking any extremes either of genius or misfortune, and almost guiltless of mistakes".

'Farm', their Sparkbrook home, now accommodates a Sons of Rest branch, and its grounds are a public park which incorporates an adventure playground. In July 1969 it staged the first sports competition between its own adventurers and visitors from another adventure playground in Handsworth. Sparkbrook and Handsworth are both intensely 'coloured' areas, and all of a summer's afternoon the grounds of 'Farm' swarmed with 1,000 ebullient children, 80 per cent of them of West Indies, African, or Indian parentage.

In 1916 Neville Chamberlain, halfway through his 1915–17 Lord Mayoralty, brought into being the Birmingham Corporation Savings Bank. It commenced operations humbly enough in a basement of the Water Department. The intention was to help the war effort by investing deposits in War Loan Stock, and the Act of Parliament setting up the bank stated: "The bank shall not be carried on . . . after the expiration of three months from the termination of the present war." Yet, when war ended, the bank was proving so successful that its winding-up could not be considered, and the city obtained a new Act establishing the Birmingham Municipal Bank on 1st September 1919. At the time of its Golden Jubilee in 1969 the bank remained unique in Britain, with total balances of £96 million due to depositors and over 40,000 mortgages granted. It had all the modern aids to banking—plus an interesting plaque on the door of Room 12 which reads: "This is to record the special wartime service given by the staff of the Birmingham Municipal Bank during the war, 1939 to 1945. After the ordinary day's work was done, members of the staff from all branches assembled in this room to inspect parts vital to the production of aircraft. They worked through blitz and quiet."

The members of the Lunar Society were generally moneyed men of good education who sought culture for its own sake, and conducted their scientific experiments as much to satisfy their enquiring minds as to advance their careers. Birmingham has never been deficient in another class of man—he who, being born in humble circumstances, has had to use his skills to establish himself, often very comfortably, and who has then become a generous patron of the culture and education denied him in a straitened youth.

A hundred years ago just such a man, a self-made Birmingham

manufacturer, put the finishing touches to a building project which had taken him nine years and cost £60,000. Twelve years later he died and was buried in a mausoleum in the grounds. Today you search in vain for that building, and the manufacturer himself was disinterred eighty years after his death, cremated, and his ashes scattered in the Garden of Rest at Perry Barr Crematorium. Consumed with him in his belated cremation were the remains of his wife and of fifty-three of their children; not natural children, but their adopted boys and girls who died in the building that is no more.

For the manufacturer was Sir Josiah Mason, and the building the orphanage he founded on the Erdington ridge which dominates Birmingham's lowest depression—the Tame Valley below Castle Bromwich. But though he and his orphanage are gone, Sir Josiah is remembered on the island at the junction of Chester Road and Orphanage Road by a bronze bust on a plinth, cast from a seated marble statue which stood in Chamberlain Place from 1885 until 1951. Before its demolition in 1964 Sir Josiah Mason's Orphanage was liberally decorated with mermaids, even on its prefects' badges. They are sisters to the mermaid on the coat-of-arms of the University of Birmingham, which began life in Edmund Street as the Mason Science College, so called after its founder, Sir Josiah, on whose 85th birthday, 23rd February 1880, it was opened. It did not long survive the orphanage in the cataclysmic bulldozing of the 1960s. As a boy in Kidderminster Josiah Mason was said to have been fascinated by a mermaid in a stained-glass window, so when with growing fame and fortune he became an armiger he incorporated the mermaid in his coat-of-arms.

Josiah Mason was born in 1795 in Mill Street, Kidderminster, the third generation of Josiahs. His paternal grandfather, a bombazine weaver, was also a mechanic, mending looms and other machinery. His father, a carpet weaver, became a clerk to John Broom, carpet manufacturer, and married Elizabeth Griffiths, the daughter of a Dudley workman. Our Josiah was their second son. His original education was in a dame's school, but it ended at the age of 8 when he began selling cakes from door to door. 'Joe's Cakes', which he bought at sixteen to the dozen, became quite popular, but the young tradesman sought other outlets, and moved on to selling fruit and vegetables from panniers slung across a donkey. At 15 he took up shoe-making in order to stay at home with an invalid brother. Working with top-quality leather, his charges did not match up to his painstaking craftsmanship. "I found I couldn't make it pay, and must become bankrupt," he explained. "So I gave it up."

He then learned to write and began writing other people's letters for cash, which he spent on books. Meanwhile he tried, and rejected, shopkeeping, baking, carpentry, and blacksmith's work before taking up carpet weaving, but the pay was at most £1 a week, and Josiah's thoughts turned northward to Birmingham and its opportunities. So at the age of 21 he paid a Christmas visit to his uncle, Richard Griffiths, in Birmingham. It was his moment of destiny. He married his cousin, Anne, at Aston Church, and took charge of his uncle's imitation jewellery business so success-fully that he hoped for a share in it. So when his uncle sold out over his head, although the buyer offered him the manager's post, Josiah declined it. It was 1822, he was 27 and unemployed.

One day a steel-toy manufacturer named Heeley, a stranger to Josiah, stopped him in the street.

"You are Josiah Mason, and out of work," said Heeley. "Meet me tomorrow at Mr. Harrison's in Lancaster Street."

Next morning Heeley told Harrison, a manufacturer of split rings and pens, "Here is just the young man you want."

Harrison was unconvinced.

"I've had many young men here," he said, "and they were afraid to get their fingers dirty."

Josiah Mason looked down at his own outspread fingers and said quietly, "Are you ashamed of dirtying yourselves to get a living?"

This impressed Harrison. He told Mason to move into the premises with his wife and furniture. A year later, on Harrison's retirement, Mason bought the business for £500. It was 1824, he was 28 and his own master in a prospering trade.

In Josiah Mason inventive genius was allied to commercial flair. Inventing machinery for bevelling hoop-rings, he made a profit of £1,000 in its first year's use. Then came the slit pen—and the jackpot. In 1825 the pen nib—plain 'pen' to the trade—was first made commercially by James Perry of Manchester, later London. He was quickly followed by the Birmingham pen-makers Mitchell and Gillott. Harrison had made barrel pens for Dr. Priestley in 1780, and Josiah Mason continued making some pens at the Lancaster Street works. Walking down Bull Street in 1829 Mason saw in Peart's bookshop window a card advertising nine pens for 3s. 6d. He bought one Peart was using for 6d., went home, made three better pens, and sent the best to the address on that he had bought—Perry, Red Lion Square, London. At 8 a.m. three days later James Perry was in Lancaster Street appointing Mason his maker of Persian and Steel B pens. Mason's improvement on Perry's own pens was to slit them with a press and die instead of cracking them with a hammer after hardening. In November 1830, with twelve workers using 1 hundredweight of steel a week, Mason supplied Perry with his first order of one hundred gross. By 1875, when Mason sold his works to a company formed as Perry and Co. Ltd., there were 1,000 workers using three tons of steel each week.

Having moved house from his works, Mason had been living at Woodbroke, a residence in Northfield. He was selling this house in 1840 when the buyer sought his co-operation in the electro-plating process he was developing. Thus began Mason's partnership with George Richards Elkington and his brother, Henry, a risky capital investment initially, as the trade and workers resented the new method, and no one would take out a licence to use the process. So the Elkingtons themselves became manufacturers, and it has been written: "What Boulton was to Watt in an earlier period of the history of Birmingham inventions, so Mason became to Elkington."

As in his Perry associations, Josiah first intended remaining anonymous, but "the great and incessant call for money in the business needed my personal care". He planned Elkington's showrooms in Newhall Street, now the Science Museum, to display the electro-plated spoons, forks, and other items made in their Brearley Street factory. The Great Exhibition in 1851 finally clinched the new method over the old hand-plating, and Elkington's went from strength to strength. Mason's partnership with Elkington was dissolved in 1856, and in 1875 he sold his Lancaster Street pen and split-ring premises to Perry and Co. Averse to the public eye, he shunned public office with the exception of a directorship in the Birmingham Banking Company, formed after a failure in 1866, and when, after the opening of his orphanage, Birmingham Town Council wanted to put a statue of him in the Art Gallery his reluctance killed the project.

On 19th September 1860, without any ceremony, he laid the foundation stone of his great orphanage after many troubles with a committee of clergymen because he wanted it to remain unsectarian. On 31st July 1869 Josiah Mason formally opened the orphanage for 200 children. It reached a peak of 350 in 1889, the number steadily declining until its final demolition in 1964, when the proud and graceful tower fell on 16th June, the anniversary of the founder's death. Mason is said to have known all his 'children' by name. His instruction to the staff was inscribed on the glass of his mausoleum:

> They will be what you will make them,
> Make them wise and make them good,
> Make them strong for time of trial;
> Teach them temperance, self-denial,
> Patience, kindness, fortitude.

Sir Josiah Mason was granted his knighthood in 1872, and though the court presentation was dispensed with because of his age and ill-health, his greatest work was still to come. Having conveyed property to the value of £100,000 to trustees, on 23rd February 1875, his 80th birthday, he laid the foundation stone of the Science College in Edmund Street, which was to blossom into the University of Birmingham. Sir Josiah died at Norwood House, Erdington, on 16th June 1881, aged 86. His personal motto was "Do Deeds of Love", and well he had lived up to it.

Barely 100 yards distant from the new Mason Science College there was, in Paradise Street, an institution which had functioned there since 1834, the Birmingham Medical School. This, in 1843, became Queen's College. It was in 1825, the year after he received his diploma as a Member of the Royal College of Surgeons, that William Sands Cox, a surgeon at Birmingham Dispensary, advertised in Birmingham newspapers that he was starting a course of anatomical lectures and demonstrations at 24 Temple Row, then a fashionable residential thoroughfare. Three years later he convened a meeting of the senior members of the medical profession in Birmingham to propose the formation of a school of medicine and surgery similar to those in Liverpool, Manchester, London, and other towns. His idea was approved, received the benediction of the General Hospital, and the introductory address was delivered on 28th October 1828. At the inception there was a panel of six lecturers from the General Hospital and the Dispensary, but in 1841 the Queen's Hospital, Bath Row—now Birmingham Accident Hospital, famed for the work of Mr. William Gissane—was established to give clinical instruction to students of the School of Medicine. In 1851 the General Hospital established its own Sydenham College, initially at 12 St. Paul's Square, later in Summer Lane, and finally, in 1869, amalgamated with Queen's College.

Towards the end of the century the number of students at Birmingham Medical School was declining because it did not confer degrees. To improve its status the school was incorporated from 1st January 1898 with the Mason University College, which had broadened its scope from the technical school of its original conception and, with its new name, had also introduced the first Chair of Brewing in Britain.

At a luncheon preceding a meeting of the Governors of Mason University College on 13th January 1898, Joseph Chamberlain suggested the possibility of a university, with Mason's and Queen's as the nucleus.

"To place a university in the middle of a great industrial and manufacturing population," he said, "is to do something to leaven the whole mass with higher aims and higher intellectual ambitions than would otherwise be possible to people engaged entirely in trading and commercial pursuits."

A Town's Meeting was called to discuss the project on 1st July 1898, by February 1899 a sum of £326,500 was raised towards an endowment fund, and the Birmingham University Act came into operation on 1st October 1900. Andrew Carnegie, the Scottish philanthropist, had offered £50,000 in a letter to Chamberlain, quoting a Birmingham steel manufacturer who had told him: "Mr. Carnegie, it is not your wonderful machinery, not even your unequalled supplies of minerals which we have most cause to envy. It is something worth both of these combined, the class of scientific young expert you have to manage every department of your works."

The Charter of the University of Birmingham was received by the Court of Governors on 31st May 1900. Mason University College was dissolved and all its property transferred to the new university. Joseph Chamberlain, appointed the first Chancellor, was indefatigable in collecting £500,000 towards the new buildings, and found himself in some conflict with Oliver Lodge (knighted in 1902), whose appointment he had sponsored as Principal. Lodge felt that people came before buildings, but Chamberlain replied, "Spend the money now, give people something to see, and I will get the other half million without delay."

A suggestion that Edgbaston Park would be the best site for Chamberlain's new buildings fell through because the resident had no wish to leave. Then came an offer from Lord Calthorpe of twenty-five acres at Bournbrook, "to be used solely for the purposes of a university for ever"—and there, during the next nine years or so, Birmingham erected the prototype of the city 'red-brick' university. Although it was in red brick, there is nothing shoddy about it, and still its buildings remain perhaps the most pleasing architectural complex in the city, rising majestically above the additional twenty acres of playing fields given by Lord Calthorpe when Birmingham Volunteers vacated their rifle range in Bristol Road. Despite the graceful Chamberlain Clock Tower, 325 feet tall and designed to resemble the Mangia campanile at Siena, the dominant feature is assuredly the Great Hall with its fine south window by T. R. Spence.

It was in the Edmund Street section, on 1st October 1900, that the University of Birmingham first began business with the opening of the inaugural session of the Medical Faculty. The Science and Arts students started work one day later. In all, the converted Mason's College had 700 students, with some seventy professors, lecturers, and demonstrators. Soon Birmingham made an innovation appropriate to a city famed for its industry and commerce when it established a Faculty of Commerce.

The Bournbrook buildings were put into service piecemeal while further work progressed, and on 7th July 1909 King Edward VII performed the opening ceremony. In the absence of

Joseph Chamberlain through illness, the King and Queen Alexandra were welcomed by the Vice-Chancellor, Alderman Charles Gabriel Beale, himself four times Lord Mayor, whose family was for long one of the pillars of the Birmingham 'Establishment'.

After serving as a military hospital during the First World War the Edgbaston buildings returned to academic life between the wars, a period of great progress with a Faculty of Law created in 1928 and the setting up of new chairs of Theology, Italian, Russian, Bacteriology, Oil Engineering, and Dental Surgery. Fronting Edgbaston Park Road at the junction of University Road is the Barber Institute of Fine Arts, opened as a completed building on 26th July 1939, by Queen Mary. Sir Henry Barber was born in Birmingham, where he practised as a solicitor, but retired before the age of 40 to Henley-on-Thames. There was nothing about his modest gift of one hundred guineas to the original endowment fund for the university in 1900 to suggest his subsequent benefactions, though he was a Life Governor of the University. In 1923 he endowed the Chair of Law with £20,000. After his death in 1927 his widow took the advice of Sir Charles Grant Robertson, Vice-Chancellor and Principal 1919–38, and of the Pro-Chancellor, Sir Gilbert Barling, on the execution of a trust deed to provide "an Institute of Fine Arts in the University for the study of Fine Arts generally; the advancement of Music and musical education in the University; and for the further development in the Faculty of Law".

Lady Barber placed securities yielding approximately £12,000 annual income with the Trustees, and specified that an institute should be erected on the university site at Edgbaston to include galleries for art exhibitions and a hall suitable for musical recitals. Among the treasures bequeathed to the Institute by Lady Barber herself were her Sheldon tapestries. The first Barber Professor of Fine Arts to be appointed was Dr. Thomas Bodkin, Director of the National Gallery of Ireland, whose white hair and neat white beard surrounding a fresh face—often to be seen as an Aer Lingus passenger on the airport bus—marked him as one of Birmingham's best-recognised characters throughout the 1940s and 1950s. It is Professor Bodkin to whom Birmingham is indebted for the equestrian statue of George I that stands on a plinth in front of the

Barber Institute, a statue that disputes with Le Sueur's Charles I in Whitehall the claim to be the most beautiful equestrian statue in Britain. When the statue of George II in Stephen's Green, Dublin, was blown up on Coronation Night in May 1937, Professor Bodkin remembered the George I statue near the Mansion House in the Irish capital. First installed in 1722 on Essex Bridge—now Grattan Bridge—it was removed to the Mansion House in 1798. Now, thought the professor, it might be in jeopardy. So, with the permission of the Barber Institute Trustees, he flew to Dublin and negotiated for it, getting it for the ridiculously low figure of £500.

On the pedestal left behind in Dublin was a loyal inscription. When one of the Trustees suggested that his might be recut on the plinth at Edgbaston, Professor Bodkin replied—and one can see his eyes twinkle—"Perhaps we ought instead to inscribe the only recorded saying of Hanoverian George about the Arts—'I 'ates all bainting and boetry: neither of them ever did any good to anyone.'" The statue is, in fact, inscribed simply "George I".

Of recent years Professor Anthony Lewis, Professor of Music at Birmingham University, who in 1968 became Principal of the Royal Academy of Music, has put on much rare sixteenth-, seventeenth-, and eighteenth-century music at the Barber Institute, specialising in Handel and Purcell.

In 1925 a committee was set up under Sir Charles Grant Robertson to review hospitals development in Birmingham and its relationship to the Medical School, which had outgrown the Edmund Street quarters, with double the students it had in 1900. Their clinical instruction was centred on the General Hospital and the Queen's Hospital, both of which, needing more beds, had prepared plans for considerable development. The Hospitals Council requested the suspension of most of these, pending consideration by Grant Robertson's committee of a scheme for a new Hospitals Centre, incorporating the medical school adjacent to the university. This became a possibility when Cadbury Bros. offered a suitable site beside the Edgbaston campus. The foundation stone of the new hospital was laid, and the first turf of the medical school site cut on 23rd October 1934, by the Prince of Wales. The formal opening was on 14th July 1938, and on 1st

Narrowboats in Gas Street Basin

March 1939, accompanied by the King, the Queen named the Queen Elizabeth Hospital.

The move from Edmund Street to the new medical school took place during the 1938 summer vacation, and students commenced the 1938-9 academic year there. The physical growth of the school is shown by full-time student numbers rising from 230 in 1930, plus 80 dentistry students, to 620, with another 300 dentistry in 1970.

The medical school is probably unique in Britain in sharing a campus with the Queen Elizabeth Hospital, the maternity hospital, and, by the mid-1970s, with the accident hospital, the eye hospital—moved from their present Birmingham sites—and a new psychiatric hospital. In this enormous complex the medical school is also in close proximity to the university for its collaboration with several departments. Various departments of the medical school are distinguished for heart and vascular surgery with artificial blood vessels and cardiac pacemakers; in respiratory and renal diseases; gland physiology and reproduction; and in virology over the whole field of life from bacteria to man.

For seven years the school, through the university, sponsored the medical school of University College, Salisbury, Rhodesia, an uneasy relationship recently, with Birmingham struggling to preserve the multi-racial nature of its protégé. The link was severed in April 1970.

In April 1966 the city's second university opened, the 'University of Aston in Birmingham', to give the new institution its correct title. Its Charter states: "The objects of the University shall be to advance, disseminate, and apply learning and knowledge by teaching and research for the benefit of industry, commerce, and the community generally. . . ." At the installation of the first Chancellor, Lord Nelson of Stafford, Chairman of the English Electric Company, the chain of office of the old mayors of Aston Manor was handed into the keeping of the new university.

Aston University is two steps removed from the 'dreaming spires' of the classical university, leaving behind also the 'red brick' for pre-cast concrete. Public technical education first began in the city in 1891 with evening classes in metallurgy at the Birmingham and Midland Institute, from which sprang the

I

Crescent Wharf

Birmingham Municipal Technical School, to become the Central Technical College in 1927, the College of Technology in 1951, and the College of Advanced Technology in 1956. At this stage 'sandwich' courses found students dividing their time between the college and the factory, thus fostering close ties with local industry. First-grade engineers, scientists, and technologists were appointed to the staff of the college, and at the time, in 1966, when they exchanged their titles of departmental head or lecturer to professor or don, some 2,000 full-time students became undergraduates.

Aston University adds nothing architecturally to the city. A massive grey barracks, it looms intimidatingly in Gosta Green behind the Central Fire Station, and its students must have been encouraged to use cars, for, while navigating a vehicle through the ever-changing intricacies of Lancaster Place was for long a daunting enough exercise, to reach the university on foot from the city seemed to be an impossibility for its first three years at least.

Aston's 2,000 students with its 1,000 part timers, added to Birmingham University's 6,750 or so, give the city a student population around 10,000. Mature citizens of Birmingham are not unique in having changed their attitude towards universities and students over the past decade. Many who regret having missed a university education themselves thirty and forty years ago are glad that their children today have been spared the dubious advantage. In January 1969 a fall of 50 per cent in offers of part-time holiday jobs to students by Birmingham firms followed the eight-day rebellion by students at the University of Birmingham in November 1968, when not only were the Vice-Chancellor's office, the secretary's office, and the Great Hall occupied during a 'sit-in' but confidential files were ransacked. Dr. R. B. Hunter, the Vice-Chancellor, said:

> On Thursday evening my confidential files were broken into by some members of the Guild of Undergraduates Executive. Some papers were removed and copied or photographed and then replaced. I therefore have to say, with regret, to all those who have consulted me about their affairs in the past two months, that I cannot guarantee that those matters are still confidential. We now know what the Executive of the Guild of Undergraduates means by direct action and no confidentiality.

The Vice-Chancellor added: "We also know of their total disregard for the interests of the majority of the University community."

There are many such suggestions that the rebellion was the doing of a minority. In my youth university students would have been the last section of society to tolerate an unsavoury minority, yet exactly twelve months after the trouble it was revealed that twenty-five to fifty former students, many of them failed, were still regularly using the Students' Union, and playing leading and influential roles in campus affairs. Not internal affairs only—one failed law student, an active member of Birmingham Students Marxist Group, organised a rent-strike of Balsall Heath municipal tenants from headquarters in the Students' Union. Four other failed students who were dead but refused to lie down, and were currently using the Students' Union, were the editor and leading feature writer of the student newspaper *Redbrick* and the editor and assistant editor of another student journal, *The Mermaid*. All had failed their English courses!

It is not necessary to be a student to share full facilities in the Students' Union building at Edgbaston. On payment of the specified fee members of the public are accepted, while sixth-formers from Birmingham schools are encouraged to become members.

Two universities or no, the King Edward VI Foundation is Birmingham's best-known educational institution within the city, comprising King Edward's School, King Edward's High School for Girls, the King Edward's Grammar Schools for Boys at Aston, Camp Hill, and Five Ways, and the King Edward's Grammar Schools for Girls at Camp Hill and Handsworth.

Since 1940 King Edward's School, with King Edward's High School for Girls beside it, has occupied spacious premises in an appropriate academic environment, facing the University of Birmingham across Edgbaston Park Road. A finely carved panel in the school "in memory of E. T. England, Headmaster 1929–41 —under whose guidance the school was moved from New Street into the present buildings" lists the twenty-one past headmasters, beginning with Thomas Buther, 1561–83. The school had received its Charter from King Edward VI in 1552, though its origins must be sought in the reign of Richard II, when four

Birmingham men endowed the Charity which became the Gild of the Holy Cross. The Gild was dissolved in 1547, but part of its possessions were granted to Birmingham with the 1552 Charter for the maintenance of a Free School—'free' probably in the sense that it was to be autonomous. This school met in the old Gild Hall in New Street until 1707, when was erected there a larger Italian-style edifice which endured to the third decade of the nineteenth century, after which it was replaced by Sir Charles Barry's famous building, occupied in 1833, which lent dignity to lower New Street until its demolition in the 1930s. The site was then sold to a syndicate which granted leases to the Odeon Cinema and several business concerns. In 1936 the school moved to temporary structures in Bristol Road, Edgbaston, destroyed by fire in the same year, after which King Edward's pupils became sojourners in other institutions until 1940.

The separate foundation of King Edward's High School for Girls dates from 1883, when it occupied rooms at New Street vacated by the Middle School, which moved out to form a grammar school at Five Ways in buildings already in scholastic use. The four other branch grammar schools date, as such, from this same period. Several King Edward's elementary schools had been started in 1837, and by 1852 there were four of them, including one at Meriden Street, Digbeth, with 125 boys and 120 girls. These became the first pupils of King Edward's Grammar School, Camp Hill, when, in 1883, it was opened with separate departments for boys and girls on a site of three acres which had been acquired in 1881 together with Camp Hill House. Hemmed in by clanging tramcars, a railway, and a saw mill, Camp Hill pupils could sing with feeling two lines of the Foundation Song—

> Here no classic grove secludes us,
> Here abides no sheltered calm.

This verse was dropped when a new Camp Hill was built in the sylvan surroundings of Cartland Priory Estate at King's Heath, acquired by the Governors in 1945.

Five Ways suffered, too, from being cheek by jowl with the funnel through which traffic entered Birmingham in ever-increasing volume, so that a move was made in 1958 to the more open countryside of Bartley Green. Aston boys and Handsworth girls have stood their ground in their original locations, though in 1948 Aston set up Birmingham's 'first boarding school within a day school' when it adapted Longdon Hall in Staffordshire, and began sending all its boys there for one term as boarders while in the fourth form.

When the branch grammar schools were fee-paying they catered for pupils from the district nearest to them. With free grammar school education, successful candidates in the entrance examination were given a choice of three schools, including, in addition to the King Edward's grammar schools, another twenty or so county grammar and technical schools, in order of preference, but many did not get to one of the schools of their choice. The result has been that each school draws its pupils from the entire city, not from a small area. Consequently, local interest in and loyalty to the nearest school has tended to die, the school-friends of pupils do not necessarily live near by—which leaves them seeking non-school interests nearer home—and school commuting adds noticeably to the city's transport problems. Difficulty is often experienced in raising school teams, while some Old Boys rugger clubs are taking members who were not pupils. The school spirit is not what it was in Birmingham, but that loyalties remain strong among older Old Boys is demonstrated by the city's stout fight to retain its grammar schools in the teeth of a Labour Government's 'comprehensive' policy. In any gathering of successful Birmingham men many memories will be unleashed by the odd name mentioned of one of our old masters—"the men who tanned the hide of us, our daily foes and friends"— men like 'Taffy' Davies of Camp Hill, Frank Jones of Aston, or 'Scrabo' Greaves of Five Ways.

Birmingham is often described as being a cultural desert, particularly when the General Purposes Committee is jibbing, as it often is, against the financial demands of the City of Birmingham Symphony Orchestra on the ratepayers. Citizens are entitled to a measure of pride in the C.B.S.O., among its past conductors being Sir Adrian Boult and the late George Weldon. When it gave a grant of £1,250 to the orchestra in 1920–1 Birmingham was the first local authority to subsidise municipal music. In 1970 the grant was £50,000, and the orchestra was asking a further £15,000, which initially the General Purposes

Committee refused. This impasse at the time of writing may well be resolved as similar situations have been resolved before. Manchester Corporation's grant to the Halle Orchestra is normally £22,000—increased on urgent occasions, while Liverpool City Council's grant to the Royal Liverpool Philharmonic Orchestra just about matches Birmingham's £50,000 to the C.B.S.O. These northern orchestras seem better at self-help than the C.B.S.O., but, playing off one cultural millstone round the ratepayer's neck against another, why not sell one of the city's pictures or other art treasures each year to meet this annual demand if we must keep an orchestra which cannot support itself?

Birmingham City Council has made a grant of £65,000 towards a new Birmingham Repertory Theatre expected to be built in Broad Street by the autumn of 1971. The 'Rep', as it is affectionately known, opened with *Twelfth Night* on 15th February 1913; its purpose, defined by the founder, the late Sir Barry Jackson, being "to serve an art instead of making that art serve a commercial purpose". Famous names of the stage have passed through the 'Rep' company, among them Felix Aylmer, Leslie Banks, Gwen Frangcon-Davies, Sir Cedric Hardwick, Robert Newton, Sir Laurence Olivier, and Greer Garson. In 1934 Sir Barry gave the theatre and all its effects to a non-profit-making company, and in the following year the balance of an appeal fund was handed over to the trustees of the Sir Barry Jackson Trust, which had been formed to hold the shares in the Birmingham Repertory Theatre Ltd.

Despite substantial help from the Arts Council, Birmingham ratepayers have been annually mulcted of £8,000 towards the 'Rep', which is now about to be demolished. In Birmingham— as in the Honours List—much more attention is paid by news media to the theatre than public support merits. Columns of newsprint are devoted to keeping the Alexandra Theatre open because its regular patrons cannot, and on the sacrilege of giving the new 'Rep', when it is built, any other name than the Barry Jackson Theatre. In 1955 the city conferred the Freedom on Sir Barry Jackson.

The hard theatrical facts are that over the past few decades Birmingham has lost the Theatre Royal, the 'Prince of Wales,' the

'Grand,' the 'Empire,' 'Bordesley Palace,' Aston Hippodrome, and the 'Gaiety', and is the worse for it only to the degree that the television which has taken their place is even more unworthy, violent, and anti-social. The Hall Green Little Theatre, the 'Crescent,' Highbury Little Theatre at Sutton Coldfield, the Birmingham Theatre Centre in Islington Row, and the Educational Drama Association keep the Thespian backcloths flapping, while the theatre in the Midlands Arts Centre for Young People in Cannon Hill Park has already put on one four-letter-word play which sent some of its young audience scurrying. It has also provided a stage for ten assorted students from Cologne University to perform in the nude, and eight Swiss actors and actresses to simulate the sex act and send a largely student audience into hypnotic staggers.

These latter capers were part of the International Drama Section of the Birmingham Festival, a charity fund-raising effort by university students—and they were repudiated by officials of the Midlands Arts Theatre.

The Arts Centre itself offers more conventional facilities for ballet, opera, puppets, films, and—completed or intended—galleries for the visual arts, an exhibition hall, lecture theatre, restaurant, library, arts club, workshops, a swimming pool, and a skating rink in fifteen acres of parkland.

In pictures of the top end of New Street between 1829 and 1913 the most prominent feature, the portico of the Royal Birmingham Society of Artists gallery, extended across the pavement. The Society was founded in 1809 in a room in Peck Lane, moving in 1814 to Union Street, and again in 1821 into a circular building where one Robert Barker exhibited a panorama on the site of the present R.B.S.A. premises. By 1829 the porticoed building had arisen on the spot, and in July 1868 Queen Victoria granted the society her patronage and the style of the Royal Birmingham Society of Artists.

Among its many illustrious members have been Peter Hollins, the sculptor, who was elected in 1826; artist Frederick Henshaw (1826); artist David Cox (1842), born in Heath Mill Lane the son of a blacksmith, but prevented by a broken leg from following his father's trade; and artist Samuel Lines (1815), once an apprentice clock-dial decorator in Great Hampton Street, who lies buried on the spot in the churchyard adjacent to Temple Row West from which he did his painting of St. Philip's.

Today the society has sixty members and forty associate members, artists in their own right, professional or amateur practitioners of the fine arts in sculpture, pottery, and architecture as well as painting. At a meeting in April each year members vote for new members, while members and associates elect new associates. The society holds two open exhibitions annually—of oil paintings in March, and of water colours and craft work in June—for which artists and craftsmen throughout the Midlands can submit work in addition to that on display from members and associates. An annual autumn exhibition is restricted to members and associates. The organisation of Friends of the R.B.S.A. puts on an exhibition in July, and the galleries are also used by the Birmingham Art Circle and the Birmingham Water Colour Society, while any artist of standing can hire them to put on an exhibition. An innovation coming up to its third winter is the series of six R.B.S.A. concerts at which talented young musicians have an opportunity to perform in public. Organisations such as the Gilbert and Sullivan Society and the Midland Arts Club both use the R.B.S.A. premises.

Without claiming any Welsh or Yorkshire fervour in choral singing, Birmingham voices are raised frequently and melodiously in many societies. The Birmingham and Midland Operatic Society takes the professional Birmingham Theatre for an annual fortnight's production, and the Forward Operatic Company for a week. Other societies put on their productions at the Crescent Theatre and local halls—the Arcadians Operatic and Dramatic Society, Bournville Musical Society, the Midland Music Makers Grand Opera Society, and the Harborne, Dunlop, Kingstanding Community Centre, Queen Elizabeth Hospital, Savoy, and Sutton Coldfield Operatic Societies.

The strength and attraction of the Museum and Art Gallery in Birmingham is its wide diversity of exhibits, and most local folk cherish their own particular memories of it. Mine is of the seascape room in impecunious lunchtimes during the late 1920s, when the boisterous salty canvases sent my vagrant mind ranging over the ocean, while my body found surreptitious sustenance in hot meat pies from John Bosley's shop near the old White Horse Hotel.

Today, in addition to its outliers such as Aston Hall, Blakesley Hall, Cannon Hill, and Sarehole Mill, the Birmingham Museum and Art Gallery has, in its city centre building, a museum within a museum. This is the fascinating Pinto Collection, comprising nearly 7,000 objects wholly or in part made of wood, a collection begun by Edward Pinto in his boyhood, and built up into probably the largest collection of domestic woodwork in the world. In 1964 Edward Pinto, and his wife Eva, allowed Birmingham to acquire it for a nominal sum, and they themselves opened the exhibition in April 1969. It is displayed under headings such as eating and drinking, children and pastimes, the tobacconist, the apothecary, candlesticks, wassail bowls, boudoir, writing, souvenirs, measurement, and others.

While the strongest feature of the Department of Natural History is its section on European birds, the Beale Memorial Gallery has a comprehensive collection of British birds displayed in their natural surroundings. A prized possession is the skull from North America of the horned dinosaur (Triceratops). Gemstones are featured in the noted Bragge and Ansell Collections, and the lepidopterist, botanist, and entymologist will all be amply repaid by long browsing over the exhibits devoted to their interests. Archaeologically the museum covers the world, with a remarkable bronze Gautama Buddha from India one of the highspots, and, nearer home, a collection of medieval pottery from kilns at Nottingham that is unique. Philatelists are catered for in the Evans Collection, which is backed up by the Thompson Collection of Birmingham Postal History.

Among its magnificent collection of pictures the Art Gallery finds most pride in the Pre-Raphaelites, of which Birmingham has the world's finest collection, with major masterpieces of Rossetti, Holman Hunt, Ford Madox Brown, and Millais. Additions are constantly being made to the collection of Old Master paintings, and the gallery has portraits by Lely, Dahl, Gainsborough, and Reynolds, with collections of contemporary art and sculpture also growing rapidly.

Regular series of lunchtime lectures by experts from all departments of the Museum and Art Gallery attract audiences ranging from 50 to 200, and lunchtime concerts are also organised by the Birmingham Chamber Music Society, groups of instrumentalists from the City of Birmingham Symphony Orchestra, and various other ensembles.

The Brummie, nostalgic for the past, can at least evoke some of its sounds in the Museum of Science and Industry, housed in Elkington's one-time plating factory in Newhall Street. Here, by pressing the appropriate buttons, he can bring back the clangour of tramcar No. 395 as it hurtled through Birmingham streets, the puffing of steam locomotives up the notorious Lickey Incline just south of the city, or the melody of old steam fair organs. Superannuated steam rollers come to life again, ancient beam engines, like the 1864 Amos, thump and thud as their huge fly-wheels revolve again, and there are working models of many industrial processes. A Hurricane and a Spitfire built in Birmingham in 1944 are great attractions in the aircraft section. There is an arms gallery of particular interest to the city, and the Charles Thomas Pen Collection. Motor cycles, remembered from a boyhood immediately after the First World War, are ranged in shiny polished array—the Saltley Villiers, Rudge Multi, Norton, Triumph, Sunbeam, Cyclone, Excelsior, Francis Barnett, many of them made in Birmingham. A Tangye steam engine and the lantern of the Longstones lighthouse, made by Chance Bros. Ltd. "near Birmingham" in 1873, are solid souvenirs of local industry, together with a thousand and one less comprehensible workshop items. Even so, the non-mechanically minded will delight in exhibits of ships' badges and the coats-of-arms of all the delightful little railways that ever merged into the countryside of our islands, including even the West Clare Railway, lampooned at once cuttingly and lovingly by Percy French.

The Museum of Science and Industry is always well patronised by earnest, wholesome, and knowledgeable men. Perhaps this is the true seat of culture in the "Workshop of the World".

VII

THE CHAMBERLAIN TRADITION

IN 1869, the same year that he became father of a son destined to be Prime Minister, he entered Birmingham Town Council. Four years later he was mayor. In 1876 he became an M.P. Four years later he held the first of the posts in the Cabinet which were to make him at times the outstanding figure in British politics. He was certainly Birmingham's greatest man. Burial in Westminster Abbey was offered at his death in 1914, but his family felt he would prefer to rest in his constituency.

Today, seeking his memorial in Key Hill Cemetery, Hockley, barely a mile from the city centre, is like looking for a needle in a haystack. You find it eventually about halfway across the base of the semicircle of catacombs. It is the third name, seemingly an afterthought, below those of his first two wives—"also of Joseph Chamberlain, born July 8th. 1836; died July 2nd. 1914."

Birmingham got its Charter of Incorporation as a Borough on 1st November 1838. The package containing it was actually opened by William Scholefield, the High Bailiff, in the newspaper office of the *Birmingham Journal,* and it was published with an invitation to the inhabitants to hear it read at the Town Hall on 5th November.

A town council was constituted by the Charter. It was to consist of a mayor, sixteen aldermen, and forty-eight councillors, to be elected by thirteen wards, only five of which still bear the same names. Each ward was to elect three councillors except St. Peter's, Deritend and Bordesley, and Duddeston and Nechells, which were given six each. So anxious was the new borough to

get off the mark that the elections were fixed for Boxing Day
1838. In Volume One of the *History of the Corporation of Birmingham* John Thackray Bunce writes that the election "was preceded
by a great deal of commotion in the political parties of the
borough, and by a division among the Liberals". *Plus ca change.* . . .

Despite this division, or because of it, the Radical section of the
Liberal Party captured all forty-eight seats, although the Tories
contested all but four of them. Still rushing on with almost
indecent haste, the new council held its first meeting on the day
following the election in the Committee Room of the Town Hall.
It at once elected the sixteen aldermen—two of them not being
members of the council. This meant by-elections for fourteen
more councillors, and Liberals mainly of radical persuasion again
swept the board.

The local radical newspaper at once suggested a Tammany
Hall approach to municipal administration: "There will be a
number of good things going under the Corporation. . . . These
offices will be in the gift of the Council—of the majority of the
Council; and the majority of the Council will not give their gifts
to neutrals . . . much less to opponents. . . . The Whigs and the
Tories laid on the shelf, there remain only the Radicals to choose
from, and from Radicals the choice will be made."

In fact, only one full-time appointment was made initially, that
of doorkeeper and messenger at £1 weekly. The town clerk was
always a solicitor who continued his private practice until 1868,
when the position became full-time with a basic salary of £1,000
per annum. Similarly, the treasurer's office was filled part-time by
a Birmingham banker until 1858, when the incumbent was
appointed Borough Treasurer at £500 salary.

William Scholefield, the High Bailiff, aged only 29, and son of
Joshua Scholefield, one of Birmingham's first two M.P.s, was
chosen as the first Mayor of Birmingham, and the members of
the council settled down to their first debates. There was none of
the dreary housing and public works development with which
the City Council is obsessed today. Nice points of principle occupied this first council—like the second oath, which bound councillors not to use their position to injure the Established Church
of England. Being more or less agreed politically, the new councillors beat out instead their religious differences. Councillor

David Barnett, a Jew, found himself unable to swear "on the true faith of a Christian", and advice was sought from the town clerks of London and Southampton, both places having elected Jews to their councils. Joseph and Charles Sturge, being Quakers, refused to swear a religious oath.

These oaths have long been discontinued, but there is still a fair measure of swearing oaths in connection with the municipal elections today. A short time before the May elections each year the 850 presiding officers, 800 poll clerks, and 700 or so counting assistants, recruited from teachers, council officials, and others for the day, attend *en masse* in three separate groups in the banqueting chamber at the Council House and swear in unison before the Lord Mayor to observe the secrecy of the ballot.

Back to that first town council. The members adopted as the town's motto the single word "Forward". One of the alternative suggestions, mercifully rejected, was "*Fortitudo et Rectum*". Then the names of magistrates were put up, twenty-five of them. In June 1839 the first rate was fixed—of 6d. in the £1. On a rateable value of £475,387 10s. 6d. the yield was £12,000. Birmingham then had a population of 170,000.

The new town council soon found itself in difficulties over the control of the police within the borough. Although the council was empowered to set up a Watch Committee which would exercise control in place of the old Street Commissioners for the Parish of Birmingham and the County Magistrates, a Tory-supported Police Bill was passed by Parliament in August 1839 vesting control of Birmingham's police in a Government Commissioner. The Tory Opposition in Parliament continued to contest the validity of Birmingham's Charter, but in 1842 Parliament confirmed the Charter and abolished the Government Police Commissioner.

Even so, Birmingham Town Council was still in competition with other local governing bodies which exercised their own powers, including the levying of rates for the maintenance of the streets, lighting, drainage, and for other functions. These bodies were the Street Commissioners for the parishes of Birmingham, Deritend and Bordesley, and Duddeston and Nechells, and the Surveyors of Highways for Deritend, Bordesley, and Edgbaston. In particular, this multiple control imposed grave sanitation hazards. The surveyor for Duddeston and Nechells was a beer-seller and saddler who proclaimed himself a 'universal genius' but saw no art in laying out sewers and could not use a spirit level. Such anomalies led, in 1849 at the request of the council, to a government enquiry, the outcome of which was the Improvement Act of 1851, which swept away these other local bodies, leaving the council at last in full control of the town's administration. In the ensuing reorganisation the committee system emerged; nine committees of the corporation each with responsibility for a specific department.

Before the opening in 1879 of the council house, built in Victoria Square at a cost of £84,000 (the art gallery, opened in 1885, cost another £45,000), the departments of Birmingham Corporation were scattered about the town—the town clerk's offices in Temple Street, the treasurer's in Waterloo Street, the Public Works and police in Moor Street, the Medical Officer of Health in Queen's College, Paradise Street, the gas department in the Old Square, and the water department in Broad Street. When, in 1875, Birmingham took over the two private gas-supply companies no fewer than four gas mains were found in one road, while a street lamp in Smallbrook Street was found to have been connected with the wrong company's main for the past eight years. The advantage of municipal control of the two companies at a cost just exceeding £$\frac{1}{2}$ million was soon apparent in a considerable reduction in price to the consumer, and a continuing yearly profit of around £25,000 passed on by the gas department to the corporation, mainly for the relief of rates.

The acquisition of the gas and water undertakings, together with the development of Corporation Street, were inspired by Joseph Chamberlain, who entered Birmingham Town Council in 1869 as a representative of St. Paul's Ward. "Birmingham," he once said, "is not my native town—I wish it were." His great-grand-father, William Chamberlain, left Lacock in Wiltshire, now acquired by the National Trust as one of England's most beautiful villages, where the family had been maltsters; became a shoe-maker in London; and attended a Unitarian Chapel there. When Joseph was 10 his parents moved to Highbury Place, Islington. Eight years later young Joseph came to Birmingham to join his uncle, John Sutton Nettlefold, in the manufacture of screws. An

American had patented an automatic method of making screws which would put hand manufacture out of business, and Nettlefold wanted to acquire the process and put it in operation. Unable to raise the necessary £30,000, he tried to borrow some of it from Joseph Chamberlain, sen., from whom it was forthcoming on the understanding that his son, Joseph, entered the business.

As we follow Joseph Chamberlain through the municipal and national political triumphs which brought such benefit and honour to the city of his adoption, we learn much of the growth of major industries in Birmingham—the screw and explosives industry in particular. The Birmingham of 1854 to which he came had known seventy years of the Industrial Revolution, during which brass and the hardware trade had become to it what cotton was to Manchester, wool to Bradford, and steel to Sheffield.

"The social and political state of Birmingham is far more healthy than that of Manchester," Richard Cobden wrote to John Bright, a Birmingham M.P. from 1857 to 1889. "It arises from the fact that the industry of the hardware district is carried on by small manufacturers, employing a few men and boys each, sometimes only an apprentice or two, whilst the great capitalists in Manchester form an aristocracy. . . . There is a freer intercourse between all classes than in the Lancashire town, where a great and impassible gulf separates the workmen from the employer."

Walking each day from his Edgbaston lodging to his Broad Street office, Joseph, as yet a clerk but destined to become one of the bosses, became familiar with some of Birmingham's worst housing, rushed up hurriedly as the skilled artisanship of the eighteenth century gave way to the mass production of the nineteenth. He talked to the slum dwellers and attained great sympathy with them. Another influence on him was John Bright, from whose speeches Chamberlain realised the power oratory can give a man. Bright's bitter enmity towards the established church and the aristocracy found a ready echo in Joseph Chamberlain, whose upbringing was to the left of nonconformity. When the Birmingham Education League was formed in 1867 to rectify a state of affairs in which only a half of the children up to the age of 12 received any education it became the vehicle for Joseph's first steps in public life.

By this time he was married—and a widower, his wife, Harriet Kenrick, having died at the birth of their son, Austen, in 1863. In 1868 Joseph was married a second time, to Harriet's cousin, Florence Kenrick, who bore him a son, Neville, in 1869, and three daughters, but died in childbirth in 1875 while her husband was Mayor of Birmingham. In 1863 Joseph Chamberlain, sen., had moved to Birmingham with his family, taking up residence in what was then a country mansion, Moor Green Hall, near Moseley. Young Joseph's double tie with the Kenrick family was further strengthened when his sister Mary married William Kenrick and his brother Arthur married Louisa Kenrick. The Kenricks, a wealthy business family living at Berrow Court, Edgbaston, were prominent Unitarians, and it was at church Joseph first met them. About this time another Unitarian, Robert Martineau, a surgeon of Huguenot descent, came to Birmingham, and his son, Thomas, who entered the legal profession, married Emily Kenrick, sister of Joseph Chamberlain's second wife. The great Chamberlain–Kenrick–Martineau 'clique', which did so much for Birmingham, was consolidating, for, to anticipate, when Neville Chamberlain became Lord Mayor in 1915 no fewer than ten of his relatives had held the office of first citizen, and at least two more have done so since. Thomas Martineau, later Sir Thomas, was three times mayor; his son Ernest was Lord Mayor twice, and Ernest's son, Sir Wilfred, once, in 1940–1. Over the fifty years 1903–53, with two short breaks, a Kenrick or a Martineau was chairman of Birmingham Education Committee—the last of the Kenrick chairmen, Alderman Wilfred Byng Kenrick (1872–1962), being one of Birmingham's great and much-loved 'characters', though in a quiet and modest way, for his spare, bowler-hatted figure, always without an overcoat, was to be seen, up until his eighties, weaving among Birmingham's thickest traffic on his bicycle in all weathers.

When Joseph Chamberlain, sen., came to Moor Green he acquired an interest in the brassfounding firm of Smith and Chamberlain. Young Joseph, meantime, had added to his interests a directorship of Lloyd's Bank, and, with the firm's output now 75 per cent of Birmingham's screw production, had become a partner in Chamberlain and Nettlefold in 1869. Five years later the complete Chamberlain interest was sold out for

The River Arrow

£600,000, of which young Joseph got £120,000, which enabled him to devote his energies to public life.

He was lucky in starting his municipal career when trade was reviving after the 'hungry forties', which enabled him to reverse the parsimonious policies of Joseph Allday and his 'economy' group centred around the Old Woodman Hotel in Easy Row; lucky, too, in his association with Dr. R. W. Dale, minister of Carr's Lane Chapel, whose practical Christianity took the form of preaching a raising of the standard of living through municipal development. The Rev. George Dawson, a clergyman of liberal views, had also been dedicated to enriching the lives of Birmingham workers by improving their environment, and Dale once said: "Mr. Dawson is the prophet of the new movement, but Mr. Dawson had not the kind of faculty necessary for putting faith into practice. . . . This was largely done by Mr. Joseph Chamberlain."

Joe's 'Improvement Scheme' involved 93 acres; the Corporation acquiring the freehold of 40 or 50 of them at a cost around £1,300,000. He pushed Corporation Street through a warren of slums at a cost around £34,000, the Corporation borrowing money at $3\frac{1}{2}$ per cent. Letting sites to builders on a seventy-five-year lease, Chamberlain believed there would be a threefold increase in their rateable value. He was enabled to proceed with the scheme through Disraeli's Artisans' Dwellings Act of 1875, which gave local authorities power over insanitary areas, and his brothers, Arthur and Richard, both now on the council, helped him see it through.

Joseph Chamberlain's high hopes were well borne out—the properties increased in value a hundredfold or more.

One of the first intentions of a city council controlled again in 1966 by the Conservatives after fourteen years of Labour rule was to dispose of these freeholds to help reduce the heavy loan charges incurred by a Labour administration, and thus make a saving for the ratepayers. Opponents of the scheme waxed eloquent about the city selling its birthright for a mass of potage, and pointed out that to retain the freeholds would enable the corporation eventually to redevelop the area without the need of compulsory purchase. They also pointed out that the rents from

K

A swim in the new Stechford Baths

the Corporation Street properties amounted to about £300,000 a year, and that a selling price of twenty-five times the annual rental would bring in around £7½ million, which would, applied to reducing the debt, save some £500,000 a year in loan charges. Subtract from this the £300,000 loss in income, and the annual saving of £200,000 would equal barely a penny rate. Selling the freeholds would, declared the opposition, be a short-sighted policy and a short-term saving.

The ratepayers, bludgeoned by constant rate increases and bemused by their sufferings in the demolition and rebuilding of Birmingham, grasped thankfully at this penny straw, and continued to increase the Conservative majority from a mere two in 1966 to eighty-four in 1969.

In the first three years of Conservative control—up to 1968— freeholds of nearly £5 million were sold—including important Corporation Street sites such as those of C. and A. Modes and the Birmingham Post and Mail Ltd.—and the selling policy continues. Alas, the rate, which was 11s. in the £1 in 1964, had risen to 16s. 7d. in 1970.

Birmingham became a city on 14th January 1889. Many believe that it takes a cathedral to make a city, but they are wrong. Birmingham had been a city for sixteen years before St. Philip's became the cathedral church of the Diocese of Birmingham in 1905. We became a city for the asking. On 4th December 1888 the town council petitioned the Queen that Birmingham had completed half a century of municipal life and was the largest borough in the kingdom not yet dignified as a city. Her Majesty speedily remedied this by Royal Charter, though it was not until 1896 that the chief magistrate was raised from plain mayor, by Letters Patent, to Lord Mayor. He was Sir James Smith.

In 1868 Birmingham's parliamentary representation had been increased from two members to three—all liberals, as the town's M.P.s had been since 1832, with the exception of Richard Spooner, a solitary Conservative who was elected in 1844 on a split Liberal vote, but unseated in 1847. With the resignation of George Dixon in 1876 Joseph Chamberlain was returned unopposed, to join Philip Muntz and John Bright as Birmingham's M.P.s. He was elected again with them in 1880, and after Birmingham had gained seven parliamentary constituencies at the redistribution of seats by the County Franchise Bill in 1885, he held West Birmingham through eight General Elections, being unopposed four times, until 1910, whereafter his son, Austen, won the seat seven times from 1918 to 1945. During this same period, 1918–45, Neville Chamberlain won Ladywood Division three times, moving for the remaining four elections to the safe Conservative seat at Edgbaston after Oswald Mosley had reduced his majority in 1924 to only seventy-seven.

Before his election to Parliament Joseph Chamberlain had been busy re-organising the Birmingham Liberal Association, of which Francis Schnadhorst, a former draper, was secretary. With the closure of the Birmingham-based Education League and the transfer of its functions to Liberal associations, a National Liberal Federation was set up with headquarters in Atlas Chambers, Paradise Street, Birmingham, and with Joseph Chamberlain as president. In 1880 he became President of the Board of Trade, with a seat in the Cabinet, and, in addition to his London residence, he set about building Highbury, his Moseley home in Birmingham, near Moor Green Hall, inherited by his brother Arthur on their father's death.

In the Commons Chamberlain began to castigate the Lords for their opposition to the enfranchisement of the agricultural workers, but found himself increasingly opposed—as one who favoured continued union between Great Britain and Ireland—to Gladstone's Home Rule policy, and by the 1886 election there was a split between Gladstone's Whig Liberals and Chamberlain's Liberal-Unionists. Chamberlain was returned as one of seventy-eight Liberal-Unionists, and Schnadhorst, a Gladstonian, took the National Liberal Federation from Birmingham to London. Joseph Chamberlain resigned and created his own National Radical Union in Birmingham.

The year 1891 saw the birth of the Unionist Party, which later became identified with the Conservative Party, though the term Unionist lasted longer in Birmingham than anywhere other than Northern Ireland. In January of that year the Birmingham Liberal-Unionists and Conservatives held a joint Town Hall meeting. Later in the year Birmingham was the venue of the Conservative National Union's annual meeting, and, at a luncheon in honour of Lord Salisbury, the Prime Minister, Chamberlain proposed the toast 'The Unionist Cause'. A national electoral arrangement was concluded, based on the 1886 election—Liberal-Unionists and Conservatives were to select the candidate in seats held by them in that year, the other side giving him their support.

Chamberlain married a third wife in 1888, Mary Endicott, an American girl. His brother, Richard, was on Birmingham Council and mayor in 1880 when the Chamberlain fountain was erected as a compliment to Joseph. Occupying the only traffic-free spot near the old register office in Edmund Street, it formed a background to the wedding groups of many hundreds who knew nothing of its significance. Now that the register office has moved to Broad Street the figures of Boulton, Watt, and Murdock steal the Chamberlain fountain's thunder as a wedding-photograph background.

Richard Chamberlain was ultimately elected M.P. for Islington—one of Joseph's Liberal-Unionists. Walter, the youngest brother, became chairman of Guest, Keen, and Nettlefolds, Avery's Ltd., and other companies, while Arthur, the brother closest to Joseph, went into Chamberlain and Hookham, the electrical engineering firm.

At the time of Joseph Chamberlain's arrival in Birmingham another young man, a Scot, George Kynoch, had come to the town, and after a spell as a bank clerk moved to a modest factory in Whittall Street making percussion caps. Shrewd, intelligent, and ambitious, he was soon in charge there, and at a powder magazine and factory at Witton, Birmingham. This latter he took over and, as Kynoch and Company, it prospered with cartridge contracts for the War Office. At 40 years old George Kynoch had his factory and a fortune probably amounting to £80,000. When his luxurious style of living brought difficulties he sold his business to a company known as George Kynoch and Company for £70,000 cash and 4,000 £10 shares. The new company slumped badly, but in 1889 Arthur Chamberlain became chairman and it prospered. The same could not be said for a sisal plantation in the Bahamas which Neville managed for his father. In five years Joseph Chamberlain lost £50,000 on the venture. Neville eventually established himself with a directorship at Elliotts Metal Company, Selly Oak, though his major concern was with Hoskins and Company, later Hoskins and Sewell, making ships' berths at Bordesley. Austen had meanwhile become M.P. for East Worcestershire—a Liberal-Unionist.

Arthur Chamberlain was a believer in the shorter working day, and Kynoch's was among the pioneers of the forty-eight-hour week. He was an enemy of trade unions, and when a union tried to make him reinstate a dismissed foreman he told them that he would not, and, further—happy days—that no member of a "trade society" would be employed at Witton. A strike did ensue, but Arthur broke it, and turned his mind to the use of cordite, a new smokeless explosive, for the production of which he built a factory at Arklow, County Wicklow. Later came the Kynoch machine-gun incorporating an invention for cooling the barrel automatically without the use of water.

In Salisbury's 1895 government Joseph Chamberlain was Colonial Secretary and Austen a Civil Lord of the Admiralty, so the Boer War brought embarrassment when Lloyd George began pointing out the Chamberlains' interest in Hoskins and Co., contractors for ships' berths to the Admiralty, and in Kynoch's, which was chosen from seven tenders to supply cordite for the War Office, despite its figure being the highest.

The war over, Joseph Chamberlain visited South Africa for two months, being seen off and welcomed back to Birmingham by torchlight processions, while the Chamberlain Clock, an archaic green-painted erection at Warstone Lane crossroads in his old constituency, still commemorates the journey. In July 1906 Birmingham went *en fête* for Joseph's seventieth birthday, with a civic banquet, mass rallies in six parks, and bunting across every street. But immediately after the rejoicings Chamberlain had a stroke, and his chief preoccupation thereafter, until his death in 1914, was the new University of Birmingham.

The political spotlight swung on to Austen Chamberlain, who was one of two obvious candidates for leadership of the Conservative Party on Balfour's retirement in 1911, the other being Walter Long. As often happens, a third candidate of lesser magnitude was selected, Bonar Law, who remained at the helm until 1921, when Austen, then Chancellor of the Exchequer in Lloyd George's Coalition Government, was enthusiastically elected party leader. The next year, however, saw the truth of what Winston

Churchill once said of Austen Chamberlain, that he "always played the game, and always lost it". When, in face of increasing Conservative distaste for the Coalition, Lloyd George offered to resign the premiership in favour of Austen Chamberlain, Chamberlain begged him not to do so. The consequence of his loyalty was that late in 1922, when the Coalition fell, Austen was set aside by the Conservative Party at the famous Carlton Club meeting, and Bonar Law, recalled to the leadership, became Prime Minister.

Neville Chamberlain had entered Parliament in 1918, and in Bonar Law's 1923 government became Minister of Health, rising to Chancellor of the Exchequer later in the year when Baldwin took over as Prime Minister on Law's resignation in face of his impending death. In Baldwin's 1924–9 government Austen became Foreign Secretary and was knighted for his work on the Locarno Treaties in 1925. Neville, as Minister of Health, had a rougher ride. Unemployment was high, retrenchment was in the air, and economy in the Cabinet Room. The unemployed were being organised by a Communist-inspired National Unemployed Workers Movement, and there were frequent processions around Birmingham after midday meetings in the Bull Ring—sad, squalid demonstrations. The politically conscious front ranks sometimes sang the "Internationale", but more frequently it was the more-easily memorised "Red Flag". Political ardour tailed off nearer the end of the processions among those who joined in from sheer boredom and desperation at their workless state. There were, however, fathers and mothers pushing broken-down prams with their children, and always, as the rabble passed Empire House, Edmund Street, the Conservative Party headquarters, it achieved a unison shout of "Who stole the mothers' milk? Chamberlain"—a reference to one of the Government's economies.

These were unhappy processions, bearing visible evidence of human misery and despair in threadbare clothing and inadequate footwear—so different from demonstrations and marches today of well-fed strikers, municipal tenants, or long-haired layabout protesters, tattered and disreputable by choice rather than from the necessity forced on them by unemployment.

Since 1918, when Birmingham electors first voted in twelve

constituencies, the Conservatives had swept the board in three General Elections, with the exception, in 1918, of a Coalition Labour candidate with Conservative support, Ernest Hallas in Duddeston. In 1924 the first breach was made when Robert Dennison (Labour) defeated Sir Herbert Austin in his own citadel of King's Norton. Even so, the city contributed two others to the Baldwin Government in Leopold Amery, that mighty atom from Sparkbrook, who was climbing considerable mountains named after him in his sixties, as Dominions Secretary; and Sir Arthur Steel-Maitland, M.P. for Erdington, as Minister of Labour. Mrs. Neville Chamberlain was the goddess of Birmingham women Conservatives, who, in her presence, invariably began their meetings with "Land of Hope and Glory" and "For She's a Jolly Good Fellow".

The phoney National Government of 1931 saw Birmingham parliamentary representation back to an unbroken twelve Conservatives after seven seats had been lost to Labour, and one, the unpredictable King's Norton, won back for the Conservatives by Major Lionel Beaumont-Thomas, in 1929. The Conservatives retained all twelve seats in 1935, but of the thirteen seats in 1945 they won only Edgbaston, Handsworth, and Moseley, a lowest ebb from which they had won back to five seats in 1964.

Birmingham has always had its peculiar electoral factors. The Chamberlain tradition and the votes of multitudes of small back-street shopkeepers helped Conservative candidates in working-class constituencies up to the Second World War. Although it involved no unexpected representation, the impact of a much-admired personality swept Miss Edith Pitt, the eldest daughter of a large artisan family, into Commons for the select Edgbaston constituency. In 1951 she polled very well against Roy Jenkins in Stechford—an intriguing confrontation of a Conservative who left school at fourteen and a brilliant Balliol man, already the interim biographer of Attlee, holding the lists for Labour. He, of course, was to become Chancellor of the Exchequer.

Edgbaston had been represented all through the twentieth century so far by Sir Francis Lowe, Neville Chamberlain, and Sir Peter Bennett, and on Sir Peter's elevation to the peerage in 1953 a Manchester businessman, Colonel Douglas Glover, was chosen as candidate by the divisional executive committee. Six hundred members of the divisional association thought differently, however, and rejected their executive's choice, selecting instead Edith Pitt, who became not only a fine constituency M.P. but held various government posts, became Dame Edith, and worked herself to an untimely death in 1966, when her friends packed Birmingham Cathedral for a memorial service.

In June 1969 Birmingham returned its first Liberal M.P. since John Bright in 1886, the tiny Ladywood Division electing Councillor Wallace L. Lawler. This was a purely personal and well-deserved triumph, a tribute to Wallace Lawler's energy and pertinacity over many years, and practically nothing at all to do with Liberalism, whatever this may be. Commenting on the Ladywood result, a *Birmingham Post* leader writer said: "Ladywood is a Lawler success, but is it a Liberal success? Modern Liberalism is not very easy to define—it covers a multitude of attitudes and, particularly among the young Liberals, some 'way-out' notions that Liberals of an older generation would unhesitatingly have repudiated." Several months later *The Birmingham Post* published a picture of seven Liberal municipal candidates and councillors in the city, their average age only 24!

In 1944 Wallace Lawler founded the Public Opinion Action Association, a forum which met weekly at Digbeth Institute, and for some years after the war gave a platform to national spokesmen for unpopular causes and a regular safety valve to those of us in Birmingham who generally could not conform to a party line, though one young member, Mr. Denis H. Howell, conformed well enough to become Labour M.P. for All Saints Division in 1955, for Small Heath in 1961, and subsequently Minister for Sport. Derided by the political parties, P.O.A.A. fulfilled a valuable function in Birmingham, with audiences of a hundred or so each week. Unhappily its rump has continued now that there seems no call for the organisation. Some of us were not interested in the 'action' side of P.O.A.A., but with the enthusiastic Wallace Lawler as the mainspring it took up causes—in housing problems, and for old age pensioners—and it was with such a rag-bag of personal service to his credit that Mr. Lawler won a seat as a Liberal on the city council in 1962. He has been followed by six others, in his own and two other wards, younger lightweights of no significance, 'back-passage' politicians.

In my early enthusiasm as a convert to Socialism—long since jettisoned—I once went canvassing in Aston Ward with a home-spun councillor. He knocked at a door in one yard and was greeted by a surly woman.

"Don't you know me?" he demanded.

"No," she said.

"I'm Councillor ——," he said. "I got a lamp put up your back passage."

Since then the do-gooder type of local representative, usually with no wider horizons at all, has to me been a 'back-passage' politician.

There are today 156 members of Birmingham City Council, thirty-nine wards with three councillors and one alderman each—he acts as returning officer for his ward. The aldermen are elected not by the voters but by the councillors, and serve for a period of six years before seeking re-election. In the council chamber our city fathers do not sit in party blocks. They mingle haphazardly, but retain their personal seats. When a newly elected councillor goes before the Town Clerk to make his declaration to serve he is shown the seating plan and takes his choice of the free seats. He gets no pay, but a modest allowance for time genuinely lost from work, and a free travel pass on city buses.

There are no Chamberlains, Kenricks, or Martineaus on the city council today. Among Birmingham's recent Lord Mayors have been a works gardener, a surveyor and auctioneer, a personnel officer, a sheet-metal worker, an insurance broker, a solicitor, a director of a fuel company, a trade-union organiser, a manufacturer, and an insurance official who got a knighthood.

Labour gained control of Birmingham City Council for the first time in 1946, but the Conservatives had a majority again by 1949. Three years later Labour regained control, and ran the city from 1952 until 1966. Since the war politics has become increasingly discredited in Birmingham. There was a record municipal election poll in 1949 of 50·7 per cent, but by 1956 this was down to 34·18 per cent, since when a steady slump brought it to a 29·18 per cent rock bottom in 1969. One factor which could cause this apathy is the death of the public meeting—advice bureaux are a poor substitute, transforming those who should be intellectual and physical leaders into mere welfare workers, just more bureaucrats in fact. Nor does television politics stimulate interest in local affairs. Candidates are of an inferior standard, less articulate because they have no actual platform, and all too often reliant for publicity on silly stunts with the Press. Perhaps the primary cause of public disinterest is the growing feeling on the part of the electorate of frustrating impotence in the face of rates which rise unchecked by the 'economy' party, the Conservatives, as steeply as they did under the 'spenders' of the Labour Party.

Birmingham's neighbour, Wolverhampton, has continued to hold its domestic rate at 11s. 8d. in the £1 for the three years 1968–70, though it must be added that over this period the municipal poll has been on average only 3 per cent higher than in Birmingham. Birmingham's rate in those three years has been 12s. 6d., 14s. 6d., and 16s. 7d., with the business rate running as high as 13s. 4d., 15s. 9d., and 18s. 3d.

The poll in the 1966 parliamentary election in Birmingham, which returned four Conservatives and nine Labour M.P.s, was 69·1 per cent. Voting in the city always shows one intriguing phenomenon. From time immemorial Selly Oak, King's Norton, and Northfield wards have polled a much higher percentage in the municipal elections than other wards, while there is always a comparatively high poll in the parliamentary constituencies including these areas. This has been put down to the political consciousness of the Austin workers who live thereabouts—though the results have not necessarily reflected the point of view they might be expected to hold. It possibly stems from the old King's Norton Division being a marginal or even unpredictable constituency, voting against the swing of the pendulum in 1924 and 1929, with Labour's 1924 victory pepping up the Conservative organisation, and the Conservative victory in 1929—one of only two Conservative gains from Labour in Britain—similarly pepping up the Labour organisation.

Forty years ago politics was fun in Birmingham. We still talk with relish of two great Rag Market meetings only two years apart. At the first of these hustings in this vast cavernous covered space, in 1929, Sir Oswald Mosley, Labour M.P. for nearby Smethwick, wiped the floor intellectually with Commander Oliver Locker-Lampson, that eccentric ultra-patriotic M.P. for Handsworth. Sir Oswald was the blue-eyed boy of the Birmingham 'Reds', and I have a vivid memory of him on polling night 1929, having retained his seat safely at Smethwick, visiting Birmingham after midnight and being tossed about on the shoulders of jubilant Labour supporters in a packed Victoria Square—flamboyant, ebullient, and victorious with flaming red rosette and waving black hair and moustache.

What a political tragedy was about to be unfolded. Within two years Mosley had found Ramsay Macdonald an impossible, incompetent, and jealous leader, had left the Labour Party, and was fighting the 1931 election as leader of the New Party with a bodyguard of ex-pugilists and rugger players. Labour supporters in Birmingham swore that their previous darling would never again be allowed a hearing in the city, and they wrecked his crowded Rag Market meeting during the 1931 campaign. It was a riot comparable with any in Birmingham's stormy political past, with fists, chairs, and bottles flying before a courageous and defiant Sir Oswald was rescued from the wreck of his platform and marched, with his supporters, up the Bull Ring to his hotel under strong police protection.

Through all its political changes, perhaps one thing has remained unchanged in Birmingham. Cobden, as we have seen, wrote over a century ago of the many small manufacturers who were the backbone of Birmingham. Half a century ago the Conservative Party made its strongest appeal to the hosts of small shopkeepers supposedly threatened by socialism. And in his maiden speech in the Commons in 1969 Wallace Lawler, the city's new Liberal M.P., made a spirited defence of the 'small man'.

Alas, Lawler's 'break-through' lasted only until the General Election of June 1970, when his parochialism fell in a close fight with the even more limited parochialism of a Labour woman candidate. He had, however, the consolation of having become an alderman of the city after the May elections.

The General Election of 1970 left Birmingham with six Conservative M.P.s to seven Labour.

VIII

THE WAR YEARS

ON 5th September 1895 a Mr. Jones presented himself at the Birmingham Small Arms works in Armoury Road, Small Heath, claiming to be the assistant secretary of the British South Africa Company. He was, he said, commissioned to buy all the Lee Metford rifles available, to be despatched from Southampton to Cape Town on the following night. Hard work and a night shift produced 2,000 rifles, while 1 million cartridges were also found. At 9 a.m. on 6th September these were put on a special train, and by 4 p.m. were aboard the S.S. *Scott* at Southampton. On 29th December 1895, the notorious Jameson Raid took place, precipitating the Boer War. It was strongly rumoured that the Lee Metfords from the S.S. *Scott* were the rifles used. Guns cannot be made without their having an occasional impact on events, whether for good or ill.

The Birmingham gunsmiths called upon by Sir Richard Newdigate to supply William III with muskets (see Chapter III) had continued to trade as a group until in 1854, their numbers swollen to fourteen, they banded together more definitely to fulfil their government contracts during the Crimean War as the Birmingham Small Arms Trade Association. On 7th June 1861 the association formed a public company, the Birmingham Small Arms Co. Ltd., "to make guns by machinery"—a break with the normal hand method viewed with some suspicion by the craftsmen of the trade. The new company's nominal capital was £55,000 in £25 shares, and by 1863 the factory had been built on 25 acres at Small Heath—on condition that the Great Western Railway should build a station near by, which it did, known as

'Small Heath and Sparkbrook'. A picture of this factory, dated about 1866, shows a hansom cab at the arched door and picnickers on the fields alongside, with a path, now Armoury Road, running across them.

Soon the B.S.A. was the largest private arms manufacturer in Europe, and world-wide fame followed. When the Prussian Government ordered 40 million cartridge cases during the Franco-Prussian War the directors acquired a munitions factory near by at Adderley Park. But peace in Europe brought crisis to Small Heath, and in August 1878 the B.S.A. closed down for a year, while the skilled gunsmiths dug the ponds and laid out flower-beds in the new Victoria Park.

Obviously the company had to find some line to tide it over during periods when swords were turned into ploughshares. In 1880 an eccentric inventor visited the factory, which had reopened on a contract for 6,000 Martini-Henry rifles. He was Mr. E. C. F. Otto, and before the astonished directors he heaved his new bicycle, with a saddle slung between two large wheels side by side, on to the boardroom table and rode up and down. From that moment the B.S.A. was in the cycle business, and 1,000 Otto bicycles were made at Small Heath during the next few years. Gunmaking continued too, and in 1881 the famous trademark of three crossed rifles was registered. Nevertheless there was a £70,000 bank overdraft, and the £25 shares were selling for £1 5s. The manufacture of 1,500 of the world's first rear-driven safety bicycles staved off disaster until, in 1888, a decision to equip the British Army with the new Lee Metford magazine rifle brought a change from cycle manufacture just two years before 1890 ushered in the pneumatic tyre.

Five years later the rifle trade slumped again, but bicycles were now the craze. In September 1893 a George Illston called at the Small Heath works to fix a game of billiards with an executive friend. Looking around the works, he saw the idle shell-making plant, persuaded the management to adapt it for cycle hubs, and became B.S.A.'s first commercial traveller at 5 per cent commission—soon, paradoxically, to fall to $2\frac{1}{2}$ and then $1\frac{1}{4}$ because of his success. At $1\frac{1}{4}$ per cent Illston made £3,000 a year.

By the turn of the century 3,000 were engaged at Small Heath. Sporting rifles were made; a record of 2,500 rifles a week was reached during the Boer War, and production of cycle fittings continued. Expansion was now rapid. Premises were taken over in Montgomery Street, and in 1908 a complete B.S.A. bicycle was again on the market. Next came the first B.S.A. motor cycle, at £50. B.S.A. entered the car industry, too. In 1910 it made a spectacular take-over, of the Daimler Co. Ltd. of Coventry, but with the First World War guns and more guns became the cry. Ten thousand Lee Enfield rifles left Armoury Road each week, and throughout the war 145,397 Lewis guns were made by B.S.A., all of which necessitated the extension of the Armoury Road works.

During the war the B.S.A. group employed 20,000, but again war was followed by depression. In the twenty-one years between the two wars B.S.A. £1 shares fell to a few shillings, and dividends were paid on eight occasions only.

The only bright spot of these days was the development of the motor-cycle trade. "One in four is a B.S.A." was the slogan. Cycles, too, boomed in the thirties. But the rifle and the machine-gun plant lay moribund, with not a single order in seventeen years from the end of the First World War until the mid-1930s, when rearmament against Germany could no longer be delayed.

The Second World War was soon going disastrously for Britain, but with the retreat from Dunkirk the Armoury Road factory went on a seven-day week, to rearm the survivors with rifles and to supply machine-guns for Spitfires and Hurricanes. Naturally the Luftwaffe viewed all this with jaundiced eyes, and after several lesser raids came the blitz of 19th November 1941, when two direct hits brought the southern end of the four-storey 1915 building crashing to the ground, killing fifty-three employees and injuring eighty-nine. Two nights later the original gunsmiths' building was bombed and the entire factory was evacuated.

By the end of 1941 fourteen factories had been requisitioned to carry on B.S.A.'s vital role, and the new factory at Kitts Green was to the fore in the production of machine tools. B.S.A.'s peak war effort involved the control of sixty-seven factories, employing 28,000, who produced more than half of Britain's small arms.

During my First World War boyhood in Small Heath the 'gun factory', as the B.S.A. was generally called, raised fears among many of us living near by that it would attract German Zeppelins. One night in April 1918 bombs were said to have been dropped in Olton Reservoir, some two miles along the railway from the B.S.A., and it was believed that the bomb-aimers mistook the moonlit water for the glass roof of the 'gun factory', both being alongside the railway.

Three times only in the First World War did Zeppelins reach Birmingham, and there was just one fatal casualty—his gravestone stands in my garden. One October night in 1917 several bombs were dropped on the Austin Works at Longbridge. During the raid, a mile away at the Manor House, Northfield, the home of Dame Elizabeth Cadbury, one of her pet monkeys died. He was duly buried in the Cadbury animal graveyard and an epitaph carved on a shaped 'headstone' of wood:

> Jacko
> A Monkey, killed
> with fright,
> Caused by a Zepp
> that came over
> one night.
> 1917.

In 1968 I acquired this historic memorial from an old gardener who unearthed it from a dusty corner of a stable at the Manor House, now a hall of residence for the University of Birmingham.

The picture in the Hitler war was a more solemn one. In seventy-seven air raids on Birmingham the death roll of citizens was 2,241, with 3,010 seriously injured and 3,682 slightly injured. A total of 140,336 dwelling-houses was damaged, 12,125 seriously; while damage was caused to 2,365 factories and workshops and 4,003 business premises. Among the 654 public buildings to suffer from German bombs were the Market Hall, completely burned out on 26th August 1940; the Empire Theatre, destroyed on 28th October 1940; the Prince of Wales Theatre, destroyed on 9th April 1941; and the regency church built by Thomas Rickman in 1826-9, St. Thomas, Bath Row, destroyed on 12th December 1940, but for the tower with its cupola and a curved colonnade, which are now incorporated in a garden of rest.

The city's worst raid on 19th-20th November 1940 blasted 23 districts with 646 heavy bombs, 48 unexploded bombs, 18 parachute mines, 243 sets of incendiary bombs, and 17 oil bombs. One hundred factories suffered damage; 150 gas mains were fractured and 58 water mains. The dead numbered 615, with 1,084 injured. On 11–12th December 1940, the longest raid, thirteen and a half hours, brought a death roll of 263, with 543 injured. Throughout this protracted raid Birmingham's anti-aircraft guns were silent, to the disgust of many citizens. The night had been chosen for an experiment in night interception by Hampden aircraft, and it was poor solace to the blitz victims throughout the city that, though the experiment yielded no 'kills', it provided the R.A.F. with valuable information, so that night interception ultimately became an exact science. A young wireless operator in one of the Hampdens, who later came to Birmingham as Flight-Lieutenant W. E. Clayfield in charge of R.A.F. recruiting, has written of his bird's-eye view of Birmingham's ordeal: "Later, through cloud gaps, we saw the city ablaze. It was a dreadful sight. Every now and then we could see fires starting up, then bigger and darker flashes followed by great spirals of smoke."

Remembering the constant recital of air-raid stories in those harrowing days, one tends to forget that many Brummies now grown into adults have never heard a bomb explode. Despite so many contemporary war scenes from far and wide on television, they find it hard to imagine their own neighbourhood the scene of horror and desolation that confronted me when I was allowed twenty-four hours' leave from the comparative safety of a country searchlight site near Stratford-upon-Avon to see how my wife and home had fared in the 19th–20th November raid. Jack Shaw of *The Birmingham Post* recalled that night in an article from which I append one incident for the edification of the under-thirties.

> I was walking down Coventry Road during the height of a blitz in November. The area was so dotted with fires that anywhere one could have read a newspaper with ease. The Civil Defence was doing its usual superhuman best, but for the moment the fires, because of a fractured water main, had won. A weary fireman stood by a hose from which only a trickle of water emerged, a mug of steaming tea in his hand. I asked him where he had got the tea.
>
> He pointed to a group of people standing at the end of a row of

A detail from the mural in Old Square

houses—at least it was the end of the row then; earlier in the evening it must have been about the middle of the row. I walked over and saw the most astonishing sight. The bomb which had torn apart the street had also broken a sizeable gas main, and a hissing jet of flame leapt horizontally from the last, tottering house, turning up at the end like a serpent's tongue. Over the upturned flame someone had erected a sort of tripod and on this was balanced an old-fashioned zinc bath. Presiding over the entire scene was my "Witch of Endor". Over her nightdress was an old black coat, tied around the middle by a bright blue and white scarf—in happier days a Birmingham City fan's scarf, I imagined—and her iron grey hair stood out in elf locks all over her head.

Her language was enough to make a Billingsgate porter blush, but people kept appearing with packets of tea, or buckets of water, which was flung or poured into the zinc bath, from which anyone could help themselves to a mug of some of the finest tea I have ever tasted.

The First World War found Birmingham still basking in the glory of a description accorded it by J. Ralph in *Harper's Monthly Magazine*, 1890—"the best-governed city in the world". The city showed that it was well on the ball, being used by the Government as a guinea-pig in one important measure—rationing—and introducing another revolutionary scheme in the Municipal Bank referred to in Chapter VI.

In December 1917 Mr. James Curtis (knighted in 1919), the Midland Food Commissioner, was asked by Lord Rhondda, the Food Controller, to inaugurate a pilot rationing scheme in Birmingham. Already, anticipating government policy by six months, Birmingham Co-operative Society had introduced sugar rationing cards for its members in July 1917, and during August Birmingham's provisional Food Committee became a statutory authority. Sugar retailers, 4,586 in number, had to register and make returns of their stock and customers, and in September 1917 sugar rationing cards had been introduced.

Lord Rhondda's request covered family ration cards for tea, butter, and margarine in addition to sugar, and before the twelve weeks' experiment was ended rationing was so successful that first other local authorities and then the Government adopted it.

It was, of course, in the production of armaments that Birmingham made its major contribution to the war effort. Sir John French said in 1915, "The issue is a struggle between Krupps and

L

Anglers start young in Birmingham
The Serbian Orthodox Church of St. Lazar

Birmingham." Among the other obvious statistics, like 15 million shells being produced in three and a half years, are the hundreds of thousands of Mills grenades—a Birmingham invention—made by the men who normally made gas meters. Those of us who were boys in Small Heath remember how we used to scramble for the parachutes which carried the experimental star-shells constantly fired from Wilder's fireworks factory in Greet. But for all Birmingham's munitions effort, 54 per cent of the city's male population of military age served in the Forces.

In 1914 the city followed the lead of Liverpool and Manchester in forming 'Pals' battalions of friends to serve together. The first week of recruiting brought 4,500 men, followed soon by £10,000 subscribed towards their equipment by well-wishers. At first styled the 1st, 2nd, and 3rd Birmingham Battalions, the 'pals' were incorporated in the Royal Warwickshire Regiment as the 14th, 15th, and 16th Battalions. All three battalions distinguished themselves in July 1916 at Longueval and Delville Wood on the Western Front. On 30th July, the first time a creeping barrage was employed, the 14th, one of the assaulting battalions, were badly mauled because the artillery preparation had been falling short. Forced to take refuge in shell holes only 50 yards from the German trenches, they were ultimately relieved by the 15th, and as the 16th came up in support all three Birmingham battalions were fighting shoulder to shoulder and in the same trenches on the same day.

The 3rd September 1916 saw the 14th fighting bravely in an abortive attack on Falfemont Farm, the 15th and 16th also being involved nearby. Later in the month these Birmingham men covered themselves with glory in the capture of Morval. Congratulating their Division—the 5th—on its brave contribution to the Battle of the Somme, General Rawlinson wrote: "The heavy fighting in Delville Wood and Longueval, the attack and capture of Falfemont Farm and Leuze Wood, and finally the storming of Morval, are feats of arms seldom equalled in the annals of the British Army. They constitute a record of unvarying success which it has been the lot of few divisions to attain; the gallantry, valour, and endurance of all ranks have been wholly admirable."

Three months earlier other battalions of the Royal Warwicks, with many Birmingham men, played an heroic part in the Battle of Beaumont Hamel on 1st July. They are commemorated in two pictorial windows of the soldiers' chapel at Knowle Church, five miles beyond the city, with a caption quoting 8th Corps Orders of 4th July 1916: "There were no cowards or waverers and not a man fell out. It was a magnificent display of disciplined courage worthy of the best traditions of the British race."

The three Birmingham battalions were heavily engaged at Polderhoek in October 1917, and during the next month they moved to Italy, where, in January and February 1918, they saw action on the Piave. Back in Flanders, they fought before Merville in April 1918 and at Cambrai in September and October 1918.

"Homes fit for heroes" was the promise made to these men, and housing was Birmingham's main preoccupation between the wars; housing, and the unemployment of the Depression years which moulded my generation so that we are not over-sympathetic to the problems of modern youth.

Birmingham's first municipal houses were built in Alum Rock in 1919. On 25th July 1930 the 30,000th municipal house was opened at Kingstanding, and on 23rd October 1933, at Weoley Castle, the 40,000th, when, performing the opening ceremony, Neville Chamberlain, Chancellor of the Exchequer, said: "Birmingham celebrates an achievement on the part of the City Council which has no parallel in this or any other country." By 20th June 1939 the 50,000th house was formally opened at Lea Hall. Statistics issued to mark the occasion were that 200,000 people had thus been housed on 5,380 acres at an all-in cost of £23,592,000. The building was spread over thirty-one estates, the largest being Kingstanding with 4,802 houses on 493 acres; Fox Hollies and Gospel Farm with 3,762 on 393 acres; Billesley Farm with 2,442 on 374 acres; and Weoley Castle with 2,718 on 312 acres.

Birmingham had sowed the wind; it has been reaping the whirlwind ever since. These pre-Second World War municipal houses never yielded an economic rent, being subsidised on average 4s. per week per house by rates and taxes. The Acts under which they were built stemmed from the early Victorian liberalism of Lord Shaftesbury—Acts for the Housing of the Working Classes at a period when the 'working classes' were synonymous with the poorest classes in a scale that rose next to the 'lower middle classes', who tended to be white-collar workers as against the manual labourers in the working classes. Time has dealt less kindly with the white-collar workers than with the manual labourers, so that the former, to the degree that they are owner-occupiers of non-municipal houses, rightly resent continuing to subsidise their less thrifty and often better-off fellow citizens. This has constituted one of the major bones of contention in Birmingham for years, and shows no sign of abating. The municipal tenants have always been the pampered darlings of Labour politicians, and, as I write, early in 1970, Birmingham's Labour M.P.s are demanding that the city's 350,000 ratepayers should pay an extra 7d. in the £1 rate to meet a housing deficit, rather than the municipal tenants pay an average rent increase of 7s. 6d. weekly.

As municipal tenants are also ratepayers, they now find themselves with a grouse. In the way that private householders subsidise them, they now have to pay for Birmingham City Council's mania for building, on borrowed loans with very high interest charges, wherever it can lay its grasp on some green and unsullied countryside.

There were extensions of the city in 1928, when a portion of Perry Barr was taken over, and in 1931 when large parts of Castle Bromwich and Sheldon were brought within the boundary. This last accretion included Bromford Bridge Racecourse, the British Industries Fair, and Castle Bromwich Aerodrome. It was significant of Birmingham's outlook that in 1937 the city council resisted a suggestion that Shirley might be transferred from Solihull. Shirley was already well built up, and Birmingham was exclusively interested in land on which it could build—and build it has, on the racecourse, the B.I.F. site, and on the aerodrome.

The new municipal estates posed problems in the 1930s because they lacked community facilities. In 1932 Kingstanding had a population of 30,000, rather more than Shrewsbury; yet against Kingstanding's one church and one hall Shrewsbury had thirty churches, fifteen church halls, five other halls, and two public libraries. The Birmingham Common Good Trust provided funds for amenities such as trees, shrubs, and allotments, but the great need was deemed to be a meeting place, and in November 1936 the first Community Centre was established by the city council, on Billesley Farm Estate with fifteen organisations ready to move in. The Birmingham Council for Community Associations, set up in 1930 to promote a community spirit between the local authority, voluntary organisations, and residents, has now changed its name to the Birmingham Council for Neighbourhood Groups, and, incorporating the Birmingham Association of Women's Clubs, it musters over eighty separate organisations, many of them on the municipal estates.

In the economic doldrums of the 1930s I was in a particularly advantageous position to watch the transition of slum families to municipal estates. I was an insurance agent with one-third of my calls in the Gooch Street and Lee Bank slums, and another third in the municipal estates. Cynics used to say that the ex-slum-dwellers kept their coal in the new baths at their municipal houses. My work did not take me into the bathroom, but in one living-room in Tynedale Road, Tyseley, I saw the legs of the dining-table completely boarded up on three sides and half boarded on the fourth as a convenient coal bunker. Calling one week on a Bishop Street slum family I was told they had "got a council house". On my first visit to the new home I found they had signalised their move by spreading a new sheet of newspaper as the table cloth. It had an attractive 'pin-up' girl; so attractive that I was reluctant to leave. I need not have worried; the same sheet of newspaper was there, increasingly gravy stained and tea-ringed, on the next Saturday, and the next. Perhaps the men of the family liked the 'pin-up' girl themselves.

Those cynics again used to say that the municipal estates would soon be slums, but in the second generation they have improved. Children born on municipal estates have never known the cosiness of the slums—for which many of their parents hankered after they had been moved to municipal houses. Distance from work and old friends, with travel costs and inconvenience, was often a plaint of the earliest municipal estate dwellers who had moved out from inner-ring industrial slums. New times, new manners—and the second generation is accustomed to and can afford travelling farther. Large aggregate wages go into many municipal houses in 1970 and large cars stand outside them.

One of the features of suburban life between the wars was the 'monkey run'—the night-time parade up and down the main street in any suburb, now no more. We lacked the money to spend on indoor pleasures, television had not come into our homes, and sound radio was in its infancy, so we walked up and down engaged, according to our intellectual capacities, in serious or banal conversation, but all eyeing the girls who chanced to please us. I met my wife on the Sparkhill 'monkey run' in Stratford Road.

Many words were wasted in pleas to 'get youth off the streets'. It was claimed that we learned our sex in the gutter. Now that young people are off the streets in the youth clubs playing poor table tennis and learning their sex from pop songs and television, society seems much less responsible, worse not better for the change, with the illegitimacy rate and venereal disease on the increase. The threat of war hung more certainly over us from 1933 on than it does over youth today, but we did not make this an excuse for vandalism and permissive behaviour. When I contemplate young people today I feel glad to have been brought up the son of poor parents during the Great Depression.

It was during the between-war years, with omnibuses shouldering it alongside the tramcars, that Birmingham's public transport system took on the form that has continued into the 1970s, though the tramcars have gone. Many are the memories they have left of invigorating journeys on open-top decks, Jupiter-like among the constant lightning flashes from the trolley pole on the wires close overhead, of the open 'birdcages' at either end after the upstairs was covered, and particularly of the bucking bronco ride to the Lickey Hills along the central reservation on Bristol Road. Not even contemplation of the pleasing country skyline, now unhappily built up, from Shenley Fields towards Frankley Beeches, could calm nerves on edge at the fear of derailment.

Until 1926 Birmingham's public transport, mainly tramcars, ran from the city centre outward along main roads to suburban termini. In April of that year an Outer Circle bus route commenced, touching all these radial routes, some at their termini. Its 25-mile circular journey took 2 hours 20 minutes—it now takes 2 hours 10 minutes except on Sunday, when it takes 2 hours. An

Inner Circle of 11 miles followed in 1928, and four years later a City Circle was inaugurated, 6¾ miles round, which intersected the outward routes about 1 mile from Victoria Square.

In January 1970 "Ex Conductor 7376" wrote to the *Evening Mail* severely criticising present-day conductors for their slovenly appearance and apparent lack of interest in their job. He, himself, had been an unruffled paragon. His letter elicited two replies which underline changing manners in Birmingham as seen from the platform of a bus. "Conductress 4773" from Kitts Green wrote: "He served on the Inner Circle Route in 1937. . . . It is a pity he is not employed by the undertaking today. . . . Gone are the days when schoolchildren boarded the bus in an orderly manner. Nowadays they would impress the All Blacks forwards by the manner in which they charge on to the platform. A week of this would put his nerves on edge." Writing from Moseley "Another Conductress" declared: "It was his pleasure to work at a time when a conductor was a person who was respected—not a target for abuse, or in some cases for assault."

The conductresses are right—but their strictures do not apply only to the Birmingham travelling public.

It was a Mr George Francis Train, an American inventor, who first suggested tramcars in Birmingham in 1860 when he sought permission to construct a tramway from New Street to Five Ways along Broad Street. He undertook to complete the work in four weeks, and to remove the lines and make good the road at his own expense whenever required. Although the Public Works Committee granted permission and even suggested an extension along Hagley Road to Monument Road, Train did not proceed with the project, and the first tramway was not completed until Monmouth Street (Colmore Row) was linked with Hockley in 1873, the line being let to the Birmingham and District Tramway Company on a seven-year lease, the corporation to keep the works in repair. Horses provided the original means of propulsion; steam engines were authorised in 1884, but were never popular, and a ground cable line once operated from Hockley Hill to Colmore Row. The proudest boast of a really old Brummie is the quavering assertion: "I can remember the old steam trams."

Electric traction driven by accumulators had a short, unimpressive trial before the Central Tramways Company, lessees of the Bristol Road track, wishing to emulate Walsall, appealed for permission to erect overhead wires. The proposal was successfully opposed at first on Bristol Road, but wires ultimately came into use on the Nechells route in 1896.

Around this period five municipalities had acquired control of their transport undertakings, and one, Blackpool, was making a good profit. Municipalisation was discussed in Birmingham, the chief alternative being an offer from a Canadian company to take over the leases. The offer fell through from disagreement on the method of traction after a corporation deputation had investigated the transport services of Paris, Vienna, Budapest, Brussels, Berlin, and other continental cities. It returned favouring an underground conduit system as against the overhead wires of the Canadians, and negotiations ceased after much controversy. The leases thus ending soon, the city's transport services were taken over piecemeal by the corporation between 1904 and 1911. Public Works control gave way to a Tramways Committee in 1900. This has since become the Transport Committee.

Omnibus services began in 1913, and in the following year the corporation purchased the interests of the Midland 'Red' Omnibus Company within the city. From 1922 some tramway routes were abandoned. In that year four-wheeled trolley buses with solid tyres and gongs replaced trams on the Nechells service, and in 1923 top covers were fitted to double-deck motor buses, both pioneering achievements in Britain.

The last tram in Birmingham ran on 4th July 1953, from Steelhouse Lane to Erdington, Pype Hayes, and Short Heath and back. By a happy coincidence the Lord Mayor of the day, Alderman James Crump, who shared the driving, was an ex-tram driver and actually drove the first overhead-cable tram in Birmingham on trial at the turn of the century. He sported his old driver's badge at these obsequies of the city's tramways on Tramcar No. 616.

This last of an honoured line had a triumphal funeral procession filled with civic dignitaries, waved on its way by schoolchildren with Coronation flags, hammered past Aston factories by workers beating hammers and steel bars on empty cylinders and drums, serenaded by motor horns and the "Last Post" on a trumpet, and followed by a motor cyclist with a wreath of laurel. With the return of No. 616 to Miller Street Depot destined for the breaker's yard, Birmingham was left without a tramcar. Twenty-three years earlier it had the largest fleet of trams in the world.

Just one of the fleet is preserved in the Birmingham Museum of Science and Industry in Newhall Street, a four-wheel non-bogie 3-foot 6-inch gauge tram, built around 1910—and with it goes a recording of the noises made by any tram as it lurched along Birmingham streets pitching like a liner in a head sea, nostalgic sounds for so many Brummies.

IX

PERAMBULATION WITH COMMENT

Approach Birmingham from wherever you will, and it is likely that an inn or an hotel will figure in your directions. Coming in from Coventry you pass 'The Swan', Britain's biggest public house when it was reopened after the Yardley underpass development in February 1967 on the site of a pub of that name for 300 years. Come in from Stratford and you make your Birmingham landfall at the 'Robin Hood Hotel', in an area with other Sherwood names but no known association with the famous archer. Come from Warwick and you join the Stratford Road in Sparkhill at 'The Mermaid'.

From Coventry, Stratford, or Warwick you all converge at Bordesley in the shadow of the first prefabricated flyover to be erected in Britain. It took only a weekend in October 1961 for Birmingham to install it, a 300-ton steel structure, and it carries outgoing traffic on to Camp Hill for the Stratford Road.

The traveller entering from Walsall in the north-west makes the acquaintance at Perry Barr of the Alexander Stadium, headquarters of Birchfield Harriers, a club which has provided Britain with many international athletes in addition to having won the National Cross County Championship more times than any other club. Continuing citywards along the Birchfield Road this traveller will pass through Birmingham's Harlem, where the coloured populations of Handsworth and Aston mingle in equal numbers with the whites.

Driving in from Lichfield or Sutton there is a glimpse on the right—if you can spare it from traffic problems—of the floodlight masts at Villa Park, where, despite their lowly position (in 1970),

Aston Villa Football Club share with Newcastle United the distinction of having won the F.A. Cup a record six times. The wearers of the claret-and-blue scarf of the Villa often taunt the fans in the blue and white of Birmingham City that Aston Villa has lost the F.A. Cup more times than Birmingham City has won it—a reference to the occasion in 1895 when the cup, held by Aston Villa, was stolen from a local shop window where it was on display, and never recovered.

Approaching the city centre from the south-west and west the way lies through Edgbaston, either by the Bristol Road or the Hagley Road. Change has treated these two aristocratic arteries somewhat differently. The spacious residences that lined Bristol Road have remained residential, if not so lavish, though some have gone from the south side, and others have added to the schools already sprawling through property originally used for dwellings. The Hagley Road mansions, together with the distinctive late-eighteenth-century red-brick terraces, have been taken over by commercial and business houses or converted into hotels, though a couple of skyscraper blocks have sprung up among them.

The Five Ways junction, at the beginning of 1970, was in the throes of underpass construction—a 1,250-foot thoroughfare with a covered middle section of 350 feet, running from Hagley Road into Broad Street. Five Ways Grammar School building had disappeared without trace, motorists were nonplussed, pedestrians petrified; but the area had retained one old statue and gained a new one. Standing stolidly on his plinth above the earthquake, Joseph Sturge still rested his right hand gently on a Bible, an inscription below declaring: "He laboured to bring freedom to the negro slave, the vote to the British workman, and the promise of peace to a war-worn world." Born in 1793, the son of a grazier in Gloucestershire, Sturge was a conscientious objector, and watched his flock of sheep driven away by government agents to compensate for his refusal to do military service. He came to Bewdley in 1818 as a corn factor and prospered. Moving into Birmingham, he was one of our first sixteen aldermen in 1838, and he took a great interest in the slave trade, ultimately buying an estate in the West Indies. A home he had at Hyde Park, London, was the resort of peace, temperance, and anti-slavery figures—one can imagine a similar do-gooder today attracting an unsavoury

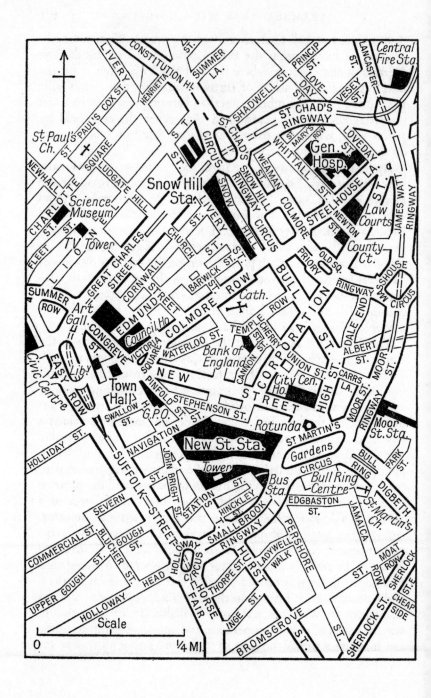

following—and as a Quaker, Sturge founded the Friends' Sunday Schools in Birmingham, which by 1898 were attended by 3,000 children each week.

Across the much-disputed no-man's-land of the Five Ways junction, Auchinleck House rises towards the clouds above the shopping piazza of Auchinleck Square, where, a pleasing bronze figure in jungle jacket and shorts, stands Birmingham's newest statue, of Field-Marshal Sir Claude Auchinleck, who shares with Bishop Gore the distinction of seeing a statue raised to him in Birmingham in his own lifetime. Perhaps it is pertinent to wonder at the legitimacy of this tribute to a soldier whose only connection with Birmingham was the speculative building by the Murrayfield Real Estate Company of which he was chairman.

Let us walk from Five Ways into Islington Row and Bath Row, past the Accident Hospital, and Davenports—the headquarters of 'Beer at Home'—with the tower blocks of Lee Bank Estate on our right, and down Holloway Head to a perambulation of the new Ringway.

We strike it in Holloway Circus at the western end of Smallbrook Ringway. Here is one of the oases round which Birmingham traffic gyrates, a walled refuge adorned by a nude reclining Hebe above the underpass now taking traffic from Bristol Street to Suffolk Street. A tablet tells that a long mosaic mural "depicts activities in the Horse Fair which took place in this area until 1911 and was the last remaining fair of the Charter granted by Henry III in 1215". The mural, designed and executed by Kenneth Budd and Associates, features Edwardian ladies in large hats and voluminous dresses seated in carriages, a flower seller, boys in sailor suits, a groom giving a horse its nosebag, ostlers showing off horses to shirt-sleeved men wearing cloth caps or billycocks, and one open-topped tramcar. A second tablet tells that "This garden was named after Alderman D. S. Thomas who was Chairman of the Public Works Committee from April 1959 to May 1966."

From 1935 to 1939 an informal discussion group met weekly, first at my home in Mansel Road, Small Heath, and later in a room above Mac Fisheries on the corner of Bull Street and Dalton Street. We were young, and predominantly Socialist. One night one of our regulars brought along a friend and told me, "He wants to learn about politics, so I thought this the best place to bring him. His name's Dennis Thomas." Dennis ultimately became a Labour councillor and then Alderman D. S. Thomas. The group had another incipient Chairman of a Public Works Committee—Councillor Bernard Arrowsmith, who became the Conservative Chairman of the Public Works Committee and later Mayor of Solihull, Birmingham's neighbouring borough. We also had John Baird, who became M.P. for a Wolverhampton constituency. One other of us became Leader of the Labour Party on the City Council, Chairman of the Health Committee, and Lord Mayor of Birmingham in 1952–3, Alderman William Tegfryn Bowen, who died in 1970 on the very day when this was being written; another became Leader of Birmingham City Council during much of Labour's sixteen years of power which ended in 1966, Alderman Harry Watton; while yet another, Alderman Jack Wood, was at times Chairman of the Education and the Watch Committees.

In fact, in terms of its contribution to the government of Birmingham our group can claim comparison with the famous Lunar Society. Even our name was comparable. A slighting reference to the group by a member's wife as "those Loonies who talk their heads off" was seized on, and we took to calling ourselves 'The Loonies'.

Although we are well aware of the personal worth of our friends and contemporaries, we tend not quite to appreciate their standing in the community. It took Alderman Bowen's memorial service to open even my eyes to the regard in which he was held, with an overflowing congregation of the Lord Mayor, ex-Lord Mayors, councillors, civic officials, business associates, and friends. It was at once a personal occasion and one that has validity in the chronicles of our city in revealing so much of the new men who have taken over from the traditional city fathers.

"This," said Alderman Victor Turton, opening the service, "is a humanist occasion, but because Teg Bowen had a Welsh love of singing we shall open with 'Cwm Rhondda'." Alderman Turton, elected to the City Council at 21, had become, in particular, an expert on civil aviation in the West Midlands. Denis Howell, M.P., Minister of State for Housing and Local Government, spoke of Teg's masterly conduct of council committees, and of his love and use of words: "With his skill in debate he would have adorned the highest assembly. Words were what mattered most to Teg Bowen because, as he said, words are the currency of our everyday life."

Alderman Harry Watton, himself a pillar of integrity, who, when once his job as a printer conflicted with his city council work, gave up his job because his civic work was so much more important, best summed up Alderman Bowen's influence. "It was Teg Bowen," he said, "who taught us and then demonstrated to us, that we of the Labour Movement could govern the city with ability and dignity."

Alderman Bowen was an incomer like so many of the builders of Birmingham in the eighteenth and nineteenth centuries. Born at Porth in the Rhondda, he worked down the pits until a miner's scholarship brought him to Fircroft College in Birmingham. Here he stayed with a clerical job at the Austin Motor Works, and was soon leading what we should call in these days an 'unofficial' strike. Thereafter jobs were hard to come by, and not until the age of 51, after his Lord Mayoralty, was his great ability recognised beyond the city council, and he was given a directorship with Concrete Ltd.

Smallbrook Ringway runs eastward out of Holloway Circus between 'The Scala', one of Birmingham's oldest cinemas, now vastly changed, and the offices of one of our new masters, the Amalgamated Engineering Union. Birmingham has lost two major hotels of recent years, 'The Queen's' and 'The Grand', and gained 'The Albany' in Smallbrook Ringway. Opened in December 1962 with 254 bedrooms, it took two years to build, with workers exceeding at one time 250, and including Pakistanis, West Indians, Ukrainians, one Russian, many Irishmen, and one squad of seven Sikhs, six of whom could not speak English—a typical Birmingham labour force.

Overshadowed by 'The Albany' in Hill Street is the grim little church of St. Jude, which was dedicated in 1851 in one of the toughest parts of Birmingham and always had a High Anglican tradition. During the late-nineteenth-century incumbency of Father Arnold Pinchard, St. Jude's was very much a church militant. Father Pinchard was an excellent lightweight boxer, and when a Good Friday procession was held up by 'peaky blinders', louts so-called because they pulled the peaks of their cloth caps over one eye, he knocked out their leaders and invited them to his boy's club for further tuition in boxing. St. Jude's has always been Birmingham's actors' church, being central for the city theatres, and the performance on 2nd October 1907, of *The Interlude of Youth* in St. Jude's Mission Hall, Inge Street, was the first public appearance of the Pilgrim Players, later to form the Birmingham Repertory Theatre. Sir Barry Jackson, founding father of the 'Rep', played the part of Riot, and John Drinkwater that of Charity. On the opening of the 'Rep' in 1913 Father Pinchard produced five of the plays in the first year, his half-brother, Father Lester Pinchard—assistant priest at St. Jude's—taking charge of the music.

Up Hill Street from this position just off the Ringway the vista leads past the back of 'The Futurist', Birmingham's last word in cinema luxury fifty years ago, to the mental picture carried by every Brummie wherever he goes, of the Art Gallery tower rising to the clockface of 'Big Brum', flanked by the Council House dome above the General Post Office bridge across Hill Street. Navigation Street crosses Hill Street above the railway as the metals enter New Street Station, and here British Rail has perpetrated the ugliest building in the city, in a signal box somehow resembling a ship's bridge aground on a pebble beach. It is surrounded by a dangerously angled conglomerate wall.

Back on Smallbrook Ringway we swing along towards St. Martin's Circus with an uninspired and uninspiring windowed wall on our right, four storeys of glass-fronted offices, a number still 'To Let', above the ground-floor shops. Only after dark does the lighting effect make this building bearable. The area had to fight hard to establish itself, for while the old Smallbrook Street previously on the site had its traditional regular shoppers from nearby streets, these have since been cleared, and the new shops did not readily take on with shoppers coming into town from the suburbs. This shift of a shopping focus has been a problem throughout the development of the new Birmingham. New Street itself, for long the city's main shopping street, showed all the signs of increasing dereliction around 1967, but it seems to have achieved a come-back by 1970. The closure of an established site, such as the Birmingham Post and Mail offices on Queen's Corner when those newspapers moved to Colmore Circus, can

Birmingham confers the Freedom of the City

bring a deserted air which deters prospective shopkeepers and shoppers, and all too soon a thriving area can die. Similarly, stagnation can come with the alteration of bus stops or the diversion of pedestrians. The funnelling of rail commuters from New Street Station in serried ranks down a ramp to Queen's Corner seems to have renewed the prosperous appearance of what was long the strong-pulsed heart of Birmingham.

Smallbrook Ringway strides across Dudley Street, named after the Dudley family, once the occupants of the medieval manor house on this site, and comes up to one of Birmingham's major traffic hazards. St. Martin's Circus poses a problem unique in the experience of several drivers who have poured out their scorn in letters to the Press. It is, they say, the only 'roundabout' where vehicles already on it do not retain right of way over new entrants, and that vehicles coming to it along Smallbrook Ringway from the west push on with undiminished speed. Who can blame them? They are on the main ring road which proceeds undeviatingly past the entrance for traffic which has come up the Bull Ring and turned left into the 'circus', so aptly named in one sense, though it certainly is not a roundabout in a road sense. The Chairman of the Road Improvement and Traffic Sub-Committee tells Birmingham motorists that they must learn to 'weave' in such situations, the great thing being to keep moving at all costs, throwing caution to the winds apparently. Even rugger three-quarters, adept at scissors movements, find scissoring blind at 30 miles per hour too risky on Birmingham roads, but everything must be subordinated to keeping the traffic moving. If you feel inclined to protest that this is what roads are for I can only quote a visiting driver who said, "You can do anything with a car in Birmingham—except stop it." Strange proposition though it may seem, it is normally when a car, and more so a bus, is stopped that it has been put to legitimate use, for visiting, for shopping, or on a business call.

The late Alderman Jack Wood, who was at the time both Chairman of Birmingham Watch Committee and of the Midland Area of the Ramblers' Association, once pointed out to the Chief Constable that cars were regularly parked partly on the pavement in a certain street to the great inconvenience of pedestrians.

M

An eastern prospect of Birmingham
A northern panorama of Birmingham

"But, Alderman," replied the Chief Constable, "what else can we do? We must keep the traffic moving on the roads."

Flaunting its flags of a red bull in a white roundel on a blue field over the bobbing and weaving traffic on St. Martin's Circus is the BULL RING SHOPPING CENTRE. If you take refuge down in the Manzoni Gardens, and bask in the morning sun on one of the many seats, you stare at that oversized legend in red letters on white panels already becoming scruffy and stained, though the centre was constructed only between 1961 and 1964. One of the city's major planning achievements, it provides two levels of shops, a retail market, a multi-storey office block and car park, and, beneath it all, a bus terminal—"like the High Street under cover" as its television publicity tells us.

By 1970 retailers trading there were at last satisfied that the Bull Ring Centre had 'arrived' in the eyes of Birmingham, and that it was a profitable venture. Its architecture is conspicuous by its absence; its market atmosphere is its great asset. Shoppers number over a quarter of a million each week, rising even higher at holidays and Christmas.

On Saturday 6th December 1969 Birmingham City Police were called to unravel a traffic jam. Not until 5.30 p.m. could they safely leave the scene. Traffic jams are daily occurrences; mammoth jams occur regularly. This, however, was a jam with a difference—it was a pedestrian jam. The message, as it came to my newspaper from the police information room, ran thus:

At 3.10 p.m. today the pedestrian subway from High Street and New Street was completely blocked by pedestrians wishing to gain access to the Bull Ring Shopping Centre. The blockage was so serious that there was a danger of injury to shoppers, some of whom were becoming distressed. The blockage extended from the steps down from New Street and High Street, through the ramp alongside the Bull Ring Open Market, and into the paved area of the Manzoni Gardens. Police control was put into operation. Pedestrians from New Street and High Street to the Bull Ring were allowed to use the subway normally. Pedestrians from the Bull Ring to New Street and High Street were routed via Manzoni Gardens to the exit near the Rotunda. This diversion operated until about 4.15 p.m. when the use of the subway was restored in both directions but Police control continued until 5.30 p.m. with the assistance of a portable loud hailer.

Trouble was not unknown previously in this part of Birmingham's pedestrian underworld. An escalator up to New Street has been known to go berserk and spew its users out too rapidly for their comfort, while on another occasion its steps developed defects and pedestrians were injured.

For all its crowds, however, and despite the continued black spiky presence of St. Martin's Church, the Bull Ring Shopping Centre lacks the appeal of the old cobbled Bull Ring. Its outdoor market stalls are gay enough, but they are continental, not 'Brummie' like the old drab tarpaulins straining in the wind. Nelson is still there, Sir Richard Westmacott's bronze statue erected on its original Bull Ring site in 1809, railed in by naval pikes and ropes. He looks down on a tumbled sea of ridged hexagonal market-stall covers, and from the corner of his good left eye he gets a glimpse of two nautical pubs, 'The Outrigger' in a Moor Street, now merely a dead end leading to its railway station, and Kempenfelt's ill-fated 'Royal George' on the corner of Park Street, where a notorious 'blood tub' cinema once stood.

The internal-combustion engine does not intrude on the present outdoor market, but it did so only at its peril in the original Bull Ring. People dominated that slope, and though they often jostled, they did not need police control and diversions. With its raucous barrow boys and girls, who drew lots each morning in a Gloucester Street greengrocer's yard for the best positions in Spiceal Street, from the 'plum' on Bell Street corner downhill—both physically and in favour—to Edgbaston Street, the Bull Ring was for every 'Brummie' a focus of affection such as we no longer possess.

But as a "much needed focal point and contrast to all the surrounding rectangular blocks" the Bull Ring area has the Rotunda, the inspiration of architect James A. Roberts, though some say his white elephant. It is undeniably the wonder of the new Birmingham, and it underlines with its gleaming sunlit curves the architectural bankruptcy of the concrete cubism which has sprung up everywhere else in the city. A cylinder of twenty-four storeys, the Rotunda rises 271 feet above the Ringway on the junction of New Street and High Street. Alexandra Wedgwood, already quoted just above from Pevsner's *Warwickshire*, describes it as "a splendid design for its position" and succinctly sums up its functional aspect. "It provides accommodation," she writes, "for two floors of shops, two floors of a bank, a floor for the bank's strong room, sixteen office floors and two floors for services, plus a parapet."

A building like the Rotunda has to be paid for, and Property and General Investments Ltd. sank £1 million in it. Twelve months after it opened only eight and a half of the available twenty floors had been let—at 17s. a square foot if an entire floor was taken.

James Roberts, chartered architect and town planning consultant, was born the son of an architect in 1922. He set up in business on his own in 1952, and thirteen years later he was occupying the top floor of the Rotunda, his most spectacular brainchild, with a staff of forty. Among his most striking projects have been the restoration of West Bromwich Manor House, and of Stratford House, Camp Hill, an early seventeenth-century farmhouse where the fields gave way to a railway goods yard. He designed the Albany Hotel, and, away from Birmingham, the Mander Centre at Wolverhampton, some town-centre redevelopment in Liverpool, and a motorway service area at Heston. James Roberts, a countryside preservationist, has earned the disapprobation of the land-grabbers on Birmingham City Council by describing the city as "a lazy-minded sprawl brought about by thoughtless and unimaginative development over the years", and by suggesting expansion upwards with such devices as flats above schools.

While James Roberts was attending Stanley House School, Edgbaston, he had a schoolfellow named John Madin who also went on to the Birmingham School of Architecture. The two of them have been the significant architects of Birmingham's redevelopment. Born in 1924, John Madin is the son of a master builder. As with James Roberts, his rise was rapid. He designed his first house in 1952 with only his army gratuity behind him; ten years later he was wielding a considerable influence on the appearance of Birmingham. Now the senior partner of the John Madin Design Group, he is also consultant architect to the Calthorpe Estate, in which capacity he has ensured the retention of much of the sylvan character of Edgbaston so near the city centre. He is in addition consultant architect and planner to the Ministry of Housing and Local Government, Telford Development Corporation, Corby New Town, the *Birmingham Post and Mail*, and the B.B.C., for which he has designed the new Midlands headquarters at Pebble Mill.

Choosing a Sunday when it is possible in uncrowded comfort to climb the steps from the Bull Ring complex into High Street, you will find, beneath the street nameplate and between the Times furnishing and the Burton tailoring emporia, one of the blue discs placed on locations of historical interest by the initiative of Birmingham Civic Society. The legend here reads: 'William Hutton, Bookseller, the first historian of Birmingham, lived on this site from 1772 to 1791." Some 30 yards distant on the frontage of Birmingham Co-operative Society's premises a neat head of George Jacob Holyoake peers from a tablet which describes him as "Social Reformer and Co-operator. Born at No. 1 Inge Street, Birmingham on April 13, 1807, died January 2, 1906." Holyoake's activities were national rather than local. He was an outspoken secularist and the chronicler of the Rochdale pioneers of Co-operation.

Beyond St. Martin's Circus, Moor Street Ringway continues with a switchback dip towards Lancaster Place, or an alternative left turn at Masshouse Circus, which takes its name from Masshouse Lane, where in 1687–8 an ill-fated Roman Catholic church was built. Among the subscribers were such noted Midland Catholic families as the Giffards, Throckmortons, Penderels, Ferrers, Blounts, and Middlemores, while James II gave 125 tons of timber which realised £180. The church was consecrated on 4th September 1688, but two months later, with James in flight and William of Orange come to take his throne, the rabble of Birmingham demolished the new church, even digging out the foundations.

The outer Ringway, having traversed Lancaster Place and enclosed the General Hospital, cuts through the old gun quarter of Birmingham and ducks beneath St. Chad's Circus. In the autumn of 1969 I almost missed a pleasant journalistic Mediterranean cruise with 1,900 Warwickshire schoolchildren because of the chaos caused by the Ringway construction around Lancaster Place. It is a fact that such upheavals bring an inertia on citizens, who eventually just cannot be bothered to find a way afoot across the sundered earth, sandpits, mudheaps, barriers, and general debris. My passport required renewing; the passport office was not five minutes walk from my office—but the Ringway construction intervened. It might have been the Atlantic Ocean. Several times I set out only to return repulsed. Ultimately I embarked on a more determined expedition, found a way through, and renewed the passport in the nick of time.

From Masshouse Circus there is a short cut to St. Chad's Circus by way of Priory Ringway and Colmore Circus with their accompanying troglodyte tunnels for pedestrians. Left high and dry beyond Priory Circus is the rump end of Corporation Street, which has practically died because, leading as it does to the seismic Lancaster Place, it has become a cul-de-sac for pedestrians. Fortunately much of it is taken up by the red-brick and terracotta Victoria Law Courts provided by Birmingham as the price for the granting of an assize. The great hall, open to the public, has the most interesting windows in the city, though they are too high for comfortable viewing. One constitutes a portrait gallery of leading Birmingham men, with Shakespeare thrown in as a Warwickshire bonus. If this book had not started with the River Rea and pursued the course it has, it might have taken a pattern from this window—a de Birmingham knight, Edward VI, Dr. Samuel Johnson, Lench, Hutton, Baskerville, Mason, Dr. Ash, Louisa Ryland, Priestley, Boulton, Watt, Murdock, and David Cox the artist. Another window is a pictorial catalogue of Birmingham's industries—pen-maker, glass-blower, iron-worker, wire-drawer, medallist, glass-cutter, screw-maker, gunsmith, and so on. Other windows show Queen Victoria opening Aston Hall in 1858 and laying the foundation stone of the Law Courts and inspecting schoolchildren in Small Heath Park in 1887. Finally, there is Prince Albert laying the foundation stone of the Midland Institute, which survived in Paradise Street from 1855 to 1969.

A congruous essay in building in the Birmingham of seventy years ago was the Methodist Central Hall, which matched the terracotta and red brick of the Law Courts across Corporation Street, its slender tower providing a prominent landmark before so much else in the city aspired skyward. Birmingham Methodism had a thorny passage from the days when Charles Wesley on Gosta Green first implored his hearers to "Repent and be converted". Preaching in the Bull Ring in 1746, he was assailed with a barrage of stones, while others of his opponents tried to drown his voice by ringing St. Martin's bells. A year later John Wesley put his life in peril to speak at Gosta Green. In 1750 there was a Methodist meeting house in Whittall Street, from which they moved to a deserted theatre between Moor Street and Park Street until, in 1783, Cherry Street Chapel opened and sustained them until it disappeared in Joseph Chamberlain's Corporation Street scheme, to be replaced in 1903 by the Central Hall.

The shopping precinct below Priory Circus is still called Old Square, and an entrancing brass-and-iron relief mural tells the story of the site from the thirteenth-century Augustinian priory to its end as a residential area in 1896. The main theme is the eighteenth-century heyday of the square designed by William Westley and built by Thomas Kenney in 1713. Most of the history and the characters portrayed appear in these pages—one amusing addition being a daughter of Samuel Lloyd eloping down a ladder into the expectant arms of her lover.

Lewis's, which rears its bulk above Priory Circus, is the store where the Brummie feels most at home—though perhaps my claim would be disputed by Grey's, long a family concern but taken over by Debenham's in 1958. Lewis's one-time roof garden, the Christmas lights in the Minories, and the seasonal window display, together with the father of all the city's Father Christmases—these things have been established long enough to enable it to keep its head well above water despite a more elegant newcomer in Rackham's.

Yet, across Corporation Street from Lewis's a Birmingham furniture firm, Kean and Scott, established for more than a century, closed in 1969. When redevelopment came they invested £60,000 in a store in Priory Ringway on a twenty-five-year lease on practically the same site as their old premises. The closure came after three years without a trading profit, and directors put the blame on inadequate car parking and the absence of other amenities for shoppers.

The Chairman of Birmingham Public Works Committee pointed out that Kean and Scott was within a stone's throw of three car parks with 800 spaces and directly above another with 260 spaces. Admitting this, a director said that the car park beneath his store charged exorbitantly at 2s. 6d. an hour, and that, having already subsidised customers' meals in their restaurant, his company could not also subsidise their car parking. So the company would concentrate on its successful business in Solihull, eight miles from Birmingham city centre. Despite an increase in central car-parking spaces from 3,400 in 1966 to 9,400 by 1970, shoppers continue in ever-growing numbers to defect to more comfortable and convenient shopping centres out of Birmingham, like Halesowen and Solihull. Housewives from Hall Green, for instance, a good-class outer suburb of Birmingham, not only find Solihull nearer; they find all they want in smaller space and without fighting their way up half a dozen floors by lift or escalator. If Solihull parking tends to be strained sometimes the turnover is quicker, with nothing so frustrating as the slow and costly procession awheel around central Birmingham, often repeated four or five times before an available meter space is found.

Beattie's departmental store reached £5 million annual sales in its Wolverhampton base, a return of 45 per cent on the capital employed. The company then opened in Birkenhead to seduce local people from shopping in Liverpool, and ultimately made a profit. Then, with the same idea—of luring Solihull shoppers away from Birmingham—it opened in Solihull, breaking even in two years and estimating a £300,000 profit in the third.

Rackham's brought a new plush dimension to shopping when they opened in Birmingham in 1960, and their sales are said to have trebled. However, with Selective Employment Tax on 1,600 employees costing £135,000 a year, and rates in excess of £200,000, profits are tending to fall.

In a praiseworthy attempt to seek solutions for our growing city centre malaise, *The Birmingham Post* invited Mr. A. A. Wood, City Planning Officer of Norwich, to lecture in Birmingham on the Norwich scheme of creating a traffic-free area of pedestrian streets in their city centre. Mr. Wood brought encouraging news. London Street, a convenient route across the city centre, was the pioneer street in this experiment, and it was closed to traffic on 17th July 1967. Little disturbance was caused to Norwich traffic generally, deliveries to shops were maintained by dropping goods at the ends of the street and conveying them to the stores by trolleys, pedestrians trebled, and thirty of London Street's thirty-two stores reported a sales increase of over $7\frac{1}{2}$ per cent.

Traders have since petitioned Norwich City Council for other streets to be made traffic-free.

Birmingham's shopping problem differs from that of Norwich in that there are so many more alternative suburban shopping centres. In discussion after the lecture the Secretary of the Great Western Arcade Tenants Association—which has for long offered traffic-free shopping in Birmingham—says that many residents in suburbs such as Northfield and Selly Oak had told him they never come into Birmingham, and he concluded that Birmingham people have lost faith and interest in the city centre.

Two interesting developments springing from the Norwich experiment were the establishment of continental-type street cafés and closely knit small-scale housing development only two minutes walk from the main shopping centre. The Birmingham City Surveyor promised that our centre would be clear, at least of through traffic, by 1972. In an editorial on the discussion *The Birmingham Post* referred to "a pleasure that our fathers took completely for granted—that of shopping in conditions in which it was possible to make a leisurely crossing at will from one side of the street to the other", and concluded that, "Readiness to experiment is the very first requirement if there is to be progress in restoring to Birmingham's centre streets their full potential as shopping areas and diminishing their role as traffic gulleys."

Colmore Circus is dominated by the tower block of dark-grey glass of the *Birmingham Post and Mail* building. Since 1965 the tower lights have been taking Birmingham into Europe by flashing the passing minutes on the twenty-four-hour system, which most people now understand, alternately with the temperature in Centigrade, which completely mystifies most of us. Equally incomprehensible are the murals in the pedestrian underpass, though one is captioned as a battle between Roundheads and Cavaliers.

The ramp leading up to the *Post* and *Mail* Office is called Feeney Subway, presumably after John Frederick Feeney, founder of *The Birmingham Post* in 1857, though his son, John Feeney, was a great benefactor to the city, making generous donations to the Art Gallery while alive, and leaving £50,000 from which the Feeney Galleries were opened after the First World War. The elder Feeney came to Birmingham in 1835, aged 27, to edit Joseph Sturge's journal *The Philanthropist*. In 1844 he bought the *Birmingham Journal*, which had begun as a weekly in 1825, but on 4th December 1857 he changed it to the *Birmingham Daily Post*. In 1869 Feeney died and the *Birmingham Weekly Post* was born, followed a year later by an evening paper, the *Birmingham Daily Mail*. The *Daily* was dropped from the titles of both the *Post* and the *Mail* in 1918.

From 1741 Aris's *Birmingham Gazette* had an unbroken life until November 1956, when it merged with the *Birmingham Post*. Its evening paper, the *Evening Despatch*, merged with the *Birmingham Mail* in 1963. The *Gazette* and *Despatch* group had a weekly newspaper, the *Sunday Mercury*, and in 1960 this swallowed up the *Birmingham Weekly Post*. So Birmingham is now served by *The Birmingham Post*, a morning daily with a readership of 220,000 adults; the *Evening Mail*, with over 1 million adult readers; and the *Sunday Mercury*, with a circulation of 230,000. There is also, from the same stable, a Saturday night's *Sports Argus*.

Birmingham city centre stands on a well-defined narrow ridge of Keuper Sandstone which is crossed at its eastern end by Priory Ringway. From Masshouse Circus there is a wide industrial view southward, and within 400 yards the land falls away northward down Snow Hill, with extensive views across Hockley and the outer northern suburbs to Barr Beacon. Its exposed position on the top of this northern slope makes the *Post* and *Mail* building a veritable temple of the winds. Braving the downdraught from its tower block, we skirt the Gaumont Cinema and drop down to St. Chad's Circus.

St. Chad's was the first post-Reformation Roman Catholic cathedral to be built in Britain. R. K. Dent describes the Consecration on 22nd June 1841 as "one of the most magnificent ecclesiastical ceremonies ever witnessed in England", with thirteen bishops and 150 priests in attendance. The design, by Augustus Welby Pugin, was deliberately intended to differentiate the cathedral from Protestant churches, and he chose a pointed Hanseatic style. Its red-brick bulk and slender blue-slated spires, which once dominated the closely packed dwellings of the gunmakers, are now themselves overshadowed by the towering concrete and glass of which modern Birmingham is fashioned. The windows of St. Chad's are good modern glass, one of them portraying four stages in the making of it by the Birmingham firm of John Hardman and Company—drawing the cartoons, cutting the shapes, painting, and firing the glass. Another group tells the exciting story of the relics of St. Chad.

He was a Bishop of Mercia with his seat at Lichfield, and he died on 2nd March 672. After two moves from local churches his bones were laid in Lichfield Cathedral, which continued to be built around them until its completion in 1420. Although Lichfield escaped spoliation under Henry VIII, a certain Prebendary Arthur Dudley secretly removed St. Chad's relics for safer keeping at the time of the Dissolution of the Monasteries, entrusting them on his death to his nieces, Bridget and Kathleen Dudley of Russell Hall, near Dudley. Being fearful of the Penal Laws, these ladies passed the relics to a Henry Hodshead or Hodgetts of Woodsetton, Sedgeley, near Dudley, who, in 1615, on his deathbed, was attended by a Father Peter Turner. Asking the dying man why he called so insistently on St. Chad, the priest was shown some of the saint's bones wrapped in buckram on a bedpost.

Father Turner took charge of the relics, and on his death in 1655 they were passed on to a John Leveson, a Jesuit, from whose care some were taken to Flanders for veneration. Those remaining were consigned to the care of Father Collingwood at Boscobel House, a Staffordshire home of the Fitzherbert family, from where they went eventually to Swynnerton Hall, near Stone, another Fitzherbert residence. For some time the relics were missing. The Fitzherberts had moved to Aston Hall, also near Stone, and a search of Swynnerton Hall proved fruitless. Then, in 1837, the Rev. Benjamin Hulme, missioner at Aston Hall, was clearing out the chapel when he found a beautiful casket with authenticated relics of four saints which had belonged to the Fitzherberts. With them were four other large bones, and these were accepted by Pope Gregory XVI as being "the relics of the Holy Bishop Chad". As the new Roman Catholic cathedral in Birmingham was about to be dedicated, the bones found a resting place there.

St. Chad's has as attractive an interior as any building in Birmingham, a soaring spaciousness springing from its slender pillars. It is perhaps the interior most worth showing a visitor to the city, and fortunately it is only a short step from another feature that should not be missed—the railway mosaics in Kennedy Gardens, exciting and colourful even to the non-railway enthusiast. In a semicircle 300 feet long and 17 feet high, one of the largest murals in the world, it tells the story of the Great Western Railway from 1847 to the closure of Snow Hill Station, just across the road, to main-line traffic. Nothing is missed, even Dash, the station dog at the turn of the century, being there, while the openings of two pedestrian subways are incorporated in the design as the portals of railway tunnels. Kenneth Budd and Partners had researchers working for six months at Swindon Railway Museum on details of the locomotives and rolling stock in the mural. Unfortunately this magnificent feature shares the gardens with an alien mosaic memorial to John F. Kennedy, President of the United States 1960–3—of which more in the next chapter. Also alien, though in name only in this predominantly Irish Catholic enclave, is the new skyscraper hotel opposite St. Chad's —'The Royal Angus'.

The underpass beneath St. Chad's Circus brings the Ringway from Shadwell Street to Great Charles Street, but after a fleeting glimpse of the 500-foot Post Office Radio Tower, Birmingham's tallest building, which is to the north of the city ridge what the Rotunda is to the south, the motorist ducks once more into the bowels of Birmingham, following the old line of Great Charles Street round beneath the new Paradise Circus, and so into Suffolk Street, completing a through route on the A38 Leeds–Exeter trunk road by the underpass beneath Holloway Circus where we began this circuit of the Ringway. This tunnel, 1,140 feet in length and costing £2¼ million, has emergency signalling systems to warn of concentrations of exhaust fumes and of vehicle breakdowns. The walls are colour-graded from off-white to charcoal to aid drivers' eyes in transition from artificial lighting to daylight, and the interior lighting can be varied in accordance with sunshine or dull conditions outside.

The main victims in the demolition for Paradise Circus were Sir Josiah Mason's College, two historic pubs—'The Woodman' and 'The Hope and Anchor', and the Midland Institute, which has contributed so much to the cultural life of Birmingham since it came into being in 1854 as the successor to the Philosophical

Institution, the Mechanics Institution, and the Polytechnic. Writing the centenary book of the Midland Institute, Rachel Waterhouse referred to "its diversity of operations, whereby anemometers may become mixed with Wagnerian trombones, or a Conversazione with a class in Old Icelandic". This is a reminder that two famous Birmingham institutions have sprung from the Midland Institute—the School of Music, of which Sir Granville Bantock was Principal from 1900 to 1934, and Edgbaston Observatory. In 1884 the Midland Institute leased Perrott's Folly or the Monument, a singular building which gives its name to Monument Road, off which it stands in Waterworks Road, Edgbaston. John Perrott raised his folly around 1758, according to some legend-spinners in order to see his wife's grave in Warstone Lane Cemetery—which was not opened for another ninety years. Others say it was to observe the home of his sweetheart at Five Ways, and that when she died he added height to see her tomb in St. Philip's Churchyard. Any suggestion that Perrott built his folly to give a view of his ancestral home at Belbroughton is destroyed by the Clent Hills, which interpose their bulk. The probability is that the eccentric slim tower was built as a folly in an age of follies, though it would have given Perrott a grandstand view of the coursing on Ladywood Fields below. Ninety-six feet high, with 139 steps, it was scheduled as an ancient monument in 1950, and as Birmingham Observatory it will always be associated with the names of Follett Osler, a considerable meteorologist, inventor of an anemometer and a rain guage, and Arthur Joseph Kelley and his son Arthur Leslie Kelley, who between them were directors of the observatory from 1917 to 1967.

Follett Osler in 1885 presented Birmingham with the Council House clock, known affectionately as 'Big Brum', just as in the 1840s he had set up, on the Philosophical Institution in Cannon Street, a clock which became accepted as the public time-keeper of Birmingham. In this present period of change in coinage and with the unfortunate coming of decimalisation, it is interesting to reflect on the manner in which Follett Osler brought about the change in Birmingham from local time to Greenwich Mean Time when railway timetables necessitated a national standard time. The changeover had caused trouble in some places, and Osler determined to avoid this.

The people of Birmingham then took their time from their local church clocks. These were wound and regulated early each Sunday morning by officials who checked their watches by the Cannon Street clock on their way to the churches. So, before sunrise one Sunday, Osler changed the Cannon Street clock to G.M.T.; the church clocks were duly adjusted, and workmen had all day on Sunday to adjust their watches in time for work on Monday without anyone but Osler realising what was happening.

With the demolition of its old home in Paradise Street, the Midland Institute proposed building a £1 million cultural centre, probably in Broad Street, including a 200-seat planetarium. Half of the cost could be raised from the Institute's own assets; for the other £500,000 it proposed launching a public appeal.

The Central Library, next-door neighbour in Ratcliff Place to the old Midland Institute, is not scheduled for demolition until 1972, when it will be rehoused, in the Paradise Circus complex, in the greatest library building in Europe, twice the size of the Town Hall with 31 miles of shelving accommodating 1½ million books.

Emerging from the tunnel beyond Holloway Circus, the motorist will at once be impressed, on his right, by the circular Roman Catholic Church of St. Catherine of Siena, built at a cost of £180,000 and opened in 1965 to replace a church of the same name which stood in the Horse Fair from 1875 until it was sacrificed to the Holloway Circus development. The enormous painted half-relief Stations of the Cross from the old church provide about the only decoration in its successor, though the bare interior is pleasing.

No book on Birmingham would be complete without reference to John Henry Newman, the convert to Rome who became a cardinal. He was born in London in 1801 and ordained in 1824 as a Church of England curate at St. Clement's, Oxford. He preached his first sermon on the text "Man goeth forth to his work and to his labour until the evening". Nineteen years later, having been associated with Keble and Pusey in writing *Tracts for the Times* and in the Oxford Movement, which revived the historical basis of the Church of England and brought ritualism into its liturgy, Newman used the same text in his last sermon as an Anglican. He was received into the Roman Catholic Church in 1845 and, coming to Birmingham, founded an Oratory of St. Philip Neri in Alcester Street, Highgate, one of the poorer quarters of the town. His co-founders, four other priests and six lay brothers, supported themselves on weekly offertories of around £4, given mainly by Irish labourers, immigrants into Britain after the great famine of 1845. Father Newman even learned to play the organ to save paying an organist. When a large money gift became available a new site was acquired between Hagley Road and Plough and Harrow Road, and there the Birmingham Oratory made its permanent home. Newman was created a cardinal in 1879 and died in 1890. He lies in a modest grave at Rednal, Birmingham, and between 1903 and 1906 the present Oratory Church of the Immaculate Conception was built to his memory on the Hagley Road site.

Cardinal Newman was a great writer, but perhaps his best-known production is the beautiful hymn "Lead Kindly Light". This he wrote during the summer of 1833 in the Strait of Boni-facio between Corsica and Sardinia while becalmed there for a week aboard an orange boat on passage from Palermo in Sicily to Marseilles.

The Ringway happens to be in Birmingham. It might be almost anywhere. I have tunnelled into Heathrow Airport and beneath the Mersey; passed under and flown over in Brussels, Paris, and Lisbon; and the skyscraper blocks of flats were one of the sights of Helsinki when we called it Helsingfors. So, for something more legitimately Birmingham, we must glance at one or two streets with which we have grown up.

Victoria Square has never been a focus of affection like the Bull Ring because traffic has discouraged any standing and staring. Sir Robert Peel, who stood staring there in effigy since 1855, was toppled from his pedestal by a passing lorry in 1926, and now, as founder of the Police Force—the 'Peelers'—has an appropriate spot outside the Police Training College in Pershore Road, Edgbaston. Edward VII was removed from Victoria Square to the obscurity of Highgate Park in 1951, leaving Queen Victoria in sole possession, seemingly in the act of lobbing a hand grenade into the general post office. Of the tens of thousands who see her there, how many know that the statue is a memorial, not to the old queen herself but to William Henry Barber, given by his son, the Sir Henry Barber of the Barber Institute? When the statue was unveiled in 1901 the Lord Mayor, Alderman Samuel Edwards, made a rash promise "that it shall be preserved in its present position for all future time". He also petitioned the Queen that Council House Square be renamed Victoria Square. Despite Alderman Edward's undertaking, Queen Victoria was removed from her square in March 1950, recast in plaster by William Bloye, the Birmingham sculptor, and from this a new bronze statue was made. This was returned to Victoria Square in 1951, but in 1970 another Edwards was on the rampage, Councillor Harold Edwards, Chairman of the Public Works Committee, and Victoria's island domain shrunk in the interests of traffic.

Another attempt to alter Victoria Square met with some opposition. Since Christ Church was demolished at the turn of the century, the site running round from the square into New Street has come to be known as Galloway's Corner after a chemist's shop of that name. Christ Church was commemorated in Christ Church Passage, a narrow flight of steps rising from New Street to Waterloo Street and islanding Galloway's Corner. The intention to demolish Galloway's Corner, while somehow preserving the steps in Christ Church Passage, was not universally popular. It may have become an accomplished fact between writing and publication. If so, and if it leaves the steps open on one side with some elevation above the traffic for a view of the Council House and Town Hall, it could be an improvement. Both buildings have suffered from overcrowding and will gain when seen from farther away, and both are well worth displaying to best advantage.

Alexandra Wedgwood saw the façade of the Council House as "jolly", an assessment which seems to damn with faint praise, though I am sure that was not her intention. Built from 1874 to 1879 to a design by Yeoville Thomason, the Council House is a dignified and attractive building worthy of a great city. Behind the balcony above the main portico is a mosaic by Salviati, and the topmost feature is a pediment showing Britannia rewarding the Birmingham manufacturers for their contribution to Britain's Victorian prosperity.

The dignified block which included Lloyd's Bank across Eden

A south-west view across Birmingham

Place from the Council House has been replaced by a modern and flimsy substitute for the old bank. Eden Place, incidentally, owes nothing to the Birmingham Conservative headquarters facing it across Edmund Street—it is an obvious name association with Paradise Street. The name of Waterloo Street dates that thorough-fare of office buildings. With Colmore Row—redesigned in the 1860s—Newhall Street, and Temple Row, it was the legal quarter of Birmingham, abounding with solicitors' offices. Today they may still be there, but the building society and insurance office palaces overshadow them. Above the site where a cherry orchard once gave its name to Cherry Street, the new Bank of England tower block rears up 215 feet towards the clouds, 15 feet taller than the Rotunda, and on higher ground. The core of this tower went up incredibly in eleven working days with nineteen men working twenty-five twelve-hour shifts, and now the new Bank of England stretches from Cannon Street to Temple Row. During those eleven days the tower grew at the rate of 10 inches each hour.

In its modernisation Birmingham has lost some interesting groups of statuary. The pediment of the Grand Theatre was one, and a delightful little 'Fairy Shoemakers' pediment over a door, originally a shoe manufacturer's, on the corner of Seymour Street another. This was the work of Benjamin Creswick, twenty years modelling master at Birmingham College of Art and Crafts, who died in 1946, aged 93, leaving the Cornwall Street exterior of the college decorated in terracotta panels. A pupil and friend of Ruskin, at once potter, metal-worker, and printer, it was written of Creswick, "He is equally at home with a colossal statue as with an ivory statuette, with a pair of gates as with an ink-stand in wrought iron." His work went all over Britain, and as far afield as Penang.

The prying eye that risks looking upward from our teeming pavements still reaps a reward, such as the little-known reliefs of Shakespeare and Sir Walter Scott above W. H. Smith and Son Ltd., Corporation Street; the mystery head above No. 4 Bennetts Hill, said most confidently to be Alexander Pope; and the roundels high on 81–83 Colmore Row with the heads of Ben-venuto Cellini, and Lorenzo Ghiberti (the clean-shaven one). The property was built in 1871–3 for a Mr. W. Spurrier, silversmith

N

The Ringway as it tunnels beneath Great Charles Street

and cutler, so he commemorated on the façade these two Florentine craftsmen in precious metals.

One colourful gain among our uniform drab and glassy modernity is the proliferation of achievements-of-arms on business houses, a delight to the enthusiast for heraldry.

X

SHALWARS ACROSS THE COLE

THE Irish have always had more than their fair share of detractors, particularly the Irish in Birmingham. Whenever anti-Irish sentiments were expressed in the city in the years just following the Second World War we were reminded that if we kicked out the Irish the entire Birmingham public-transport system would grind to a halt. More recently the recruitment of coloured bus conductors and fearfully ebullient West Indian drivers has ensured that this would not be the case.

Birmingham has an estimated Irish population of 110,000, about 60,000 being Irish born, and they tend to retain their national identity at the Irish Community Centre in Digbeth, in their county associations, and with Irish dancing schools and a Gaelic Football League. Before committing myself I must declare an interest. My love for Ireland is such that I have visited that exquisite land sixty-two times and slept in all thirty-two counties. So I have never been a 'kicker-out'; in fact, I have leaned over backwards even in defence of the predominantly Irish tinkers and itinerant scrap-metal merchants who have caused much trouble, especially in Sparkbrook. Two recent cases of Irish betrayal of Birmingham's hospitality have, however, incensed me and many other citizens.

At the height of the Civil Rights disobedience in Northern Ireland in 1969 the Birmingham Irish community called a strike of Irishmen in the city in support of their rebellious compatriots in Northern Ireland. Its effect on public transport was negligible.

The other Irish solecism is not so transient, and it brings us back to the Kennedy Gardens and that mural to John F. Kennedy, which cost £5,000, raised by the city's Irish community. The proximity of St. Chad's was the obvious place for the Roman Catholic Irish to site a memorial to one of their own persuasion—but is it justified in Birmingham at all? Described by one of Birmingham's leading sculptors, Mr. Bryan Bulmer, as "a vulgar picture postcard" and "politically tendentious", it depicts, all too plainly, the naïve ex-presidential features rising above a score of ugly toothily grimacing faces of coloured and white people trying to shake Kennedy's hand. To the left, more restrained pastel tints show his widow playing with children against the background of an Irish church. To the right, however, beyond a caption: "There are no white or coloured signs on the graves of battle," is a scene which makes that noble integration sentiment appear rather sick. Deliberately obscurely, as though it lacks the courage of its convictions, it shows American police clubbing coloured people—a grossly offensive portrayal of the police force of a friendly country. Can one invoke the Race Relations Act against this monstrous attempt to blacken a section of the white race? Perhaps not; so I must content myself by reminding the Irish perpetrators of this memorial that most American policemen seem to be Irishmen.

These things apart, the Birmingham Irish bring colour to the city with their annual St. Patrick's Day parade. They even brought a 'first' to Birmingham on 16th March 1952, when they stole a march of forty-five minutes on London to make Birmingham the first English city to hold an Irish parade. Usually some 5,000 or so fall in behind their county banners on the Sunday nearest 17th March, and march round the town preceded by flags bearing the three gold crowns of Munster, the golden harp of Leinster, the demi-eagle and upraised sword of Connacht, and the red hand of Ulster. I wonder how many of them know that the father of one of their martyrs, Patrick Pearse, proclaimed President of the Provisional Government of the Irish Republic in Easter Week 1916, came from Birmingham.

Irish children, going piously to their first Communion in white, have replaced the Nonconformist children who half a century ago flocked in their white dresses to the annual anniversary services at their chapels.

One January evening in 1970 I arrived home from my office

with a glum face and told my wife that I had seen an Indian or a Pakistani family shopping "on our side of the River Cole". Earlier in the day, with great solicitude, I had helped to her feet a West Indian woman who had fallen heavily on a treacherous ice-covered ramp in Colmore Circus, and, after retrieving her hand-bag and umbrella, I had laughed cheerily with her when she said: "Lord, man, it's a good thing I'm black so the bruises won't show."

This about sums up the colour problem in Birmingham: a human acceptance of and sympathy with individuals, but an ever-present fear that the coloured tide will engulf our own homes.

Hall Green, the outer suburb where I live, has remained free from coloured immigrants longer than most districts. On the five-mile journey from the city along Stratford Road the bus to Hall Green passes first through Sparkbrook and then Sparkhill. Elegant in Edwardian days, and eminently respectable until the late 1930s, Sparkbrook is now one of the 'twilight areas', with as many coloured residents as white. I lived a happy, spacious, and dignified life in Grantham Road, Sparkbrook, from 1920 to 1934. In 1963 I revisited my old home to write a nostalgic story, and found it occupied by seven families, one per room, four of them coloured, two Irish, and one English. After a fatal stabbing in Henley Street in November 1969 a magistrate said that Sparkbrook was a place where it was unsafe to walk about after dark. Yet I still do so, unmolested.

Sparkhill, outward from Sparkbrook, never had the latter's elegance, but it was a suburb of good-class artisan and white-collar homes between the wars, returning 100 per cent Conservative councillors—the hallmark of respectability. Today it has a large Indian and Pakistani population, an outward-bound colour wave which turns back, so far, at the River Cole; and I am not the only Hall Green resident who watches anxiously for signs of encroachment on "our side of the river". Residents in other colour-free suburbs have the same preoccupation. It is only incidentally to do with colour. We are equally worried about skinheads, leather-jacketed ton-up boys, mods, rockers, or any other group which would lower the value of our property or depress our living conditions.

Birmingham first appointed a Liaison Officer for Coloured

Immigrants in 1954, and the city has had one ever since. He became obligatory under the Race Relations Act of 1968, and is now known as the Community Relations Officer. His salary is paid to the city council by the Community Relations Commission of the Home Office, but his offices and staff are provided by the city council. His function, he points out, is as concerned with integrating the whites in their own communities as with integrating the coloured races, first among themselves and then with the whites. His office problems are almost entirely with the coloured population, and the "Please Enter" notice on the door is repeated in Urdu for the Pakistanis, Hindi for the Indians, and Punjabi.

Pamphlets are issued in these languages on such subjects as tests for cervical cancer and on the safe handling of heating appliances, the misuse of which has caused so many fire tragedies in immigrant homes and lodgings. The principal advice sought of the office concerns immigrant entry and passport difficulties, particularly getting dependants into Britain. A full-time case worker is employed, an Indian woman M.A. of an Indian university, a former teacher and lecturer, who can speak to Asians in their own languages. Where organisations of a neighbourhood-group type already exist the office is happy to co-operate with them. One difficulty it finds in setting up local organisations is in identifying someone who can speak authoritatively for immigrants of different origins. In 1970 one immigrant became a candidate in the municipal elections when Mr. Ralph Farrier, a 48-year-old gold assayer who came from Jamaica in 1942 to join the Royal Air Force and stayed in Britain in 1946, fought Soho Ward as a Liberal. He would have been following only one coloured person on the city council had he been elected—Dr. Dhani Ram Prem, who was a councillor from 1945 to 1950.

Birmingham's non-white population is approximately 85,000, of whom about 50,000 were born outside Britain. One in twelve of the inhabitants of Birmingham is coloured—8 per cent as against 2 per cent throughout Britain as a whole. Of the city's 85,000 coloured population, around 45,000 come from the Caribbean area; 34,000 from India and Pakistan; and 6,000 from Africa and elsewhere. The years 1958–63 saw by far the largest influx, six years when coloured immigrants were being cajoled into transport, nursing, and labouring—the chairman of a smelting works where I saw a number of Indians told me apologetically that they are much better workers than whites, though I have heard contrary opinions. Apologists for coloured immigration point out that from 1964 to 1968 inclusive, the average surplus of emigrants from Britain over immigrants into the country has been 71,200 annually. While this might pacify Britons who worry solely about overcrowding our islands, it will only further alarm those who are concerned with quality and the continuance of numerical white supremacy.

Mr. Enoch Powell, M.P., speaking on 17th January 1970, and telling his audience of Young Conservatives of the large correspondence he gets from the elderly "who rejoice that they will not live to see the England which they believe will be yours", gave some startling figures. He said, "In the city of Birmingham, which has been keeping birth figures for as long as eleven years, we know that the proportion of coloured births rose from 6·8 per cent in 1958 to 21·2 per cent in 1968. Thus, of the population now between 1 and 12 years of age which was born here, we know from these figures that about 15 per cent is coloured. To this must be added those of the same age group who were not born in Birmingham. The percentage of 15 would be raised to 20 if there were an average annual immigration during the period of rather over 2,000 children aged 12 and under."

Birmingham's Community Relations Officer told me that the main problems facing the city's coloured population concern housing and 'social deprivation', which would exist without immigrants. Brummies, however, feel that numbers inevitably exacerbate housing and social problems. The white population of the city felt considerable sympathy for the Wolverhampton Housing Committee when it was accused by the unpopular Race Relations Board of "unlawful discrimination" because of its rule that housing applicants from outside Britain must wait twice as long as local families before their claims are considered. Birmingham does not discriminate, the qualification for a council house being a minimum period of five years' work or residence in the city, come ye from Antigua, Allahabad, Alloa, or Armagh.

Housing is a key problem in Birmingham, particularly in immigrant areas. When some residents formed the Sparkbrook

Association in May 1961 its first meeting discussed overcrowding, neglected houses, vandalism, elderly people living alone, and overseas immigrants. The association flourished, and by 1970 the Chairman of Birmingham's Children's Committee could say: "Since the creation of the Sparkbrook Association our problems in the area have definitely dropped. The Association is making a very positive contribution to racial harmony." Apart from a corporation grant towards services considered worthwhile, the Sparkbrook Association is financed by members' subscriptions, private gifts, and grants from charitable foundations and trusts.

Because Sparkbrook had many large decaying houses forsaken for more modern property in the outer suburbs, it was an ideal area for immigrant lodging houses, but the Sparkbrook Association is not an organisation dealing solely with immigrants. "Whenever tension is mounting on any concrete issue," the director told me, "we bring together residents who have complaints and the civic officials who can remedy them, by providing, say, more dustbins and better refuse collection." The Sparkbrook Association organises such amenities as eight play centres for 3- to 5-year-olds, and a housing advice bureau. It nourishes some racial groups such as an Indian Music Group, and it helped some West Indians organise a Sparkbrook Caribbean Carnival in 1969.

A more elaborate 'carnival' was organised in 1969 by the Sparkbrook Association's near neighbour, the Balsall Heath Association, a four weeks' Festival of Fun, which brought a joyful summer month to the area with processions and celebrations in the parks. Two years younger than the Sparkbrook Association, its Balsall Heath counterpart also finds much of its work concerned with white residents. Whereas Sparkbrook has its own premises, Balsall Heath finds office accommodation in the Mount Pleasant Community Centre sponsored by Birmingham Education Committee. This centre provides a meeting place for a formidable array of immigrant organisations—the Arab Association; Arab Workers' Association; Association of Pakistani Women; Pakistani Institute; Afro-Caribbean Association; Barbadian Association; Diwana Indian Dance Group; Gambian Association; Nigerian Association; St. Kitts, Nevis, and Anguilla Association; Sierra Leone Students' Union; and the Balsall Heath Social Workers' Group.

Similar groups meet all over Birmingham, a random selection being the Asian Music Circle; the Pakistan Pathans Association; the Guru Nanak Gurdwara Punjabi School; the Guyana Association; the All-Pakistan Women's Association; the Hindu Volunteer Corps; the Indian Christian Group; and the Jamaica Industrial Apprentices' Association.

By 1970 Handsworth had become the coloured powder keg of Birmingham. The unsavoury cloak of prostitution had moved from Varna Road, Edgbaston, to Heathfield Road, Handsworth, and all-night parties constituted a grave nuisance to the remaining white residents. The police came in for some criticism based on alleged discrimination, but it is significant that this was voiced by young immigrants. This has little to do with the colour problem, for the generation gap knows no distinction between black and white. The police authorities recognise this, and the problem of the young has been discussed at several conferences called by the Chief Constable on relations between the police force and immigrants, and attended by all shades of immigrant opinion. "Community Relations" forms part of the force's regular training programme. The subject features in the syllabus for cadets and new recruits, and also in refresher courses for constables, sergeants, and inspectors. Many police officers give voluntary service in immigrant youth organisations, and in general, Birmingham's force can claim, in this very difficult field, to have kept up the splendid highly tolerant tradition of the British police.

The watchword of the social workers in racial matters is 'integration', but it becomes increasingly obvious that not only are Birmingham people opposed to integration but so are the immigrants themselves. Intermarriage is practically unknown. White women form associations with coloured men, but few white men marry coloured women. In fact, it is quite obvious that coloured immigrants want to live their own lives inside their own community.

Suggestions are frequently made that schools used mainly by coloured pupils should become Britain's first all-coloured schools so that the special needs of immigrant children can be met and the overall standard raised. By the end of 1970 Grove Lane Infant School, Handsworth, had six white pupils out of 280; the Junior School there had 15 out of 384, while Wilkes Green School, also in Handsworth, after only two years' existence, had 25 per cent white children in its total of 360. In schools where colours and races are more evenly mixed there is considerable evidence that must surely give pause to the most ardent apostles of integration. The 17-year-old English head boy of a multi-racial school in Edgbaston wrote a revealing letter to the Press in which he said: "Let me state most definitely that I believe on the whole the majority of the immigrants—thinking at the moment of the West Indians and Asians—do not want integration. In my opinion matters will not improve with the next generation. . . . This is pure rubbish about children disregarding colour. Even at school immigrants, especially the Asians, keep in close and separate groups away from the rest of the school. Girls at school may come in a nice school uniform, but at four o'clock ,when they get home, it is immediately changed for their traditional clothing."

The headmaster of a Small Heath secondary modern school with 30 per cent coloured pupils, mainly West Indian, was more optimistic of what is achieved in school. "Our only salvation in Birmingham is to retain in adult society the acceptance of each other as people that we achieve in school," he told me. He showed me that in school the West Indian and white children choose their own places for meals and apparently integrate completely. Furthermore, he assured me that calf-love affairs are as customary between black and white children as among boys and girls of the same colour. At this school considerable help is given towards finding jobs for immigrants, particularly Pakistanis. "The Youth Employment Office does a lot," the headmaster told me, "but we have a master who regards it as part of his school function to get them jobs. Proportionate to numbers, more immigrant parents than white attend parents' nights. They see in education the key to their children getting out of their deprived social situation, and we have one girl who came from St. Kitts in 1967 already with a place at Aberystwyth University."

Warwickshire County Cricket Club has done as much for integration as any institution in Birmingham, with more coloured players from east and west of recent years than any other county.

Our Asian and West Indian immigrants have made life in Birmingham much more colourful. Walking about the streets and the parks—particularly Cannon Hill and Handsworth—one constantly gasps with admiration at the beautiful saris of Asian women. In the Muslim religion the legs are an area of modesty and their shape must be hidden by the all-embracing sari or the shalwars—baggy trousers of cotton or silk. No such inhibition relates to the midriff, the shoulders, or the bust, but few eyes will wish to stray beyond the exquisite beauty of the Indian women's faces, even in Birmingham, which has a very high standard of indigenous female beauty.

Some Hindu foreheads bear the red spot, or 'bindhi', which, with gold or glass bangles, denotes marriage. So, too, does make-up. The Hindu woman is not expected to make herself attractive for any man, but may do so for her husband, and a daughter's marriage is still generally arranged by the parents just as in India. The stone or ring worn in the nose, pierced or on a clip, is purely decorative, and again is normally affected by a married woman, though discarded in widowhood. Broadly, the sari denotes a Kenyan Asian or a better-class woman from India, and it is more often worn than shalwars by a married woman. In rural areas of the Punjab where Hindus and Moslems live together the sari is less convenient for outdoor work, so shalwars may denote rural peasant stock rather than town dwellers.

The astrakhan cap of Moslems from Kashmir is a common enough sight in modern Birmingham, as is the turban of the Sikh, though many Sikhs regard it as a mark of freedom to cut their hair and dispense with the turban, particularly when they come to live in a Western country. There was initially some opposition to Sikh bus conductors in Birmingham wearing the turban instead of the uniform cap, though this was eventually resolved by their wearing blue turbans. At times left-wing democratic toleration breaks down before left-wing agnosticism, and it was a prominent Labour alderman who led the opposition to bus conductor's turbans. In nearby Walsall a headmaster suspended five Moslem girls for wearing shalwars. Surely it is only the outright opponent of immigration who can consistently dictate what immigrants shall wear once they are here.

With their love for bright orthodox clothing, West Indian women and girls bring a sudden joyful rainbow of colour to the occasional wedding, or when dressed in their best for church. One point readily conceded to the West Indians in Birmingham is that they turn out their children impeccably, putting many local parents to shame, and, mercifully, male Negro hair does not lend itself to the scruffy styling of white heads.

Birmingham has a large number of immigrant cultural organisations together with a Vedic Centre, a Hindu Temple, and Sikh temples. There are over 12,000 Sikhs in the city, with up to 300 at each service in their Mary Street Temple at Balsall Heath. Also in Balsall Heath, a 3,400-square-yard plot was set aside in 1963 for the erection of a Moslem mosque. By 1969, when the Moslems had raised only £60,000 towards the £300,000 required, the site was taken back by the city council for other purposes.

A community of Birmingham Serbs worships at the new Serbian Orthodox Church of St. Lazar in Cob Lane, Northfield. Builders from Yugoslavia came here in April 1966 to start work on the church, and were helped by the local Serbs. A design based on the Eastern style of Serbian churches makes this the only Serbian Orthodox church of its kind in Britain. Mostly wartime refugees, the Birmingham Serbs are ministered to by Father Milenko Zebic, whose 'parish' takes in his countrymen as far apart as Bristol and Derby.

Birmingham has, too, a Polish community of some 3,000, almost all of them soldiers of the Second World War. Their number was larger, but many have emigrated to Australia, Canada, and New Zealand. Those remaining are mostly Roman Catholics, and they share St. Michael's Roman Catholic Church in what was Moor Street, but hold separate services. They have a Polish Catholic Club in Bordesley.

In 1969, discussing race relations, the *New Statesman* described the West Midlands as a "volcano" faced with "the prospect of a vast dissident conurbation of warring communities stretching from Coventry to Telford". My belief is that this unhappy outcome, in so far as it means physical violence between white and coloured, can be avoided only by retaining the present disparity of numbers between them. Integration appears increasingly unlikely; racial differences are too great initially. It has been proved over and over again in Birmingham that black and white make uneasy neighbours. A form of domiciliary apartheid seems to be the only possible solution—an apartheid not of superiority and inferiority but of difference in outlook and behaviour.

Coloured and white can work together; they are less good at residing together. Many coloured people in Birmingham would like immigration stopped; they see in its continuance an unnecessary irritation of the normally tolerant and good-natured Englishman, and a threat to whatever comfort they have achieved.

This applies too to the activities of the ineffable Race Relations Board, such as its arraignment of Mr. Jess Wragg, a white newsagent in Lozells, who allowed a rooms-to-let card to appear in his ninepenny advertisement case offering "one double room for two white gents and one single for one white lady". The advertiser, said Mr. Wragg, when accused of racial discrimination, was a Pakistani, Mr. Williyard Ali. Said Mr. Ali: "I asked for white people because I have found them prompt payers."

So far we have laughed, but tolerance is being worn very thin on racialism in Birmingham and elsewhere, not by the coloured people in our midst, but by the white opponents of apartheid and their violent demonstrating friends who, with the help of television, keep racialism before the public.

These are the meddlers most likely to cause an explosion.

XI

THE OCTOPUS

RICHARD TAPPER CADBURY, descended from a line of West
Country yeomen and woolcombers, started business in Birmingham as a silk mercer in 1794. He and his son, John, both Street
Commissioners, were members of the committee which arranged
the transfer of the commissioners' powers to the town council.
John had a tea and coffee business in Bull Street, but later he
established a cocoa and chocolate factory in Crooked Lane, moving
on to Bridge Street, off Broad Street, where eventually his sons,
George and Richard, took over. In 1879 they erected a larger
factory 4 miles from the city centre, calling it Bournville, a name
which Cadbury's chocolate and cocoa have made famous throughout the world.

It was a revolutionary move to take industry out of industrial
surroundings, but for a food factory this semi-countryside was
the right place. The Cadbury brothers were model employers
paying more, giving shorter hours and a weekly half-holiday,
and pioneering medical and dental services, sport facilities, pensions, and paid holidays.

Riding on horseback to a Men's Adult School in Severn Street,
off Suffolk Street, early every Sunday morning, George Cadbury
saw very bad housing and learned something about the unhappy
human outcome of restricted home conditions. He concluded
that a man and his family would lead happier, healthier, and more
useful lives if their homes were more spacious and provided with
gardens. So he began building such houses at low rents for his and
other workers on land near the Bournville factory. In 1900 he
founded the Bournville Village Trust, the trust deed decreeing

that a house should occupy only a quarter of its site, the remainder being garden; that no factory should occupy more than a fifteenth of the site where it was built, and that roads should be wide with ample open spaces in the area. Bournville was incorporated in Birmingham in 1911, and a charming sylvan place it is, with its famous carillon tower facing the factory across the smooth greensward of extensive playing fields.

Over 9,000 are employed at Bournville, and it is doubtful if any factory in Britain entertained more visitors at the height of Cadburys' hospitality. They came in a constant procession of coaches, up to 100,000 annually, a policy that was being steadily curtailed as the firm reviewed any possible benefit that accrued from it, so that such visits ended completely in 1970. The Cadburys were teetotallers, and intoxicants are not allowed in the Bournville Works, where—very civilised indeed—the smoking which is naturally banned on the production lines is also prohibited in the offices. Bournville Estate is without a pub, and not until 1969 was permission granted to the four residents' associations to apply for an occasional liquor licence for certain functions.

March 1969 saw a merger resulting in the name Cadbury Schweppes Ltd.—an alien sound to one brought up anywhere within sniffing distance of Bournville chocolate, which pervades the air for miles around in the right conditions of humidity and wind direction.

In 1943 Cadbury Bros. Ltd. published an educational booklet *Our Birmingham*, which asserted, "We have shown that Birmingham is already too big. It must not be allowed to grow still bigger. Further building on the outskirts of Birmingham should be forbidden, and a green belt of fields and farms should be preserved." Excellent, but instead, said the booklet, new towns of 30,000–50,000 population might be built beyond the green belt, complete in themselves with industries, amusements, and schools, and linked with Birmingham by fast roads and trains.

This parochial passing of the buck; this attempt to sweep a city's urbanisation far beyond its boundaries, might be all right with a fixed population nationally, but not with one rapidly increasing. Birmingham's experience subsequent to 1943 has shown that the rape of the immediate green belt goes hand in glove with the establishment of overspill towns some distance away.

The Bournville Estate house occupying a quarter of its site; the Birmingham council house built fifteen to the acre. Lowering of the density of housing reached its apotheosis in three inner-ring redevelopment areas after the Second World War. Lee Bank's original population of 15,000, inhabiting a maze of back houses, is now 6,500, living mainly in tall rectangular blocks, with three twenty-storey towers; Newtown's population is reduced from 28,000 to 15,500; and Ladywood's from 25,000 to 12,500.

"At present it looks bleak and draughty," writes Alexandra Wedgwood in Pevsner's *Buildings of Warwickshire* of Ladywood's brave new world. This goes for Newtown, too, dominated by the parent factory of Joseph Lucas Ltd., one of Birmingham's industrial giants, whose 'King of the Road' cycle accessories and electrical equipment for cars are world famous. Lee Bank is the most attractive of these three slum clearances, possibly because it is more hummocky. The central green with its tiny pond among the curvaceous green mounds is a pleasant focal point to the estate. There are, too, several children's play areas, one a particularly intimate little den for the hatching of childhood plots. For those no longer children, as they sit around the green, there are glimpses, between the ring of skyscrapers, of the Birmingham they knew as children—St. Alban's tower up Conybere Street, Moseley Road library and baths, St. James's spire in Edgbaston, and, nearer, their own steeple of St. Thomas the Apostle. Lee Bank slopes upward to an elevation open enough once to have had a windmill, its sails revolving merrily over the Guinea Gardens, where, for an annual rent of one guinea, a workman could once have his allotment. Windmill Street, off the Horse Fair, still recalls those days.

In its great twenty-storey blocks of flats, each accommodating 116 tenants and approximately 300 souls, Lee Bank has gone very pretentious—Chatsworth Tower and Longleat Tower bringing to Birmingham the mansions of the Duke of Devonshire and the Marquis of Bath, while Charlecote Tower takes its name from the home of the Fairfax-Lucy family near Stratford-upon-Avon. Two six-storey blocks bring good Warwickshire names to Lee Bank in Avon House and Packwood House, one of the county's loveliest houses, near Knowle, given in 1941 to the National Trust. How long, I wonder, will it be before the last surviving tower block of flats is handed over to the National Trust.

A court in Small Heath

Alderman Francis Griffin, Conservative leader of Birmingham City Council, has said, "To develop a worn-out area means a loss of 20 per cent land because we have to build more garages, widen roads, and leave more space. We can rehouse only up to 55 per cent of the population on the original site even though we build towers." Birmingham having done this in these three areas of Ladywood, Newtown, and Lee Bank, some 33,000 have had to be housed elsewhere. Moving them has not given us back any of the pristine countryside. Rehousing them on new peripheral estates, like Kingshurst, Castle Vale, Druids Heath, and Chelmsley Wood, has swallowed up green belt, farmland, and virgin countryside. On the other hand, figures given by Birmingham's Medical Officer of Health show that in the inner zone of the city thirty-one babies out of every 1,000 born in 1968 died before the age of one, while at Sheldon, on the outer ring, the corresponding figure was two per 1,000. As we solve one problem we are creating others.

One Tuesday afternoon in July 1938 I was cycling home from Sutton Park past Castle Bromwich aerodrome. Across the Chester Road was the site of the Nuffield shadow factory, acres on acres of white ox-eye daisies. We were off to Ireland on holiday on the Friday, but I told my wife: "If you can get down there before, you must. It's a marvellous show." She did not, but on the Saturday night, in the cinema at Enniskillen, we saw in the news Sir Kingsley Wood cutting the first sod at the shadow factory— and there was that magnificent expanse of ox-eye daisies.

That shadow factory, now Pressed Steel Fisher Ltd., turned out 11,555 Spitfires, and towards the latter part of the war it had the biggest output of any Allied factory—320 Spitfires and twenty four-engined Lancaster bombers monthly. They were test flown at Castle Bromwich aerodrome, across the Chester Road.

Birmingham's first flying demonstration, including passenger flights, was given in 1911 by B. C. Hucks with a Bleriot mono-plane when Castle Bromwich was known as the Playing Fields. During the First World War the S.E.5 and the Handley Page0/400 were tested at Castle Bromwich. In the early 1930s the Great Western Railway Air Service flew from Castle Bromwich to Cardiff, the fare of 30s. single, 50s. return including transport between the aerodrome and New Street or Snow Hill Station.

o

The Bull Ring Market and St. Martin's Church

By 1934 the 'Great Western' had been dropped from the title and the service was extended to Liverpool, London, and Brighton.

From 1926 Castle Bromwich was the home of 605 (County of Warwick) Squadron, which flew Hurricanes from Croydon in the Battle of Britain, and was captured when Batavia fell to the Japs. Re-formed after the war, the squadron flew from Honiley, near Birmingham, but Castle Bromwich remained with the Royal Air Force, and on 7th June 1955 the Queen approved a unit badge for the station including a sprig of broom which once bloomed there in profusion—hence the 'Bromwich'. The 'Castle' was a small Norman structure, now gone, on the mound overlooking the area from south of the River Tame.

The last R.A.F. plane took off from Castle Bromwich in 1958, and in 1964 work commenced on the Castle Vale Estate, the intention being to build a town of the same size as Stratford-upon-Avon in four years. By 1968 this was an accomplished fact, 20,000 people being housed in nearly 5,000 homes, eleven- and sixteen-storey blocks of flats, four-storey maisonettes, and 1,750 houses, with a comprehensive school and a primary school, and a shopping centre. As usually happens in such a development, people were moved in from slum-clearance areas like Highgate too soon among the inevitable mud of construction work, and without sufficient amenities. In 1966, for instance, there was one doctor but no chemist shop to dispense his prescriptions, no pubs, no clubs, and no post office for old-age pensioners to draw their pensions. These deficiencies have been remedied, but one early deprivation has left an unhappy legacy in those growing up on the unfinished estate. There was no police station and insufficient police patrols, so that, encouraged by poor lighting in pioneer days, gangs of vandals went on the rampage. This has happened with other new estates, and any pleasure residents have found in their new, more spacious, environment has been spoiled by the bad language and bad behaviour of young people, by the uprooting of saplings, and the breaking of windows.

These things did not seem to have happened in the slums, and it is a fact that new buildings and larger windows tend to become cock-shies for stone-throwing youths where the old familiar ones do not. In January 1969 the priest-in-charge at Chelmsley Wood new town said: "Delinquency here could reach a fantastic level unless we get a youth centre." There is a touching faith in youth centres, but though youth clubs have proliferated in Birmingham since the war, so, too, has juvenile delinquency.

To be fair to Birmingham it must be added that this problem of teenage vandalism is not peculiar to the city, in fact Birmingham football fans have a less fearsome record than many on their travels. The problem is, however, rife in towns and cities, and therefore has a place in a true portrait of Birmingham.

The residents of Castle Vale will never be allowed to forget the former purpose of Castle Bromwich. The visitor, forgetful of the name of the road he is seeking, but remembering that it is named after a civil airport somewhere in Britain, will be in a quandary. Many of the roads have such names, Turnhouse Road, Sumburgh Croft, Dyce Close, Renfrew Square; many more are named after R.A.F. camps and airfields, Tangmere Drive, Upavon Close, Padgate Close, Manby Road, and the eleven-storey blocks of flats after types of aircraft, Hampden House, Trident House, Comet House, Lysander House. One of the public houses on the estate is 'The Albatross', named after the bird on the R.A.F. badge. This badge itself, erected over the entrance to the officers' mess at Castle Bromwich in 1938, is preserved on a plinth in the central gardens at Castle Vale, as is the nameplate of the 605 Squadron. A second public house recalls the most famous of all wartime bombers, The Lancaster.

A smattering of Castle Vale names have no connection with aircraft. The haphazard windings of Watton Green bear little resemblance to the straightforward uncompromising politics of Alderman Harry Watton. Thomas Walk and Bond Drive honour recent chairmen of the Public Works Committee and the House Building Committee.

Having built part of Castle Vale where it had demolished the British Industries Fair, Birmingham received government permission in 1970 to proceed with the new National Exhibition Centre at Bickenhill. While city councillors and some industrialists congratulated themselves—and B.O.A.C. put on a four-times-a-week service from Birmingham to New York in April 1970—the man in the street remained unimpressed by this boost to the city's prestige. Complaints were quickly voiced at the further intrusion into the countryside, objections were raised to the night

clubs, and ungrateful citizens bombarded the Press with suggestions that a city which could invest £3 million in an exhibition
site could surely, with greater credit to its reputation, spare the
£15,000 currently needed to keep the City of Birmingham
Symphony Orchestra in being.

In the Druids Heath Estate between King's Heath and King's
Norton, Birmingham brought the town to the country with one
surprising result. Mr. Howard Aucote, tenant of the 100-acre
Moundsley Hall Farm, had to give up growing cereals when the
skyscrapers of Druids Heath came up to his northern boundary.
"The sparrows that came with the buildings ate up all my seed,"
he told me. "So we had to concentrate on eggs and milk."

Read back into the history of King's Norton beyond the time
when a Roman community was jettisoning its broken pottery
near the top of Parson's Hill, and you find no Druids. Look at a
tithe map of 1840, and though it records West Heath, Walkers
Heath, King's Heath, and Highters Heath, it has no Druids Heath.
But a Mr. Drew seems to have had a meadow thereabouts in 1843,
and in time the lane beside it became corrupted to Druids Lane.
So Mr. Drew has something to answer for in the nomenclature
of Druids Heath Estate. True, he is remembered in Drew's
Meadow Close, but most of the other names, like the inevitable
Stonehenge Road, come from Druid country in Wiltshire—
Netheravon Close, Idmiston Croft, Larkhill Walk, Winterbourne
Close, and others. Pegleg Walk could be a memory of a Rev.
John Pegler, a considerable local landowner in the mid-nineteenth
century.

Druids Heath Estate, built in the middle 1960s, houses 8,000—
many from the Balsall Heath slum clearance—in what was at the
time of building the largest completely industrialised housing
project in Britain, the walls and floors of the flats, maisonettes,
and houses being made in factories.

When I was a boy in Small Heath, Birmingham, we played on
Heather Road fields and Monica Road fields, soon to be completely built up with the terraced houses that were already started.
Chelmsley Wood was some distant fairyland deep in the Warwickshire countryside east of Birmingham, to be visited only on high
days and holidays, and yielding armfuls of bluebells in season.
Chelmsley Wood today is gone in all but name, its site and much

other countryside obliterated by a Birmingham overspill town. Said to constitute the largest housing project in Western Europe, within five years of the area being woodland and green fields it is intended that 70,000 people will be living in Chelmsley Wood. Is this cause for jubilation, apology, or shame? Many of the new residents come from the demolished Highgate area in Birmingham's inner ring, where courts on which the sun never rose have gone the way of the empire on which the sun never set. These old back-to-back houses are razed to the ground, and the vista down Belgrave Road from Moseley Road has become a panorama across a wide grass-sown area which is, however, unlikely ever to revert to the type of pristine woodland we knew in Chelmsley Woods, swept every May by a sea of bluebells.

In the past the first essential in governing a city seems to have been, right or wrong, to provide a home for every citizen. Today, in our overcrowded island, I suggest that the chief concern of any local authority should be to ensure the preservation of every field, tree, and hedgerow around its boundaries. During 1969 an idea was propounded by the Chairman of Warwickshire County Council that the charming village of Henley-in-Arden, 9 miles from our city boundary, might well be developed for Birmingham overspill population. Among many protesting heartcries was a letter to *The Birmingham Post* from a reader at Ullenhall, near Henley. "Birmingham's greedy eyes appear to roam over wider and wider tracts of country," it said. "There is Telford New Town, Redditch New Town, Chelmsley Wood, Daventry, proposals to build at Wythall, talk of building at Bromsgrove, rumours about Meriden and Tanworth-in-Arden, and now Henley-in-Arden. . . . It is time it was stated that many people living outside Birmingham do not view Birmingham's housing problem entirely with sympathy."

Neither, of course, do tens of thousands living in Birmingham —members of the Ramblers Association, the Countrywide Holidays Association, the Holiday Fellowship, and other walking clubs, who meet on Saturday and Sunday mornings around the Civic Centre to board coaches for a day of fresh air among lovely Midland landscapes. Less ardent, perhaps, but ready to spring to the defence of any threatened countryside, are the hordes who regard the Lickeys and the Clent Hills as their open-air playground, and who sign petitions against opencast mining on the wild Clee Hills in Shropshire.

Birmingham first reached out its tentacles seriously at the beginning of the twentieth century in search of water. On 21st September 1904, thanks to the engineering genius of James Mansergh, the first Welsh water came into Birmingham through a 73-miles-long aqueduct from the Elan Valley in central Wales. The scheme involved more than reservoirs, and Edward Lawley Parker, Chairman of the Water Committee from 1893 to 1908, said: "We have learned how to manage an estate of 43,000 acres one hundred miles away ... we have founded a colony and managed a public house and the schools, and have learned also something of the value of land and water and the fish contained in the water."

The city had reached out a long way beyond its boundaries. It had to. A daily consumption of $8\frac{1}{2}$ million gallons of water in 1876 had risen by the Second World War to 35 million gallons. One of the city's first concerns after the war was more water, and in 1952 the Queen inaugurated the Claerwen Dam with its new reservoir impounding 10,625 million gallons. This gave the Birmingham water undertaking a total catchment area of seventy-one square miles, almost all of it owned by the Corporation, which thus becomes possibly the largest landowner and sheep owner in the Principality, owning about one-half of the 45,000 sheep grazed in the area. In addition, some 900 acres are devoted to the dark forestry coniferations which so despoil the Welsh hillsides.

The city also takes water from the Severn, water said seventy years ago to be too dirty to be cleaned economically for drinking. With eleven other water authorities the Corporation Water Department flooded the Clywedog Valley in Montgomeryshire during the 1960s, constructing a dam to impound 11,000 million gallons, thus enabling the flow of the River Severn to be regulated. Then in 1968 a further small reservoir was inaugurated on farmland at Trimpley, near Bewdley, in Worcestershire, where the water is extracted from the river. By 1970 another Welsh valley, the Dulas, was under attack.

So it was for water that Birmingham first reached beyond its own boundary, but it has since been for housing, peripheral and distant, that the city has eaten up land. The estate development

already mentioned has been in the city or adjacent to it, and nowhere has this lust for land been more persistent than in North
Worcestershire. In September 1969 a twenty-four-day enquiry,
the fourth, began at Bromsgrove into Birmingham's repeated
attempts to acquire green-belt land for housing around Wythall.
The first enquiry, in 1959, decided that Wythall development was
unnecessary if overspill could be unloaded on Coventry, Redditch, Kidderminster, and Droitwich. The second, in 1961, gave
priority to the retention of green fields over Birmingham's
proposal to build on 2,000 acres; and the third, in 1964, rejected
an application to develop 420 acres west of the Alcester road
because it would bring the city boundary too close to the urban
area of Redditch.

Undeterred by these rebuffs, Birmingham came up again in
1969. Alderman Griffin circulated his "private thoughts" to his
party group, explaining that he wanted "to extend our boundaries to take additional countryside to provide housing or amenities for our people", and that Birmingham "must expand by
taking land and retaining population and industry". He pointed
out that Birmingham loses certain government grants if it loses
population, and that a population loss of 27,000 denied the city
£3 million in various grants over the three years 1967–70, and
should we continue to lose grants we could not be expected to
provide regional amenities like the C.B.S.O., the Repertory
Theatre, car parks, and the projected £3 million Central Library.

The plea in 1969 was for planning permission to build 11,000
homes across the North Worcestershire border in three areas,
together with three balancing lakes to control surface water running from the proposed housing. Among nearly 500 objectors
was Worcestershire County Council, opposing the lakes and one-
third of Birmingham's building requirements—3,600 proposed
homes at Moundsley—to the disgust of some Birmingham councillors, who argue that because the city provides such a huge
market for Worcestershire farmers and horticulturists the county
should reciprocate with some land for our housing.

During the enquiry it emerged that standards laid down in
Birmingham required 5 acres of open space to each 1,000 of
population in the inner zone, rising to 7 acres in the outer zone,
a total of 6,979 acres. On these figures the city faced an open-

space deficiency of 1,543 acres by 1971, while all significant virgin land available for housing in the city would be exhausted by 1975.

Well might *The Birmingham Post* declare in a leading article: "If Birmingham is to continue to expand, the Midlands will face the risk of becoming one vast, built-up megalopolis. . . . We believe that everything points inflexibly to the fact that Birmingham's expansion will have to be stopped at some point or other."

Whatever the outcome, the enquiry was a gold mine for a legion of lawyers, and it was estimated to have cost Birmingham ratepayers at least £15,000, and ratepayers in Bromsgrove Rural District £3,500 in legal fees, with £300 costs for playing host to the enquiry.

But while North Worcestershire was holding up Birmingham's repeated attempts to urbanise Wythall, the 1960s saw a constant overspill of the city's population to more distant regions. This term 'overspill' has to be defined, and generally it stems from two factors: (1) people who firmly believe that any local authority in which they live, or to which, willy-nilly, they care to go, owes them a home, and (2) the readiness of local authorities, because of their mania for building houses, to pander to such people. So, having used up all the building land in its own area, it seeks some elsewhere within the boundaries of another local authority which is anxious to increase in size, prestige, and rates income. Along with its surplus population, the shedding authority must also provide jobs, so it encourages some industry to move to overspill areas.

In January 1963 Dawley New Town in Shropshire was designated to accommodate 55,000 people from Birmingham and the Black Country in 9,100 acres. Added to an indigenous population of 20,000, this was expected, by natural increase, to give a population around 100,000 in twenty years. The countryside conservationist could raise little objection to much of the type of land devoted to housing development in this new town, it being largely on derelict mining and industrial terrain, though Shifnal Rural District Council protested unavailingly at the inclusion of 3,000 acres of good agricultural land from its area.

Then in December 1968 the Minister of Housing and Local Government made an Order extending Dawley New Town, and designated an additional 10,143 acres, including the existing towns

of Oakengates and Wellington, and renaming the entire area
Telford New Town after Thomas Telford, who was Surveyor of
Public Works for Shropshire and a great canal engineer who con-
structed, among other famous waterways, the Shropshire Union
Canal, and an iron bridge across the Severn at Buildwas. More
good farmland was included in the boundaries of Telford New
Town, and from his 300 acres at Leegomery House, Wellington,
Mr. David Needs said on 23rd October 1968: "I am so close to
Wellington that I am bound to be included in the new town. I
came here six years ago to take over what was virtually a derelict
farm and now I am getting it back into production. But this news
means it is six years of my life wasted. I shall not be able to continue farming here." Not satisfied with its juggernaut march over
farmland immediately surrounding the city, Birmingham, the
octopus, was reaching out twenty-five miles into Shropshire.

The newly concieved Telford would provide for an influx of
100,000 from the West Midlands conurbation over a period up
to twenty years, doubling the intake originally proposed for
Dawley. It was estimated that by 1990 the population of Telford
New Town would be 220,000—and an urban sprawl would half
surround the Wrekin. By February 1969 over thirty firms, some
of national repute, had begun production on the Telford industrial estates of Tweedale and Halesfield, and work was in progress
on the third industrial estate of Stafford Park, astride the A5.

In June 1964 a Redditch Development Corporation was established to plan for the movement of Birmingham overspill into
7,180 acres already occupied by 34,000 'natives' in the Worcestershire needle-manufacturing town of Redditch. It operates an
industrial selection system whereby vacant jobs in Redditch are
offered to qualified workers who are on Birmingham's housing
register, provided, of course, that they move into one of the new
houses at Redditch. By 1976 it is intended to house 70,000 in
Redditch New Town, which should increase by natural means to
90,000 at the turn of the century. Each year until 1976 will see
1,600 new dwellings making inroads into the once pleasant valley
of the River Arrow. Three industrial areas are being developed to
balance the housing increase and to provide jobs for the new-
comers, the 110-acre Washford Industrial Estate in particular
having obliterated a sylvan countryside between Mappleborough

Green and Studley. From the centre of Birmingham to the centre of Redditch is 14 miles, with the green belt between the built-up perimeters now reduced to four miles and likely to diminish further, while the road between the two is rendered more and more hideous and hazardous by the 40 per cent of Birmingham's overspill into Redditch commuting daily back to work in Birmingham whence they came.

Until the mid-1960s there was a delightful country-lane walk of nearly two miles between Droitwich and Salwarpe some 20 miles from Birmingham. Then came the Birmingham overspill, and one side of the walk is now built up with the barracks-like Chauson Estate. The overspill plan is to treble the population of once-attractive Droitwich by building 6,000 new houses; 4,000 by private enterprise, and 2,000 council houses for tenants nominated by Birmingham City Council, which will contribute £12 annually for ten years towards the rent of each house occupied by an overspill tenant.

At Daventry, Northamptonshire, too, is caught up in Birmingham's tentacles. During the years 1970–5 around 1,600 houses will be provided there for Birmingham people, and it is planned that in the decade of the 1970s the population of Daventry will grow from 6,200 to 25,000. In both Droitwich and Daventry sites are provided and industry is encourage to move from Birmingham.

There are other enclaves of Birmingham overspill in the Midlands—at Burntwood, near Cannock Chase in Staffordshire, for instance. Yet despite all this shedding of population into all these distant 'new towns' forecast by the Cadbury's 1943 publication, Birmingham has continued to grow peripherally also, grasping out with fingers of brick and mortar to sterilise the green belt. Ever since William Blake envisaged building Jerusalem "in England's green and pleasant land" someone has been seeking to emulate him until England is less green and far less pleasant.

XII

FORWARD—AND UPWARD

THE working day begins and ends for far too many Brummies huddled bleary-eyed and choking on the upper decks of corporation buses which have not yet outlawed tobacco smoking. Alternatively, they sit fuming and frustrated—and possibly smoking—in their cars in heavy slow-moving traffic to and from work. In either case their tobacco pollutes air already foul and noxious from petrol and diesel fumes. Meanwhile the petrol shareholders rub their hands in mercenary glee, and the surgeons sharpen their scalpels.

Birmingham is not unique in this respect among cities and towns, but a long inherited legacy of chest trouble from industrially polluted air has made bronchitis peculiarly the 'Birmingham disease', and not all the smoke-abatement schemes—in which the city lives up to its "Forward" motto—will ameliorate it while citizens compulsively reach for their cigarettes and their ignition keys. The problem is aggravated by the constant expansion of our boundaries and the correspondingly greater time spent travelling to and from work. Forty years ago I walked morning and evening the two miles between my home in Sparkbrook and a city office in thirty-five minutes. I tried the experiment recently of driving over the route at the same time of day in my car. By the time I had solved my parking problem it had taken forty minutes on the townward journey. Homeward took just thirty-five minutes. So I tried walking as near the old route as modern development allows—fifty minutes to town, much of the extra time spent kicking my heels and enveloped in petrol fumes at road crossings.

Today the journey to work in the city from the suburbs is no joyride, and having accomplished it, the city worker is haunted at times throughout the day by thoughts of the journey home, and by the realisation that it has all to be repeated tomorrow . . . and tomorrow. My home now is five miles from my office in Birmingham—ten minutes drive by car on a quiet Sunday. So, ideally, having to be at my desk by 9.30 a.m. I should leave home at 9.15. In fact, I board a bus at 8 a.m. and alight from it at 8.45. That bus, capable of the speed limit of 30 m.p.h., does the journey at little more than 5 m.p.h. on some mornings. The driver is allowed thirty-seven minutes on the route. Birmingham is slowly strangling itself with traffic.

The younger generation excuse many of their shortcomings because, they say, they live in the shadow of the 'Bomb' thought up by my generation. If that were their main worry they would be on Easy Street. First and foremost they should blame their forebears for the motor car, and wherever he goes, unless it be Coventry or Detroit, the Birmingham man should feel apologetic to admit that he comes from this centre of the car industry. Another aspect of living in such a place is that the cost of living is geared to the inflated wages earned on the assembly line at Austin, Rover, and elsewhere, and industrial ethics too often take their tone from those peculiar to car workers, who are more prone to strike than most.

My own office, in a glass palace with all modern conveniences including too-generous heating, is on the second floor. It is a practical impossibility to have the window open because of diesel fumes from the street below, a large proportion of them from lorries with engines left running at a warehouse across the canyon. The higher one goes in these twelve- or twenty-storey blocks, the purer the air becomes as the building thrusts upward into less restricted atmosphere, and the purer it need become. We have seen frightening television pictures of Tokyo police coming off traffic duty and resorting automatically to oxygen masks. The point-duty policeman had disappeared from Birmingham's automated crossings by 1969, but long before this there had been a case or two of policemen needing treatment after too long exposure to traffic fumes. I sometimes wonder if these fumes will breed mutations in city dwellers. On most days a sudden close whiff of diesel fumes makes me begin breathing less deeply out of concern for my lungs, and having begun, I feel that subconsciously I continue shallow breathing, perhaps until indoors away from the immediate danger. Shall we gradually become a flat-chested race? Happily there is little evidence of this yet among Birmingham's lovely girls, the vast majority of whom continued through the winter of 1969–70 to flout fashion and shame their maxi-skirted sisters by remaining loyal to the mini-skirt.

Not only the nostrils and the lungs but the eyes are offended by the constant movement of vehicles in Birmingham, with nowhere offering them a moment's rest. Even St. Philip's Church-yard is increasingly violated by cars belonging to cathedral dignitaries and servants, and it is rapidly taking over from the old Bull Ring as the scene for long-haired demonstrations, often centred round a kiosk soliciting support for a variety of doubtful causes. In the better suburbs of Birmingham, with grass verges between pavement and carriageway, the more socially conscious residents have constantly to remain vigilant to prevent these being converted into churned-up mudheaps by their less considerate neighbours parking cars on them.

The car may be a leading item of export from Britain, but it also leads to an enormous number of us taking in one another's washing unproductively—giving Ministry of Transport tests, testing one another's tyres, keeping cars on the move as traffic wardens, packing them into car parks and issuing licenses and insurance on them. If you live in a town or city you are well aware of this; if in the country you would be astounded by Birmingham's preoccupation with the motor car. The amount of space covered by row upon row of cars at second-hand dealers could help considerably to solve the housing problem if used for building.

Birmingham has always been something of a hotbed of tenants' agitation, often with left-wing politicians leading the tenants' associations. In Alderman Anthony Beaumont Dark, Chairman of Birmingham Housing Committee in February 1970, they had an outspoken opponent, who, to the great pleasure of responsible citizens, revealed something of those who prey on the sympathy of do-gooders.

Hearts had been set bleeding by the publicity accorded an Aston woman, kept in hospital with her ninth baby because doctors felt she should not return to her bad home conditions. Alderman Beaumont Dark made it known that her family owed £92 in rent on their £1 9s. 3d. a week 'sub-standard' home. Announcing that the family—which he named—had been re-housed, he added: "Let there be no doubt that if this family falls into arrears again they will be left on the street." Of the mother he said: "She has said she wants sixteen children, which is the most irresponsible thing I ever heard."

When the Licensing Justices of Birmingham refused to allow Anna Pavlova to dance bare-legged over forty years ago they made the city a music-hall joke, and gained it an image of puritanism from which it took long to recover. Its lack of night life has always upset those who imagine that visitors, on business or pleasure, must stay awake at night clubs into the small hours—a fate I have strenuously avoided over years of foreign travel with groups of pressmen and travel agents. Today Birmingham is amply provided with night clubs and gambling houses, many of them in trouble with the law from time to time. The newspaper entertainment columns reveal that night-time Birmingham has sufficient simulated sex on the screen and the night-club stage, and that fans of 'groups' have plenty of discotheques to sample. It is not without significance that advertisements for 'self-defence' through such alien means as karate and judo appear in the very columns that advertise the 'with it' forms of entertainment.

What is the Brummie today? A proud inheritor of the Chamberlain tradition? An offspring of the genius of Boulton? An ambitious incomer like our industrial pioneers of the eighteenth century?

Certainly the average age of a city councillor is lower than ever it was; the apprentices in city firms seem the hardest working and most worthy of the young people within our boundaries; and I was taken to lunch at the Albany Hotel recently by a man who came to Birmingham fifty years ago, an orphan with a single silver threepenny-bit in his pocket, who now has a printing business with an annual turnover of half a million pounds.

The Brummie today might be a shop steward pondering his next move against his employers, or he could be a reluctant trade unionist hoping the brothers will not be picketing his place of work. Most likely he is a bemused little man, trying vainly to cross the road; a householder watching his property depreciate in value because of immigrant expansion in his district; or a rate-payer furious that he will have to continue subsidising municipal tenants because the City Council's latest application to the Government for powers to increase rents on municipal houses has been rejected. He could, of course, be a municipal tenant delighted to know he is still to be the beneficiary of these exactions from private householders. He could be a small shopkeeper deprived of his livelihood by diversions due to road construction, and suffering the while clouds of dust, mud, and lack of footpaths for months at a stretch, danger, and loss of amenities in general. Alternatively, he could be a successful manufacturer who commutes in a large car from a country home outside the city, perhaps on a farm which he runs as a hobby.

The time-honoured notion that an Englishman's home is his castle has become a sour joke to many Birmingham householders. If housing emerged from the previous chapter as the city's sacred cow, there is one more sacred by far, before whose progress homes are scattered like chaff in the wind—road construction. Even property built as recently as between the wars has been compulsorily acquired, and thousands of residents have been dispossessed, while many of those left in occupancy fervently wish that they had been moved, suffering, as they do, a new flyover eight feet from their back gardens, or finding their access to shops and their children's schools barred by a new roaring trunk road or expressway.

Walking about Birmingham, the pedestrian cowers beneath the monster cranes which have been the presiding genius of the city for some years, and will be for years to come, thrusting up from building sites into aerial regions where the homing flocks of starlings wheel their evening flight, tenacious birds we have failed to scare by placing electrified wires, repellent gum, or even dummy hawks on the ledges where they roost. The cranes, fitted with whirling anemometers to warn of wind speeds in which they become dangerous, inspired the children of one Erdington school to a long-term project on their usage.

If the cranes reach up to the clouds in Birmingham the excavators probe down deep into the earth, the protective boards round redevelopment sites constantly pushing the pedestrian off the pavement. Notices regretting any inconvenience are displa yed on the hoardings, while appeasement platforms, giving bird's-eye views down into their fearsome foundations, are there to placate the harassed pedestrian. With thousands of cobra-headed parking meters and other instructions to motorists disputing his right of way on city pavements, the pedestrian's lot is not a happy one. His ears are assaulted by the periodic crash of good buildings, his eyes by storms of grit, and his nostrils by smoke from the burning of the shattered woodwork. Goering never did to Birmingham what the bulldozer has done. One January afternoon in 1970 I watched practically the entire dignified façade of Snow Hill Station knocked down while I waited for a 32 bus. The tears in my eyes sprang half from the dust, half from the sad-sweet memories of assignations beneath the clock in the booking hall, a favourite place for lover's meetings in bygone years.

Throughout history contemporary generations have always suffered that posterity may benefit. In Birmingham since the Second World War we have not merely suffered, we have been crucified in the interests of posterity—and all too often with the feeling that the amenities built on our sufferings will be out of date by our children's and grandchildren's day, and that they will not thank us for leaving them the burden of interest charges on the loans we have borrowed to rebuild the city.

I can sum up only by writing that if life in Birmingham during the past decade has been purgatorial it has been no more so than in any other town or city where the motor car and the concrete tower block have taken charge.

I had written thus far when a voice came out of Birmingham's past to chasten me for my seeming disloyalty to the city. Over the last fifty years Birmingham has had its share of 'characters'. Among the upper crust were Alderman Byng Kenrick, the bowler-hatted cycling septuagenarian; Henry Whittaker, a Quaker, who boldly carried his bare knees into his eighties, and still addressed his friends in the quaint second-person singular; Councillor William Blackwell of the Dickensian collar; Canon G. N. H. Tredennick of Sparkbrook, a tall, upright, bearded Tory who once said from the pulpit that "all pacifists should be shot on sight"; and solicitor Herbert Willison with inevit- able top-hat and button-hole. Much more homespun were

Thomas Larvin, alias 'Tommy Tank', who would run considerable distances with a large stone on his head for a pint; the irreverently dubbed 'Jesus', a Bull Ring evangelist, and his competitor for public notice, the escapologist who, like the workers of the world of the adjacent Communist orators, had nothing to lose but his chains—and the pair of old trousers in which he performed, his torso naked. There was, too, Ernie McCulloch, that 'Prince of Beggars' on others' behalf, his accent homespun Brummie enough, but his black Homburg hat and impeccable suits stamping him the dressiest 'character' in Birmingham. Then, sprawling for years among the pigeons on the back steps of St. Philip's Cathedral, was old Ben, bearded, bright-eyed, and gentle.

And there was one other, an elderly woman with bonnet, shawl, and cracked boots—no one seems to have put a name on her—who shuffled great distances about the city centre and suburbs begging between the wars, singing in a throaty voice of minimal range over and over again, just one hymn.

"Count your blessings," she would croak, "count them one by one,
And it will surprise you what the Lord has done."

This was the voice which came, ghostlike, from the roar of Corporation Street traffic, to set me counting my blessings as a resident of Birmingham for more than half a century.

What can one city bestow in purely concrete terms that another cannot? Any hospital anywhere might have given me the past thirteen years of life through brilliant surgery—it just happens the Queen Elizabeth, Birmingham, did it. Any school might have given me pride in being a pupil—I'm proud to be a Camp Hill Old Edwardian of the great Birmingham foundation. Any city would have given me friends, but it is against Birmingham backgrounds I recall them. Wherever I had lived I should have sought happiness walking the countryside of England and Wales, but no city could have given me such easy access as Birmingham to the Shropshire hills, the Welsh mountains, the Wye valley and lovely quaint Herefordshire, the upland Cotswolds, Derbyshire's hills and dales, Worcestershire lanes, and the Shakespeare country of Warwickshire. Birmingham's central position is unsurpassed among British cities, and I can be in Ireland within the hour.

I am assured by a journalist colleague who specialises in welfare

P

that Birmingham is outstanding in the provision it makes, both on a civic and a private plane, for the elderly, and I know for myself that the city was a pioneer in such welfare services as meals on wheels and free bus passes for old-age pensioners. Although I disagree with much they have done, my friends largely have been aldermen, councillors, and lord mayors of Birmingham, and this gives the civic image a more personal meaning to me. To watch an old friend with whom one learned one's politics receive the freedom of the city, as I watched Alderman Harry Watton on 2nd May 1970, involves me even more deeply in Birmingham.

Any man likes to feel he is a citizen of no mean city; that his city makes a contribution throughout the world. Not in the big things only, but in lesser items the name of Birmingham confronts the travelling Brummie—earlier in the week when this was written I casually saw the name of Birmingham on the hinges of my hotel door at Cavan in the Republic of Ireland, and at an Enniskillen hotel across the Border my 'personal bath mat' bore the imprint of a Birmingham firm making sanitary and toilet requisites.

But the blessings that crown a lifetime are not counted in concrete, material things. They are measured rather in memories, in friendships, and in associations which keep a man rooted, in retirement, to the place where he has lived. They are the things which give a sense of continuity to his life, often the smaller incidents. The Birmingham City Police Band, for instance, no longer plays on summer Saturday evenings in Cannon Hill Park, but from beneath the trees around the bandstand I can still look across a stretch of greensward, past a last-wicket stand in a cricket match, to dappled sunlight falling through the branches, and set rippling by rowing boats on the pool. This was the particular memory of Birmingham that sustained me throughout my war service. The city is well blessed with parks, and the Lickey Hills provide a 'little Switzerland', particularly in the winter.

Digbeth Institute, the Art Gallery, and the Town Hall are the Birmingham buildings that have impinged most closely on my life—those contentious debates at Public Opinion Action Association in Digbeth Institute, with the tower of the Meat Market darkening against summer skies beyond the window; lunchtime sandwiches in the seascape room at the Art Gallery when first I

worked in town; and symphony concerts and political meetings
in the Town Hall, with speakers such as Baldwin, Birkenhead,
Churchill, Woolton, Wilson, and the finest orator of them all,
Sir Oswald Mosley.

When I visited Birmingham relatives as a child over half a
century ago my particular impression was of the half-dozen or so
groups of pigeons seen wheeling against the wide skyscape from
Bordesley Station. They fascinated me. The station is now closed,
but those pigeons are still there, seen from the Camp Hill flyover
as they spiral into sunlit skies from the back courts of Small
Heath. Into that same sky rise the floodlights from Birmingham
City's ground, St. Andrew's—after the nearby church. I have not
been on that ground since players have worn long hair and bawdy
songs been bawled from the terraces, but vivid in my mind's eye
is the sudden flicker of a smoker's match among the crowd in the
December gloom of the dying minutes of a game before the
floodlit era. Older supporters will recall with some nostalgia from
the days of steam the clouds of smoke that often obliterated play
as a goods train chuffed slowly past.

Despite their brash new cubic neighbours, the Art Gallery tower
and the Council House dome still dominate the skyline on my
journeys into the city as they did so long ago, while on still days
the sonorous booming of Big Brum surprises me far from the city
centre.

And, as I leave the office of an afternoon, dare I admit that the
Post Office Tower, an infant still in its first decade, already strikes
a chord from my heart, standing sharp against a blue summer sky,
silhouetted against a frosty winter afterglow, or, at any season,
capped by the clouds to which it aspires?

INDEX

(Figures in italics denote pages facing illustrations)